AMERICA'S GILDED AGE

AN EYEWITNESS HISTORY

AMERICA'S GILDED AGE

AN EYEWITNESS HISTORY

JUDITH FREEMAN CLARK

 Facts On File, Inc.

America's Gilded Age: An Eyewitness History

Copyright © 1992 by Judith Freeman Clark

Facts On File, Inc.
11 Penn Plaza
New York, NY 10001-2006

Library of Congress Cataloging-in-Publication Data
Clark, Judith Freeman
    America's gilded age : an eyewitness history / Judith Freeman
Clark
        p. cm.—(The Eyewitness history series)
    Includes bibliographical references and index.
    Summary: Traces the history of the United States from 1865 to 1901
through such primary sources as memoirs, diaries, letters,
contemporary journalism, and official documents.
    ISBN 0-8160-2246-1 (alk. paper)
    1. United States—History—1865–1921—Sources. [1. United
States—History—1865–1921—Sources.] I. Title. II. Series.
E661.C57   199 2
973.8—dc2 0   91-31178

Facts On File books are available at special discounts when purchased in bulk quantities for businesses, associations, institutions or sales promotions. Please call our Special Sales Department in New York at (212) 967-8800 or (800) 322-8755.

You can find Facts On File on the World Wide Web at http://www.factsonfile.com

Jacket design by Keith Lovell

Printed in the United States of America

VB VCS 10 9 8 7 6 5 4 3

This book is printed on acid-free paper.

for my mother,
Lillian Elizabeth Bartlett

Contents

Acknowledgments

Many people assisted me in various ways as this book progressed from idea to completed manuscript. I am indebted to Edward Knappman, who first suggested that I contribute to the Eyewitness History series, and to my literary agent, Elizabeth Frost Knappman, for her interest and enthusiasm. My editor, Nicholas Bakalar, lent an expert hand and gently suggested ways to improve each chapter.

As in the past, I was warmly encouraged by several members of the history department at my *alma mater*, the University of Massachusetts at Amherst. In particular, I would like to thank Professor Gerald Mc-Farland for his counsel and helpful suggestions. Also, my gratitude goes to Emeritus Professor Miriam U. Chrisman for her many kindnesses through the years.

Thanks also to Kate J. G. Madson, Lora Moore, Susan Carter Sawyer and Barbara Stowe for their encouragement along the way, and to my children, Timothy and Stephanie Hawkins.

Finally, my husband, Robin, deserves special mention for his support, patience and editing skills. I place the highest value on his advice and opinion.

The Eyewitness History Series

Historians have long recognized that to truly understand the past we must relive it. We can only see past eras and events clearly when we free our minds from the knowledge of what unfolded between then and now and permit ourselves to experience events with the fresh vision of a contemporary participant or observer.

To stimulate our powers of historical imagination we must begin by immersing ourselves in the documents of the period, so that we can view events as eyewitnesses. THE EYEWITNESS HISTORY SERIES offers readers and students the opportunity to exercise their historical imaginations by providing in a single volume a large collection of excerpts from what historians call "primary sources," the memoirs, diaries, letters, journalism and official documents of the period.

To give these historical raw materials a framework, each chapter begins with a brief summary of the "Historical Context" followed by a detailed "Chronicle of Events." However, the bulk of each chapter consists of a large selection of quotations from eyewitness accounts of the events of the time. These have been selected to give the reader the widest range of views possible. Each has a specific source in the Bibliography to facilitate further study. To further stimulate the reader's historical imagination, a selection of contemporary illustrations is included in each chapter. Modern maps have been included in an appendix for the convenience of readers.

Rather than interrupt the main text with lengthy official documents, we have included them in an appendix. Another appendix includes brief biographies of the major personalities referred to in the text.

EYEWITNESS HISTORIES are intended to encourage students and readers to discover the powers and the pleasures of historical imagination, while also providing them with comprehensive and self-contained works of reference to significant historical periods.

Preface

United States history often is written in small portions that detail a single life, a limited chronology, or a specific event. This approach may reflect a historian's interests and also can provide a convenient context within which a subject can be described and analyzed. But a "tidy package" approach to writing history contrasts with the reality of human experience. Average Americans struggling with the day-to-day problems of immigration, labor unionism, westward expansion or cultural pluralism did not define the years in which they lived. This task was left to critics and historians. Labeled with lively or eponymous terms, such as the "Progressive era" or the "McKinley years," these capsules of history may be aptly named but usually derive from assessments made after the fact, rather than from the views of those living through the period.

To better understand the latter, primary sources (first-hand accounts of issues and events) are by far the most useful. Reviewing dates or details of accomplishments in the words of those who recorded them permits a reader to enter history and absorb the pace and tenor of a time. People whose lives were touched by events remarked on them in ways that vividly illustrate the significance of those happenings. An understanding of individual or national experience is enriched immeasurably by reading someone's candid views on a subject. Often, these views were recorded privately, in a journal or in letters to friends and family. Sometimes they were meant to be shared publicly, in speeches, editorials and news articles.

However, they all comprise the eyewitness descriptions so critical to making facts, statistics and analyses of events come alive. Personal observations emphasize the importance or insignificance of issues or people; they are invaluable in helping us better understand that Americans who lived a century ago were a lot like we are today.

AN ERA KNOWN BY ITS EXCESSES

Inevitably, there must be a context within which these contemporary sources and vivid anecdotal accounts can be described. For the period 1865 through 1901, the context has become known as the "Gilded Age." Unlike many other such historical nicknames, it was an era christened by someone who lived through it: the writer Mark Twain. A master storyteller known for his biting satire, Twain coauthored *The Gilded*

Age with Charles Dudley Warner. In this book, they mercilessly exposed the manners and morals of the years following the Civil War.

The title became a byword for the excesses of the postwar era, suggesting that underneath the glitter was much baser stuff. Corruption and self-interest seemed prevalent then among both politicians and private citizens. Personal gain was the fuel that drove most industrial or commercial efforts; there appeared to be little altruism and only a small number of folk who dedicated themselves to solving society's many problems. But despite the era's title, for a majority of Americans, it was anything but golden. It was a time during which entrepreneurs, industrial go-getters and government officials concentrated on making a fast dollar—frequently at others' expense. A handful made a fortune—a few did so honestly, more often the wealth was acquired by means that provoked scandal. At the same time, untold millions of Americans spent their health and well-being in menial labor—often working 16-hour days—and ultimately lost everything to the vicious economic downturns that plagued the nation between 1865 and 1902.

A Period of Innovation and Reform

While these were years of both extravagance and crushing poverty, there were individuals who stood out in sharp contrast to the rest. Their unusual commitment to civic responsibility, their willingness to search for ways to end the misery of immigrants in American cities or their interest in furthering public education and bettering international relations made them heroes in their own time. Opportunity abounded for the clever and the ambitious but also for the selfless. Those willing to take reasonable, but honest, risks made legitimate fortunes and countless contributions to American culture and society derived from them. Too, technological innovation and scientific discovery were hallmarks of the late 19th century. The "safety" bicycle, the Pullman railroad car, electric lights, the internal combustion engine, as well as the automobile, barbed wire, the telephone, motion pictures, the gramophone and the X-ray machine were only a few developments fueled by the synergy of the period we now call the Gilded Age.

Congressional action of this period is especially notable for its impact on the nation's economy, society and culture. The postwar years held particular opportunity. Many people sought and accepted new ways of solving America's problems in the hope that change would encourage national unity. Constitutional amendments sent on for states' ratification, and legislative initiatives enacted after 1865, set the stage for the America of the modern era. The 20th-century United States benefited, for example, from the goals of Reconstruction laws aimed at empowering African-Americans with greater economic and political parity. It is certainly true that these laws did not quickly transform institutions or popular attitudes, and Supreme Court decisions of the time often worked against those who fought for civil rights. But while nearly 100 years would pass before African-Americans could enjoy even limited power or equality, it is clear that visionary Gilded Age legislators made possible the later gains of millions of citizens.

THE RISE OF BIG BUSINESS

Federal legislation affected the business environment as well. During the Gilded Age, government in general allowed a degree of private sector expansion that would be unheard of only a few decades later. There was little, if any, local, state or federal regulatory activity immediately following the Civil War. In fact, most politicians appeared willing to permit any business activity whatsoever as a means of advancing the nation's economic development—even at the expense of other aspects of American society.

One way of encouraging this development was through protective tariffs on foreign imports. Senators like Republican Orville H. Platt of Connecticut, who supported protective tariffs—ensuring that American goods were favored in the marketplace—were staunch backers of federal help for business. Platt, James G. Blaine (R-Maine) and Nelson W. Aldrich (R-Rhode Island) each came from heavily industrial states and believed that laws imposing limitations on business, such as the Sherman Anti-Trust bill, would lead to national ruin.

The growth of railroads provides an example of how business expansion affected the whole nation. Following the Civil War, railroads were hailed as progressive, beneficial and a great boon to society. They soon crisscrossed the country with a vast and complex network of track. By the 1890s, the U.S. could boast that it had 33% of all the world's railroad mileage.

Railroads in America enjoyed almost unlimited opportunity and license to branch into whatever territory was most profitable for their owners. As a result, Native Americans were pushed from their ancestral lands, and the country's great western regions were invaded by the "Iron Horse." Farmer and ranchers, who had appeared to be beneficiaries of railroad expansion, found that prohibitive costs imposed by greedy railroad owners limited access to railroad transport. So, while increased availability of transportation to and from markets presented a source of potential income, farmers and ranchers seeking a cheap means of carrying agricultural products and beef cattle revolted against the railroads. They formed political alliances to oppose railroad and other business growth favored by the federal government.

A cattle drive from Texas. Courtesy of the Library of Congress.

For years, these alliances pressured lawmakers and chief executives to curtail the railroads' power. As a result, by 1887 President Grover Cleveland had established the Interstate Commerce Commission (ICC) to oversee and regulate railroads. The ICC was the first effort to place the federal government in the role of watchdog over private business.

THE TRANSFORMATION OF SOCIETY AND CULTURE

Social and political reformers were active during these years, although their most effective efforts would be associated with the Progressive movement of the early 20th century. The Pendleton Civil Service Act exemplified the type of reform aimed at government cleanup. Passed in 1883 during President Arthur's administration but given force later by President Cleveland, the Pendleton Act established federal civil service examinations and eliminated the unqualified from government jobs they held only due to patronage. Among social reformers, the best known may be Jane Addams, founder of the Chicago settlement, Hull House. With her unique brand of commitment and service to immigrants and the urban poor, Addams set new standards for social responsibility and personal activism. Along with activists like Richard T. Ely, founder of the American Economic Association, and the educator John Dewey, Addams articulated a better understanding of the relationship between progress and prosperity.

Politics in Gilded Age America was marked by the bitterness of Reconstruction, the sophisticated apathy of millionaire Congressmen and the gross and outright corruption among party bosses. Too, the Gilded Age witnessed a slowly but steadily growing controversy focusing on overseas expansion. Beginning in the 1880s, imperialists and anti-imperialists in Congress clashed time and again. They devised ways of helping America find markets for the products of its expanding industries and farms, and not incidentally sought greater territorial rights that could lead to increased global stature for the U.S. The imperialists would eventually win—if the war against Spain could be considered a victory.

Finally, immigration in the Gilded Age transformed America no less completely than industrial development, political corruption and reform or territorial expansion. In fact, immigration could perhaps be counted the single most important factor in social change of the period. Between 1860 and 1890, 10 million Europeans arrived in the United States, where they hoped to find economic opportunity, enjoy religious freedom or discover the other assurances promised by democratic government. The arrival of these immigrant groups made a sustained impact on America, providing a steady supply of inexpensive labor and creating instant markets for food, housing and clothing.

Some immigrants fled to the nation's interior, where they broke up the prairie, built farm communities and planted an entire region in wheat, rye, oats and other crops. Others swelled the population of cities like New York, Boston, Chicago and San Francisco. There, they placed enormous strain on municipal systems, causing tenements and ethnic ghettos to mushroom almost overnight. These devolved into great, sprawling slums awash with sewage and prone to every imaginable health hazard, slums that brought the combined difficulties of poverty, illiteracy and disease to their unsuspecting inhabitants. It was this urban nightmare that, in turn, provoked the remarkable and ambitious reform efforts of the period.

Embodied in this wave of foreign immigration was an inexhaustible reservoir of energy, creativity and truth. Immigrants believed strongly that through hard work and determination they could change their lot in life. And by doing so, they transformed America. Without the contributions of Germans, Poles, Italians, Swedes, the Chinese, the Eastern European Jews, the Irish and countless other nationalities and ethnicities, the United States would have grown more slowly, without the enhancement of diversity. The skills and abilities of transplanted citizens were the key to building our nation through farming, manufacturing, commerce, mining, banking, the arts, architecture, medicine and the myriad other attributes of modern society. It is these accomplishments and the human resources that made them possible that acted as a counterbalance to the meanness of political life, the sordid racial and ethnic incidents of the period and the corrosion of wealth in the Gilded Age.

1. The Challenge of Reconstruction: 1865–1867

THE HISTORICAL CONTEXT

The mid-1860s were a turning point for the United States which would, during the next three decades, witness federal legislation, bold economic strategies, and a myriad of social reforms that completely transformed the 3000 mile Atlantic to Pacific expanse.

The country's chief focus in 1865 was continued—albeit declining—resistance put forth by the Confederacy. The rebels clung to dwindling hopes for victory against the stronger Northern forces, as federal soldiers moved into strategically important regions in the South to ensure a Union victory. General Sherman's troops laid to waste urban centers and important agricultural areas in the South until the region's spirit was broken.

The destruction of Southern property had a predictable impact: it inhibited prompt economic recovery and deepened the rift between Northerners and Southerners following the war, making reconciliation more painful and less complete. In January 1865 Fort Fisher—located on the Cape Fear River in North Carolina—fell into Northern hands and Confederates lost control of their last remaining port. Some weeks later, General Lee surrendered to General Grant at Appomattox Courthouse, Virginia, and the war ended.

But Americans had only a brief time to contemplate the much-anticipated peace before another national tragedy struck. On April 14, President Abraham Lincoln was shot by John Wilkes Booth while attending the theater in Washington, D.C. Lincoln died early the next morning, and Vice President Andrew Johnson was then sworn in as the 17th President of the United States.

As the nation struggled to overcome its sorrow, major legislative efforts at the federal level were aimed at promoting a stronger economic base nationwide. In part, Congress sought to achieve this by strengthening the South's social and economic base. Key attempts to knit together the various factions in former Confederate states included passage of several constitutional amendments and a series of Reconstruction Acts. A strongly worded postwar agenda would ensure that control of the South remained in Northern hands. Congress passed numerous bills designed to control readmission of former Confederate states into the Union, and President Johnson fought these congressional efforts. This rift between the executive branch and the Congress stalemated all attempts to heal the nation through carefully guided policy-making, and meant another decade of division at the government's highest levels.

Certain pieces of legislation passed through Congress quickly as Radical Republican zealots devised swift, effective means of punishing Confederates and preventing civil rights abuses from occurring in the South. When the Freedmen's Bureau was established in 1867, its aim was to strengthen the position of former slaves by protecting their civil rights. Force had been given to these intentions in late 1865 with passage of the Thirteenth Amendment, which formally abolished slavery and set the stage for laws that would help achieve the amendment's goal. The Fourteenth Amendment, giving full citizenship to former slaves, was another means to this end.

The federal government worked to encourage the nation's agricultural development, particularly in the vast regions opening up for settlement west of the Mississippi River. One way of assuring this was through education. The Morrill Land Grant Act, passed in 1862, remained virtually unused throughout the Civil War. Yet only two years after the war ended, many states had established agricultural colleges under the terms of this act. Maine State College of Agricultural and the Mechanical Arts, Indiana Agricultural College and the Agricultural and Mechanical College of Kentucky were all founded in 1865 under the terms of the Morrill Act.

As the nation pushed further into its frontier, it acquired territory not part of the contiguous United States. By 1867, plans were under way for a survey of Panama so that a canal could be built connecting the Atlantic and Pacific oceans. The U.S. also annexed the Midway Islands in the Pacific in a move that would be later applauded by expansionists as a key means of preserving U.S. naval superiority.

But the most striking example of expansion came with the purchase of Alaska from Russia in 1867. Bought at the urging of Secretary of State William Seward, the Alaska Territory became part of the United States on October 18. Popularly known as Seward's Folly, or Seward's Icebox, its purchase price was two cents per acre.

Perhaps as a response to the civil enmity that had gripped the nation since the late 1850s, there was an upsurge in the growth of labor, fraternal and secret societies during the first years after the war's end. The Knights of Labor was founded in 1867, one of the earliest of labor unions. The secret society, Patrons of Husbandry, founded in 1867 by Oliver Kelley—an advocate of farmers' rights and agricultural interests—was known also as the Grange. It would later join forces with the Farmers' Alliance to become an important political force in the

Midwest. And the National Labor Union was founded in 1866 by William Sylvis and Richard A. Trevellick. Sylvis served as chief executive officer of the NLU until his death in 1869.

Women became politically stronger in the immediate postwar years, due in part to their experiences in the abolition movement during the war. Seeking a greater articulation of equality during the ensuing decades, more women sought careers and diversions outside the home. A growing number entered colleges and universities—some of which were founded by and for women. Women's political and reform organizations grew in number as well. The Young Women's Christian Association (YWCA), established in 1866, was typical of the period, with an emphasis on both religion and social responsibility.

Finally, following the war, the country's rail networks were slowly combined to provide an effective way of transporting the nation's agricultural output. The Union Stockyards in Chicago became the terminus for beef cattle and other livestock and produce shipped from the West and Southwest to eastern markets. All major rail lines in the United States connected with this center at Chicago and by the next decade, the nation would be joined by a coast-to-coast railroad system.

CHRONICLE OF EVENTS

1865:

January 15: Union forces take control of the Cape Fear River in North Carolina as Fort Fisher falls. This action blocks the last rebel port and spells disaster for the Confederacy.

February 3: President Lincoln meets with a Southern peace contingent at Hampton Roads, Virginia.

February 17: A fire in Columbia, South Carolina, nearly levels the city as General Sherman's troops draw closer.

March 3: The Freedmen's Bureau bill is passed by Congress to protect the civil rights of former slaves. Existence of the bureau is authorized for 12 months after the end of the Civil War.

March 4: President Abraham Lincoln is inaugurated for his second term of office.

April 2: Richmond, Virginia, is evacuated and Confederate President Jefferson Davis removes the rebel government to Danville, Virginia. Union troops enter Richmond the next day.

April 9: At Appomattox Courthouse, General Lee surrenders to General Grant.

April 14: President Lincoln is shot while attending the theater in Washington, D.C.

April 15: President Lincoln dies of gunshot wounds at age 56. Vice President Andrew Johnson is sworn in as the nation's 17th president.

New York theaters are closed for over a week in observance of President Lincoln's death.

April 26: In Vicksburg, Mississippi, Confederate Memorial Day is celebrated for the first time.

April 27: The Mississippi River is the site of a steamboat explosion. The *Sultana's* boilers explode, killing 1,547 people, the majority of whom are Union soldiers released from Confederate prisons.

April 29: By an executive order signed by President Johnson, commercial restrictions are lifted in the South. Texas is not included in this decree.

May 2: New York City forms the nation's first paid fire department.

May 5: In North Bend, Ohio, a railroad train is held up for the first time.

May 9: President Johnson recognizes the government of the state of Virginia.

May 10: Former Confederate President Jefferson Davis is captured by Union troops at Irwinville, Georgia.

May 29: Building on a plan issued in 1863 by former President Lincoln, President Andrew Johnson issues a Reconstruction agenda in which he outlines conditions for granting amnesty to Southerners. He appoints William W. Holden as provisional governor of the former Confederate state of North Carolina.

June 19: Texas announces that all slaves in this military district are now free.

July 21: Poet James Russell Lowell addresses Harvard College graduates and commemorates slain President Lincoln.

August 14: Mississippi votes to prohibit slavery in the state.

November 9: North Carolina votes to prohibit slavery in the state.

December 2: By ratifying an anti-slavery amendment to the U.S. Constitution, Alabama becomes the 27th state to approve the measure, ensuring its adoption by two-thirds of the states in the Union.

December 4: President Johnson appoints the Joint Committee on Reconstruction.

December 18: The Thirteenth Amendment to the U.S. Constitution is adopted. It abolishes slavery in all states and empowers Congress to enforce the constitutional article with appropriate legislation.

December 24: The Ku Klux Klan is founded in Pulaski, Tennessee.

December 25: Chicago's Union Stockyards open.

1866:

January 1: As part of the Black Codes in force during the period known as Radical Reconstruction, all persons in Mississippi who are not employed are to be charged with vagrancy and fined $50.

February 12: In Washington, D.C., the first commemoration of President Lincoln's birthday is held.

February 19: An act of Congress increases the power and expands the tenure of the Bureau of Refugees, Freedmen and Abandoned Lands. The Freedmen's Bureau, as it has been known, is to be given more extensive powers to protect the civil rights of blacks in the South. President Andrew Johnson vetoes the bill. He reasons that it is unconstitutional to give the federal government legal jurisdiction in states that have no representation in Congress.

February 22: In Washington, D.C., a group of politicians demonstrates support for President Johnson's February 19th veto. During a speech, the president exhibits behavior considered outrageous by some, calling his congressional opponents traitors. This incident causes the president to lose face among the general public.

March 2: The Joint Committee on Reconstruction passes a resolution stating that former Confederate states may not be admitted to Congress except by the express authority of that body.

April: As credit grows scarce and deflation increases, Congress passes a law to speed repayment of the nation's war debt.

April 1: The U.S. Telegraph Company is taken over by Western Union, forming a huge company providing communications services to the entire nation.

April 2: By presidential declaration, the Civil War is ended in the Confederate states of Alabama, Arkansas, Florida, Georgia, Louisiana, Mississippi, North Carolina, South Carolina, Tennessee and Virginia.

April 10: After minimal debate in Congress, the Civil Rights Act is passed, granting full citizenship to all persons born in the United States, regardless of race or color. President Johnson does not support this constitutional amend-

ment and vetoes it, only to be overridden by Congress, which passes the bill by a two-thirds majority on June 13. Most observers feel the debate and disagreement over this issue to be a critical negative turning point in President Johnson's on-going struggle for executive power.

In New York City, the American Society for the Prevention of Cruelty to Animals is founded.

August 20: The National Labor Congress meets for the first time, in Baltimore, Maryland.

August 29: The Mount Washington Cog Railroad, in New Hampshire, is opened for public inspection. The steepest of its type, the railway is not completed for another three years.

October 3: A steamer, the *Evening Star*, is lost at sea during a voyage from New York to New Orleans, Louisiana. The death toll is 250 lives.

1867:

January 8: In the nation's capital, black citizens are given the right to vote.

January 23: In New York City, the East River freezes over.

February 14: In Hartford, Connecticut, the first

General Ulysses S. Grant. Courtesy of the Library of Congress.

boiler insurance company issues a policy.

February 25: Congress gives approval for a survey in Panama in order to make possible the construction of a canal connecting the Atlantic and Pacific oceans.

March 1: Nebraska is admitted to the Union as the 37th state.

March 2: Over the president's veto, Congress passes the first Reconstruction Act, which divides former Confederate states (which already have had provisional governments established) into five military districts in order to ensure more efficient governing of these areas. These districts are to be under the jurisdiction of the General of the Armies Ulysses S. Grant, not the president of the United States.

Congress passes the Tenure of Office Act. Among other things, this legislation prohibits the president from dismissing any members of his cabinet without prior Senate approval.

The U.S. Department of Education is authorized.

President Andrew Johnson. Courtesy of the Library of Congress.

African-American male voters during Reconstruction in the South. Courtesy of the Library of Congress.

Howard Theological Seminary is founded at the nation's capital. It is later known as Howard University.

March 7: The Congress forms a committee to look into President Johnson's possible impeachment for "high crimes and misdemeanors." Johnson will be found in violation of the Tenure of Office Act for dismissing Secretary of War William Stanton.

Shoemakers in the U.S. form the Order of the Knights of St. Crispin in order to provide for wage stability.

March 15: In Michigan, the first state university in the nation is authorized to be supported by direct property taxes.

March 21: The New York Philatelic Society is organized in New York City.

March 23: Congress passes the second Reconstruction Act. It is a supplement to the legislation passed on March 2 and outlines specific details governing states' readmission to the Union. President Johnson once more vetoes this bill.

The Patrons of Husbandry, or the "Grange." Courtesy of the Library of Congress.

The first state forestry inquiry commission is established in Wisconsin.

March 25: In Chicago, Illinois, the first water supply conduit constructed for city use begins operation.

March 30: The United States purchases the Alaska territory from Russia for two cents per acre. The total cost is $7.2 million. Secretary of State Seward is responsible for the negotiations, which are carried out with great secrecy.

April 9: The Senate ratifies a treaty with Russia concerning purchase of the Alaska territory.

April 12: The United States Plate Glass Insurance Company is incorporated in Philadelphia, Pennsylvania.

April 23: W. E. Lincoln, of Providence, Rhode Island, patents the nation's first animated film machine, called the Zoetrope.

June 15: The nation's first gallstone operation is performed at Indianapolis, Indiana.

July 2: The first elevated railroad opens in New York City.

July 16: In Newburg, Ohio, the first ready-mixed paint is patented.

July 17: The Harvard School of Dental Medicine is founded by Harvard University at Cambridge, Massachusetts.

July 19: Over another presidential veto, the third Reconstruction Act is passed by Congress.

August 20: The first cartridge belt is patented by Anson Mills.

August 27: The first railroad crossing gate is patented at Boston, Massachusetts.

August 28: The United States annexes the Midway Islands in the Pacific. This is the nation's first noncontiguous acquisition of territory.

October 9: The Alaska territory becomes a U.S. possession.

October 18: Transfer of the Alaska Territory, known as Seward's Folly, occurs.

October 25: Maimonides College opens in Philadelphia, Pennsylvania. It is the first rabbinical school in the nation.

November 2: Harper's Bazaar is published in New York City under the editorship of M.L. Booth. It is the nation's first fashion weekly.

December 2: Charles Dickens gives a reading in New York City for which people stood in a mile-long line to purchase tickets.

December 4: The Patrons of Husbandry, a secret agricultural society, is founded by Oliver Hudson Kelley. Soon known as the Granger movement, it becomes a strident and powerful voice in support of farmers' interests throughout the nation.

December 29: The nation's first telegraph ticker is installed by a New York brokerage house.

EYEWITNESS TESTIMONY

Go to your homes and resume your occupations. Obey the laws and become as good citizens as you were soldiers.

General Robert E. Lee, to his former troops following the surrender at Appomattox, Virginia, April 9, 1865, in Schlesinger's Almanac of American History *(1983).*

Sic semper tyrannus! [Thus be it ever to tyrants!]

John Wilkes Booth, to the audience, after shooting President Lincoln at Washington's Ford Theater, April 14, 1865, in Schlesinger's Almanac of American History *(1983).*

I suppose you have learned even in the more secluded portions of the country that slavery is entirely abolished—a most unprecedented robbery, and most unwise policy. So it must appear even to the ignorant. I know it is only intended for a greater humiliation and loss to *us*, but I should think that even the powerful and unconscious conqueror would reap the ill effects of so unguarded a movement.

Eva B. Jones of Augusta, Georgia, to her mother in Atlanta, letter of 1865, in Myers's The Children of Pride *(1972).*

I am in distress and perplexity, and write to ask your help. The authorities here promised me transportation for the freedmen who wish to go from this to Savannah. Now, on the eve of leaving, they inform us that it can only be obtained through the bureau in Augusta. Will you be kind enough to obtain from General Tilson the necessary papers for me? These people are really in distressing circumstances. They are without means, and wish to return home where they can obtain an honest livelihood.

Mary Jones, of Atlanta, Georgia, to her daughter-in-law, letter of 1865, in Myers's Children of Pride *(1972).*

I am in favor of elevating the negro to the extent of his capacity and intelligence, and of our doing everything in our power to advance the race morally and mentally as well as physically, also socially. But I am opposed to making this advance by correspondingly debasing any portion of the white race.

General George Armstrong Custer, to a friend, letter of 1865, in Slotkin's The Fatal Environment *(1985).*

General Robert E. Lee. Courtesy of the Library of Congress.

I am sorry to say that I do not feel myself capable of being a landscape gardener—properly speaking—but I have a better and more cultivated taste in that department of art than any other . . .

. . . I can do anything with proper assistants, or money enough—anything that any man can do.

. . . I dont [*sic*] feel strong on the art side. I dont feel myself an artist, I feel rather as if it was sacrilegious in me to post myself in the portals of art.

Frederick Law Olmsted, architect and landscape planner, to a friend, letter of 1865, in Zaitzevsky's Frederick Law Olmsted and the Boston Park System *(1982).*

If America is ever ruined, the Methodist Church will be to blame. For she is the strongest and most influential Church on the continent of America today.

Joseph Cook, Boston minister, decrying the evangelical nature of the Methodists, 1865, in Ahlstrom's A Religious History of the American People *(1972).*

Young men, this duty [of supporting Radical principles] devolves to you. Would to God, if only for that, that I were still in the prime of life, that I might

Republican Thaddeus Stevens. Courtesy of the Library of Congress.

aid you to fight through this last and greatest battle of Freedom.

. . . The whole fabric of southern society *must* be changed, and never can it be done if this opportunity is lost . . . How can republican institutions, free schools, free churches, free social intercourse exist in a mingled community of nabobs and serfs; of the owners of twenty-thousand acre manors with lordly palaces, and the occupants of narrow huts inhabited by "low white trash"? If the south is ever to be made a safe republic let her land be cultivated by the toil of the owners or the free labor of intelligent citizens. This must be done even though it drive her nobility into exile!

Representative and Radical Republican leader Thaddeus Stevens (R-Pennsylvania), in a speech at Lancaster, Pennsylvania, September 7, 1865, in Josephson's The Politicos 1865–1893 *(1963).*

. . . seventy years of government, during which many and fierce conflicts over the rights of federal and state governments, and of resistance by large masses of men to the authority of the former, show that all these differences may be adjusted without resort to arms. Nay further they convince me, after looking at the tariff agitation, and its result, nullification, that no question of less force and power than the slavery question ever could have produced armed rebellion against federal authority, of any serious extent.

Supreme Court Justice Samuel Freeman Miller, to a friend, letter of 1865, in Fairman's Mr. Justice Miller and the Supreme Court *(1939).*

In commenting a few weeks ago upon the course which the South is pursuing, we spoke of it as "a display of consummate political ability" and so we still consider it. At no time in its history have its leading men given stronger proofs of proficiency in the political art than during the last six months. A stupid, inexperienced, or clumsy-minded people would, after such a conflict as they have just gone through, have done what their admirers in England expected them to do—kept up an irregular warfare, or displayed their passion and mortification in sullen, passive resistance to Federal authority. But Lee had hardly laid down his arms when their leaders seemed to take the whole situation in at a glance, and decide upon their course with that swiftness, precision, and unanimity which won them so many Congressional victories in by-gone days, and are, in our opinion, destined to win them many more. Northern fury was at once disarmed by loud protestations of submission and resignation. No pride, or sentiment, was allowed for one moment to stand in the way of any declarations which appeared to be necessary to appease the conqueror. And what has been more remarkable—and it furnishes a striking illustration of the extraordinary political discipline which is still maintained amongst the Southern population—whatever the leading men of each State decided upon was unhesitatingly supported by the whole people, without any preliminary agitation or discussion, without even meetings or newspapers.

E.L. Godkin, editor of The Nation, *in the October 26, 1865, issue of that magazine.*

They are self-sustaining, capable of selecting their own employment and their own places of abode, of insisting for themselves on a proper remuneration, and of establishing and maintaining their own asylums and schools.

President Andrew Johnson, in a public statement concerning his unwillingness to back the aims of the Freedmen's Bureau due to its implied federal powers over the South, 1866, in Kelley's The Shaping of the American Past *(1978).*

Every unregenerate rebel lately in arms against his government calls himself a Democrat.

Every bounty jumper, every deserter, every sneak who ran away from the draft calls himself a Democrat. Bowles, Milligan, Walker, Dodd, Horsey and Humphreys call themselves Democrats. Every "Son of Liberty" who conspired to murder, burn, rob arsenals and release rebel prisoners calls himself a Democrat.

. . . In short, the Democratic party may be described as a common sewer and loathsome receptacle, into which is emptied every element of treason North and South, and every element of inhumanity and barbarism which has dishonored the age.
Republican Governor Oliver P. Morton of Indiana, in his "Bloody Shirt" speech at Indianapolis, Indiana, June 1866, in Johannsen's Reconstruction *(1970).*

The laws proposed by Mississippi, Alabama, South Carolina, etc. do but change the form of slavery. As it *was*, the individual slave belonged to, and laboured for the individual white man. As it is *proposed to be*, the whole body of the negro race in each state, must belong to and labour for the whole body of the white people of that state, under compulsion of law.
Supreme Court Justice Samuel Freeman Miller, on Radical Reconstruction, 1866, in Fairman's Mr. Justice Miller *(1939).*

It seems to me that it ought to be an easy thing for the better elements of society to associate together and rescue politics from the degradation which in our large cities is becoming such an open scandal.
Henry C. Lea, scholar and publisher, of Philadelphia, Pennsylvania, to Charles Eliot Norton, letter of 1866, in Morgan's The Gilded Age *(1970).*

The people . . . demand such a reconstruction as shall put an end to the present anarchical state of things in the late rebellious States,—where frightful murders and wholesale massacres are perpetrated in the very presence of Federal soldiers. This horrible business they require shall cease. They want a reconstruction as will protect loyal men, black and white, in their persons and property; such a one as will cause Northern industry, Northern capital, and Northern civilization to flow into the South, and make a man from New England as much at home in North Carolina as elsewhere in the Republic. No Chinese wall can now be tolerated. The South must be opened to the light of law and liberty, and this

session of Congress is relied upon to accomplish this important work.
Frederick Douglass, former slave, speaking in December 1866, in Johannsen's Reconstruction *(1970).*

Most of the members of the Cabinet acquiesced or submitted to the usurpation. No appointments or nominations to office made by the Executive . . . were confirmed by the Senate, except the nominees first recommended or indorsed [sic] by Radical members of Congress. Some of the Cabinet under these circumstances surrendered and made terms.
Gideon Welles, secretary of the Navy, in his personal journal, commenting on the power that the Republican Party had over President Johnson, 1866, in Josephson's The Politicos *(1963).*

. . . I could easily convince any man, who does not allow his prejudices to stand in the way of his interests, that it will probably make a difference of at least $1,000,000,000 in the development of a national debt, whether we reconstruct on the basis of loyal white and black votes, or on white votes exclusively, and that he can better afford to give the Government at least one-quarter of his estate than have it try the latter experiment.
Elizur Wright, inventor and manufacturer, letter to the Boston Daily Advertiser, 1866, in Davis and Woodman's Conflict or Consensus *(1963).*

I have changed my ideas respecting tariffs and protection very much since I came to Washington and am coming over to the ground you occupy. I am utterly disgusted with the rapacity and selfishness which I have seen displayed by Pennsylvania people and some from other sections on this subject.

I get so despondent at times in view of the manner in which legislation is conducted, that I feel as though it was no use, and that I had better retire.
Economist David A. Wells, to fellow economist Edward Atkinson, letters of 1866 and 1867, in Degler's The Age of the Economic Revolution 1876–1900 *(1977).*

Demagogues who hope to rule the country by the passions war had engendered don't want a finality. The return to questions of economy and finance would expose their ignorance too soon.

Men's minds become familiar with revolutionary thoughts when they do not see established laws regulating every part of their concerns.

*Jacob D. Cox, Ohio politician, to future U.S.
President James Garfield, criticizing supporters
of Radical Reconstruction, 1866, in Degler's*
Economic Revolution *(1977).*

. . . went by invitation to the Broker's Board . . .
a full session, and much excitement. I had scarcely
taken my seat when a member unknown to me rose
and stated that they had present "one of the bravest
and most gallant generals of the War," and pro-
ceeded to compliment your boy, by proposing three
cheers for Major-General Custer.

*General George A. Custer, to his wife, letter of
1866, in Slotkin's* Fatal Environment *(1985).*

The people of the North honestly love the Constitution, but the leaders there hate it and intend to
destroy it, and the convulsion through which we
have passed has thrown the opportunity of making
the effort into their hands, and the present military
bills, and the one which is not yet promulgated as
law, are the means adopted to accomplish their design. These bills are proposed for our acceptance.
There is a remarkable feature in these measures, that
while force is employed to execute them, they are
yet nominally submitted to us for our acceptance or
rejection.

I object to the whole scheme, because it is unconstitutional. A distinguished man—pardon me, I ought
to say a notorious individual—said to me a few days
ago, that I ought not to waste time to prove the
unconstitutionality of these measures—a thing which
every man, woman, and child in the country knew—
and yet he was for accepting! He spoke truthfully.
That tottering, gray-haired candidate in Pennsylvania
for perpetual infamy [Thaddeus Stevens (1792–1868)]
who is building for himself a monument of malignity
that will overtop the pyramids of Egypt, said the
Constitution had nothing to do with it. I shall never
get done shuddering and horrors will never cease to
rise up in my mind, when I see men taking an oath
to support the Constitution, and then legislating to
put in force measures which are outside of it.

*Benjamin H. Hill, a member of the Confederate
States Senate, and later U.S. Representative
(1875) and Senator (1877), from Georgia,
speaking in Atlanta, Georgia, July 16, 1867, in
Johannsen's* Reconstruction *(1970).*

. . . we have been wading knee deep in words,
words, words, for a whole week, and we are but
little more than half way across the turbid stream.

*Representative James A. Garfield (R-Ohio), re-
marking on lengthy impeachment proceedings
against President Johnson, 1867, in Josephson's*
The Politicos *(1963).*

What bad news, sad news tonight. Pennsylvania
and Ohio gone Democratic and the sad lessons of
the war all forgotten. Well, God reigneth. His will
and purposes will all be made known and enforced
in good time.

*Jay Cooke, financier and Republican Party sup-
porter, commenting on the returns during the
off-year elections, 1867, in Josephson's* The
Politicos *(1963.)*

I very much regret that the organization in the
interest of the banks of which you spoke to me a
year ago has not been quietly effected ready for
action. The banks need to bestir themselves to avoid
hostile legislation and yet any organization effected
now would . . . perhaps do more harm than good.
This universal suffrage country will never see the
end of attempts of demagogues to excite the poor
against the rich, labor against capital, and all who
haven't money against the banks who have it.

*William E. Chandler, assistant secretary of the
Treasury, to Republican financier Jay Cooke,
letter of December 1867, in Josephson's* The
Politicos *(1963):*

Tell Gen'l Grant from me that we'll all look to him
to save to the country the legitimate results & fruits
of the War.

*Jay Cooke, Republican financier, to his brother
Henry, letter of 1867, in Josephson's* The Politicos *(1963.)*

After looking carefully over the field I know of but
one man that in my humble judgement can beat this
repudiation platform and that man is General Grant
. . . If we run Grant, we can generally count upon
the soldiers' vote—they will vote for him to glorify
themselves—feeling that to place him in the Presidential office will be an additional recognition of their
own services . . . that is to say, they will prefer glory
to repudiation. But with Chase or any of that school
of politicians we will certainly be beaten . . . The
people are uneasy . . . and inclined to try a change.

Supreme Court Associate Justice Samuel Freeman Miller. Courtesy of the Library of Congress.

M.P. Brouns to Elihu B. Washburne, December 1867, in Josephson's The Politicos *(1963.)*

Mr. Boutwell who is perhaps the ablest member of the Judiciary Committee, declared last summer that the President must be removed, because what the radical majority wants to do cannot be accomplished while he remains. Now in all this I understand you to concur, and to be impatient at the delay of your representatives, in Congress, in putting it into execution.

Samuel Freeman Miller, Supreme Court associate justice, to supporters of President Johnson's impeachment, 1867, in Fairman's Mr. Justice Miller *(1939).*

The condition of the civil service of the United States is deplorable. Even in the early days of the Republic, although great care was taken to select for office only men of respectable character and qualifications, the need of a system of competitive examination was felt. But no such system was established, and, as far as the holders of office were concerned, a change for the worse took place in proportion to their increasing numbers and the vast increase of public business consequent to the rapid strides of our progress. Nothing was done to adapt the civil service to the exigencies of the new times.

Mr. Jenckes's bill deserves the warmest support, as much for the improvements which it actually proposes to enact by the introduction of open competitive examinations in the subordinate branches of the home civil service, and by the abolition of the system of irresponsibility and patronage, as for the way in which it prepares for the adoption of reforms in the foreign services and in all other administrative branches of the government.

Julius Bing, aide to Congressman Thomas A. Jenckes, 1867, in Hoogenboom and Hoogenboom's The Gilded Age *(1967).*

2. Economic Opportunity and Trade Unionism: 1868–1870

THE HISTORICAL CONTEXT

As the end of the decade drew near, the nation sought consensus. It hoped to achieve this by electing another Republican president, Ulysses S. Grant. By so doing, it was also assumed that a quick end would be made to the uncomfortable division between the Congress and the executive branches. This divisiveness had been fueled by bitter enmity between President Johnson and Radical Republicans in Congress right from the start of his term.

National growth flourished, however, and took many forms. Additional agricultural colleges were founded under the terms of the Morrill Act, and several influential newspapers were established—notably the *Atlanta Constitution* and the *Louisville Courier-Journal*. *Scribner's Monthly*, a new literary magazine, was founded in 1870.

Urban growth and development thrived, symbolized, perhaps, by the nation's first office building with an elevator, constructed in New York City in 1868. But as cities grew in size, problems in municipal government increased. Political party bosses established elaborate networks of support among their constituents and then coerced them into voting the party ticket. While some of these leaders were honest, many grew corrupt as their influence widened. New York City's William Marcy "Boss" Tweed was one of many whose villainy was concealed initially by his generosity and apparent competence. He was praised by news editors for his largess, particularly among the immigrant population. But by the mid-1870s, Tweed's double-dealings transformed positive publicity into lurid headlines exposing his dishonesty.

By 1870, Congress convened with a full complement of states represented for the first time in 10 years. Readmission to the Union of all former Confederate territory had been duly accomplished under the terms of Reconstruction legislation. And in one of his last official acts, on Christmas Day 1868, President Johnson declared a general amnesty for all who had fought against the Union.

With charges of treason against former Confederate President Jefferson Davis dropped, Johnson sought to heal the injuries the nation had suffered during the Civil War. In doing so, however, he brought down around his own shoulders the wrath of Radical Republicans in Congress whose goal was to, literally, "reconstruct" life in former Confederate states. The unwillingness that President Johnson displayed, most obviously by vetoing radical legislation, rendered Johnson politically ineffective. It also led to his own near-impeachment by angry Radical Republicans who controlled Congress.

The relative ease of peacetime permitted Americans to develop and indulge a passion for sports and from 1868 through 1870, professional sports gained a wider following. Baseball's popularity skyrocketed; it would come to be the nation's favorite sport. The Cincinnati Redstockings were the first team to don official uniforms and they began the first professional baseball tour in the U.S. in 1869. A year later, pitcher Fred Goldsmith first demonstrated the curve ball in Brooklyn, New York.

The New York Athletic Club held its first indoor track meet and the first intercollegiate football game was held in New Jersey. An American defeated a British boxer in the first international bare-knuckles tournament at St. Louis, Missouri, and the world heavyweight boxing championship was held at Kennersville, Louisiana.

This emphasis on leisure pastimes was counterbalanced by an upsurge in inventiveness and entrepreneurial spirit. In 1868, the first refrigerated railroad car was patented. Railroad air brakes were patented by George Westinghouse and a year later the vacuum cleaner was patented in Chicago. The process of making celluloid—which would be used in a range of products from men's shirt collars to explosives—was patented in 1870. That same year John D. Rockefeller incorporated Standard Oil of Ohio, forerunner of the one of the nation's earliest monopolies. These and other inventions and manufacturing efforts would put U.S. production ahead of any other industrialized nation by the end of the century.

Taking advantage of the spirit of the time which encouraged risk-taking, women sought an expanded role in the nation's political life. Some worked quite publicly to advance the cause of equality; in New England, the first Woman's Club was organized by Carolina Severance. In 1869, Elizabeth Cady Stanton was elected president of the National Woman Suffrage Association, and in January of that year the American Equal Rights Association met in Washington, D.C. In both the Utah and Wyoming territories in 1870, women were granted voting rights. Earlier, in 1869, the nation's first woman lawyer was admit-

Elizabeth Cady Stanton, president of the National Woman Suffrage Association. Courtesy of the Library of Congress.

ted to the bar in Iowa. On Wall Street, two of the more notorious women of the period—the sisters Victoria and Tennessee Woodhull— became the first women to open a brokerage house. They had full financial support in this venture from Cornelius Vanderbilt.

Perhaps the most notable national achievements during these years was the completion, in 1869, of the country's first transcontinental railroad. At Promontory Point, Utah, the Central Pacific and the Union Pacific railroads connected there, joined by a golden spike.

Construction of the Union Pacific Railroad, which would be part of the nation's first transcontinental railroad system. Courtesy of the Library of Congress.

The sleeping car. Courtesy of the New York Public Library Picture Collection.

Unification of U.S. rail systems meant continued expansion—and economic prosperity—for cities and towns all along the route. Without access to coast-to-coast rail shipping, the greatly accelerated growth in the country's western regions would have been less likely. This growth helped spur the organization of groups such as the Union of Railway Conductors, founded in 1868 by railroad workers seeking some control over their labor conditions. Technologically, railroads advanced so that they could travel faster and more quickly and safely.

The nation's fledgling railroad system speeded up western settlement and agricultural growth of areas west of the Mississippi. Railroads provided opportunities to ship livestock and produce and to carry supplies and items otherwise unavailable on the frontier. In fact, so complete and thorough was this western expansion that, by the end of the century, no less an authority than historian Frederick Jackson Turner declared that the American frontier was "closed."

CHRONICLE OF EVENTS

1868:

January 14: The nation's first African-American lieutenant governor is nominated in the state of Louisiana.

January 16: A patent is granted to Detroit fish market owner William Davis, for the first refrigerated railroad car, which Davis manufactures in 1869.

January 19: The first stamp collectors' organization adopts its constitution as the New York Philatelic Society.

February 4: Congress passes an act that forbids cancellation of greenbacks and delays the federal debt-funding program.

February 16: The Benevolent Protective Order of Elks is founded in New York City.

February 24: Acting on behalf of Congress, Thaddeus Stevens charges President Andrew Johnson with violating the Tenure of Office Act because of his actions concerning Edwin Stanton. These are the first impeachment proceedings ever to begin against a U.S. president.

February 24: In Mobile, Alabama, the first parade to feature float tableaux is held.

March 1: The American Journal of Philately is published for the first time by the New York Philatelic Society.

March 5: The impeachment trial of President Johnson begins.

March 11: The fourth Reconstruction Act passes Congress, despite President Johnson's veto.

March 16: In casting the deciding vote of the Johnson impeachment trial, Senator Edmund G. Ross (R-Kansas) states "not guilty." With this, Congress fails to obtain the two-thirds majority it needs to impeach the president.

March 17: The first machine to cancel postage on letters is patented.

May: The American Journal of Obstetrics, the first such professional publication devoted to diseases of women and children, is published in New York City.

The impeachment trial of President Andrew Johnson. Courtesy of the Library of Congress.

May 20: The Republican party's national convention opens in Chicago, Illinois. Ulysses S. Grant wins the nomination for president on the first ballot, with Schuyler Colfax as his vice-presidential running mate.

May 28: The impeachment trial of President Andrew Johnson formally comes to an end without his removal from office.

May 30: Decoration Day is celebrated throughout the nation for the first time.

June 1: Former President James Buchanan dies.

June 23: A workable typewriter is patented by C. L. Sholes.

June 25: Congress enacts a law providing for an eight-hour workday for government employees.

July: The nation's first cattle club, for owners of Jersey cattle, is formed in Newport, Rhode Island.

July 4: In New York City, the Democrats hold the opening of their national convention. Hor-

Workers strike in support of an eight-hour workday. Courtesy of the Library of Congress.

atio Seymour is nominated as president, with Francis P. Blair as the vice-presidential nominee.

July 14: The first tape measure is patented by A. J. Fellows at New Haven, Connecticut.

July 20: Congress passes legislation that imposes a cigarette tax.

July 25: The Wyoming Territory is created by an act of Congress.

July 28: The Fourteenth Amendment is ratified. It guarantees equal rights for all citizens in any state.

August: In Pittsburgh, Pennsylvania, the nation's first commercial high school is established.

September: In Georgia, African-Americans are expelled from the state legislature, which causes martial law to be re-established there. Georgia must now ratify the Fourteenth

Amendment prior to its readmission to Congress.

September 8: The New York Athletic Club is organized.

October 6: A process for nickel plating is patented by W.H. Remington of Boston, Massachusetts.

October 7: At Cornell University in Ithaca, New York, the nation's first veterinary department offers courses.

October 21: In San Francisco, California, a strong earthquake causes over $3 million in property damage.

October 31: The U.S. Postal Service authorizes that uniforms be issued to postal letter carriers.

November 3: With an electoral college vote of 214–80, Republicans win the election, sending Ulysses S. Grant to the White House.

November 11: The New York Athletic Club

Ulysses S. Grant, elected U.S. president in 1868.

holds the first indoor amateur track and field meet.

November 13: The American Philological Society is organized in New York City.

November 14: In Manhattan, Kansas, the first farmer's institute sponsored by a college is held.

December 3: At the federal circuit court in Richmond, Virginia, former Confederate President Jefferson Davis is brought to trial on charges of treason.

December 5: As an outgrowth of the new cycling craze sweeping the nation, the first bicycle school is opened in New York City.

December 25: President Andrew Johnson declares a general amnesty for all those who had fought against the Union in the Civil War.

1869:

January 19: The American Equal Rights Association meets in the nation's capital.

January 23: The first bureau of labor is established, in Massachusetts.

February 6: A whiskered cartoon drawing of Uncle Sam appears in *Harper's Weekly*. This figure becomes widely employed by satirists who see the character as synonymous with national interests and ambitions.

February 15: After President Johnson's announcement of a general amnesty, the treason charges against former rebel leader Jefferson Davis are dropped.

The University of Nebraska is chartered; classes will open in 1871.

March 4: The nation's 18th president, Ulysses S. Grant, is inaugurated.

March 15: The Cincinnati Red Stockings become the nation's first professional baseball team as they begin an eight-month national tour.

April 10: The states of Georgia, Mississippi, Texas and Virginia ratify the Fifteenth Amendment, which requires voting rights for all, regardless of race, color or previous condition of servitude.

May 10: The nation's first transcontinental railroad is completed as the Central Pacific and the Union Pacific lines are connected at Promontory Point, Utah.

May 15: The National Woman Suffrage Association is established, with Elizabeth Cady Stanton as its president.

June 8: A patent is awarded to a Chicago inventor for the first suction-principle vacuum cleaner.

June 15: Mike McCoole wins the first international bare knuckles boxing championship, defeating British boxer Tom Allen, in St. Louis, Missouri.

September 6: In Avondale, Pennsylvania, 108 coal miners are suffocated in a mine collapse.

September 12: The Prohibition party is formed

The completion of the transcontinental railroad at Promontory, Utah, May 10, 1869. Courtesy of the Library of Congress.

in Chicago, Illinois, at the National Temperance Convention.

September 24: After President Grant belatedly approves the release of $4 million in federal gold reserves, the price of gold plummets. This situation contrasts sharply with a previous frenzy of gold purchasing among small and large investors, and many are left bankrupt as a result of "Black Friday" conditions.

October 8: Former President Franklin Pierce dies.

November 6: In New Brunswick, New Jersey, the first intercollegiate football game is played between Rutgers and Princeton. The final score is 6–4.

November 27: The case *Hepburn v. Griswold* is brought before the U.S. Supreme Court. A decision in the case will determine the legality of

paper money issued by a government in lieu of hard currency.

December 6: The Colored National Labor Convention meets in Washington, D.C.

December 10: The Wyoming Territory grants voting rights to women.

December 28: The Noble Order of the Knights of Labor is founded in Philadelphia, Pennsylvania, by Uriah S. Stephens. The secret organization is originally established by garment-cutters.

1870:

January 2: Construction starts on the Brooklyn Bridge in New York City.

January 4: The nation's telegraph operators go on strike.

Beginning construction of New York City's Brooklyn Bridge. Courtesy of Smithsonian Institution, Photo Number 48618.

January 6: The Knights of Labor meets again to elect its first officers.

January 10: In Cleveland, John D. Rockefeller incorporates the Standard Oil Company of Ohio. This later will become the Standard Oil Trust, a virtual monopoly of the oil-refining industry.

January 15: Harper's Weekly uses a donkey to symbolize the Democratic party.

January 26: Virginia is readmitted to the Union.

February 7: With reference to the Legal Tender Act, the U.S. Supreme Court, in *Hepburn v. Griswold,* declares that debts incurred before 1862 and 1863 (when provisions of the act were adopted) are not redeemable by the federal treasury in paper currency.

February 9: Congress establishes the National Weather Bureau, which in 1891 becomes part of the Department of Agriculture and subsequently, in 1940, the Commerce Department.

February 12: The Utah Territory grants full suffrage to women.

February 23: Mississippi is readmitted to the Union.

February 25: Having been appointed to the vacant Senate seat of Jefferson Davis, Hiram R.

Revels of Mississippi becomes the first African-American to sit in the U.S. Congress.

March 30: The Fifteenth Amendment is ratified and protects the right to vote, despite race, color or previous condition of servitude.

April 27: The floor of the state supreme courtroom in Richmond, Virginia, collapses, killing 61 and injuring over 100.

May 10: Tom Allen fights Englishman Jem Mace for the world heavyweight boxing championship at Kennersville, Louisiana.

June 22: Congress passes a bill that creates the Justice Department, under the direction of the attorney general of the United States. The Justice Department will have jurisdiction over the Federal Bureau of Investigation as well.

June 30: A tie vote in Congress disapproves a treaty of annexation with the Dominican Republic submitted to Congress by President Grant.

July 8: The U.S. Senate signs a joint treaty with Great Britain to stop the sale of African slaves.

Oil magnate John D. Rockefeller Sr. Courtesy of the Library of Congress.

July 12: The process for producing celluloid is patented by the Hyatt brothers of Albany, New York.

July 14: Congress enacts the Internal Revenue and Tariff Act, protecting industrial production by sustaining high tariffs on imported goods.

July 15: Georgia is readmitted to the Union.

August 1: Women in the Utah Territory vote for the first time.

August 14: Admiral David G. Farragut dies at Portsmouth, New Hampshire.

August 16: Pitcher Fred Goldsmith demonstrates the curve ball in Brooklyn, New York.

October 3: Secretary of the Interior Jacob D. Cox resigns under pressure from industrial interests that seek freer access to the country's extensive natural resources.

October 4: Benjamin H. Bristow is appointed the first solicitor general of the U.S.

October 8: A young woman schoolteacher in Canton, Massachusetts, Miss Etta Barstow, is stoned to death by unruly students.

October 12: General Robert E. Lee, the former commander in chief of the Confederate army, dies in Lexington, Virginia.

December 5: At the convening of Congress, each state is represented for the first time since 1860.

December 5: Governor William Woods Holden of North Carolina is impeached by the state legislature there and replaced by Governor Tod R. Caldwell.

December 16: In Jackson, Tennessee, the Colored Methodist Episcopal Church is founded.

EYEWITNESS TESTIMONY

. . . [the Republican party] totally abandoned all relations to the white race of the ten states. It resolved to make the black race the governing power in those states, and by means of them to bring into Congress twenty senators and fifty representatives—practically appointed by itself in Washington.

Samuel J. Tilden, chair of the New York State Democratic party, 1868, in Kelly's The Shaping of the American Past *(1978).*

Like all parties that have an undisturbed power for a long time, it has become corrupt, and I believe it is today the most corrupt and debauched political party that has ever existed.

Senator James Grimes (R-Iowa), concerning the Republican party, 1868, in Cashman's America in the Gilded Age *(1984).*

You in Massachusetts are not in the Union. Butler is the only man who understands his countrymen and even he does not quite represent the dishonesty of our system.

Historian Henry Adams, to E. Atkinson, regarding election of Richard Henry Dana to the U.S. Senate in place of Ben Butler, 1868, in Morgan's The Gilded Age *(1970).*

This whole question of Slavery, so-called, was but one relating to the proper *status* of the African races as an element of a society composed of the Caucasian and African races, and the *status* which was best, not for the one race or the other, but best, upon the whole, for both.

Over these questions, the Federal Government had no rightful control whatever. They were expressly excluded, in the Compact of Union, from its jurisdiction or authority. Any such assumed control was a palpable violation of the Compact, which released all the parties to the Compact, affected by such action, from their obligation under the Compact. On this point there can be no shadow of a doubt.

Alexander H. Stephens, former vice president of the Confederacy, 1868, in Garraty's Labor and Capital in the Gilded Age *(1968).*

Most of the difficulties between whites and blacks resulted from the inevitable awkwardness of tyros in the mystery of free labor. Many of the planters seemed to be unable to understand that work could be other than a form of slavery, or that it could be accomplished without some prodigious binding and obligating of the hireling to the employer. Contracts which were brought to me for approval contained all sorts of ludicrous provisions . . . The idea seemed to be that if the laborer were not bound body and soul he would be of no use.

William DeForest, concerning his experience working for the Freedmen's Bureau, 1868, in Johannsen's Reconstruction 1865–1877 *(1970).*

Our Indian troubles commenced in 1864 and lasted until the tracks joined at Promontory. We lost most of our men and stock while building from Fort Kearney to Bitter Creek. At that time every mile of road had to be surveyed, graded, tied, and bridged under military protection. The order to every surveying corps, grading, bridging, and tie outfit was never to run when attacked. All were required to be armed, and I do not know that the order was disobeyed in a single instance, nor did I ever hear that the Indians had driven a party permanently from its work . . .

From the beginning to the completion of the road our success depended in great measure on the cordial and active support of the army, especially its commander in chief, General Grant, and the commander of the Military Division of the West, General Sherman.

Grenville M. Dodge, chief engineer of the Union Pacific Railroad, in Senate Document No. 447, 61st Cong. 2d. sess., "How We Built the Union Pacific Railway . . . ," (1910).

To the Indian, destruction is gain.

Herald (Kearney, Nebraska), account of 1868, in Slotkin's The Fatal Environment *(1985).*

Our cause is a common one . . . Go ahead in the good work that you have undertaken, until the most glorious success crowns your efforts . . . monied power is fast eating up the substance of the people. We have made war upon it, and we mean to win it. If we can we will win through the ballot box; if not, we will resort to sterner means. A little bloodletting is sometimes necessary in desperate cases.

William Sylvis, National Labor Union founder, to Karl Marx, 1868, in Dubofsky's Industrialism and the American Worker, 1865–1920 *(1975).*

Railroads encouraged western settlement. Courtesy of the Library of Congress.

. . . five out of six of the great fortunes are made rapidly, by happy hits or bold and ingenious combinations.

E. L. Godkin, in the North American Review, *1868, in DeNovo's* The Gilded Age and After *(1972).*

There is a large class of persons in this country called *middlemen,* who operate in all communities, and who are of no benefit whatever. They are nonproducers, deriving their sustenance from the labor of others, like a parasitic plant . . .

If the producers and consumers could be brought more directly together, so as to save the large profits of the middlemen, it would be greatly for the interests of both, and there would be less reason for bewailing the small profits of the one, and the high prices of products by the other.

George Brackett, about problems facing farmers, 1868, in DeNovo's Gilded Age *(1972).*

Still a hue and cry was raised, through the influence of the Indian ring, in which some good and pious ecclesiastics took part, and became the aiders and abettors of savages who murdered without mercy, men, women and children.

Secretary of War Philip H. Sheridan, in an attempt to persuade against implementation of President Grant's peace policy with the Indians in his annual report, 1869, in Slotkin's Fatal Environment *(1985).*

[The critic's test of a novel is to ask if it] was true to the motives, the impulses, the principles that shape the life of actual men and women.

William Dean Howells, novelist and critic, in Degler's The Age of the Economic Revolution 1876–1900 *(1977).*

Now, in two points at least, it may be said with certainty that the American character differs from the English—in being less brutal, and in being more fond of novelty, of change, of the excitement which novelty and change produce.

A. Sedgewick, in The Nation, *on the differences between American baseball and the British game of cricket, 1869, in Bowman and Zoss's* Diamonds in the Rough *(1989).*

While suppressing so rigorously all offences to the sight and smell, and punishing in general all disturbances of the peace, it would be only consistent to include in the proscription the still greater plague of noise.

Editor of the Cleveland Leader, *on the problem of urban noise pollution, 1870, in Callow's* American Urban History *(1973).*

. . . a member of this Assembly has the privilege to reveal his membership in this organization to those he desires to obtain for members; provided always, however, that he does not reveal the name or names of any other persons who are members of this organization, according to the terms of the obligation.

Robert McCauley, to the Knights of Labor, his member's motion at meeting in 1870, in Powderly's Thirty Years of Labor 1859–1889 *(1967).*

I returned from Georgia yesterday. My visit to Montevideo was very pleasant but very sad. My beloved mother was not there, and my dear father—he too was gone! . . . Everything was in much better order than I expected to find it.

Charles Colcock Jones, son of Mary Jones of Montevideo, Georgia, in a letter describing his return to his family home, 1870, in Myers's The Children of Pride *(1972).*

Senator Tweed is in a fair way to distinguish himself as a reformer . . . From beginning to end the Tweed party has not manifested the slightest disposition to evade or prevaricate . . . As a whole, the appointments of the heads of the various departments of the City Government . . . are far above the average in point of personal fitness, and should be satisfactory.

New York Times, editorial published prior to widening scandal over "Boss" Tweed, 1870, in Callow's Urban History *(1973).*

I want to know what the ladies are doing in the way of taking stock for our company. We are getting started now. We have enough subscribed to begin with, and we are starting up with a good prospect

of getting a quick sale for our goods as soon as we have got them ready for the market. Of course, we depend altogether on the working people of the country, and on the people who are able and willing to help working girls and wish to see them get along.

The stock is five dollars per share, and is only an investment, which will directly benefit working girls, not a charity . . . Any person wishing to subscribe for one share or more can address a note to [me].

Kate Mullany, president of the Laundry Union and Co-operative Collar Co., Troy, New York, 1870, in Baxandall's America's Working Women *(1976).*

Seven years ago an institution arose in our midst, which sprang into being at once to answer to the necessities of the working-women of New York . . . This new organization was given the name of the Working-Women's Protective Union and its rooms are now to be found at 38 Bleecker Street.

Perhaps no association in our city has done more for humanity in the last seven years than this.

Though it is supported entirely by private contributions, it cannot be called a charity. It is really a beneficial society, organized for the relief of women making honorable employment in trades, at wages proportioned to the cost of living.

The very existence of such an association . . . has acted as a check upon employers, and materially increased the pay of women as a class of workers. It has also lessened the hours of labor, but has lacked activity in this respect also. Statistics show that some of the women toilers of New York, the hoop-skirt factory girls, for instance, labor fourteen hours out of twenty-four, and, in times of press, eighteen hours a day . . .

Emily Verdery, writing in Woodhull and Claflin's Weekly, *1870, in Baxandall's* Working Women *(1976).*

It is practically certain that the Boston of today is the mere nucleus of the Boston that is to be. It is practically certain that it is to extend over many miles of country now thoroughly rural in character.

Frederick Law Olmsted, Architect and landscape planner, 1870, in Zaitzevsky's Frederick Law Olmsted and the Boston Park System *(1982).*

Too much education of a certain sort, such as Greek, Latin, French, German, and especially book-keeping, to a person of humble antecedents, is utterly demoralizing in nine cases out of ten, and is productive of an army of mean-spirited "gentlemen," who are above what is called "a trade," and who are only content to follow some such occupation as that of standing behind a counter, and selling silks, gloves, bobbins, or laces, or to "keep books."

Were the power lodged with me, no boy or girl should be educated at the public expense beyond what he or she could obtain at a grammar school, except for some useful occupation . . .

Were I in the position of General Eaton [U.S. Commissioner of Education], I would commence a crusade against the ignorance of our educators, and I would bring the people to a proper recognition of *"what knowledge is most worth,"* as Herbert Spencer has so well and truly sung, or these ignoramuses should have the satisfaction of lopping off my official head.

Henry Carey Baird, Philadelphia businessman, 1870, in DeNovo's Gilded Age *(1972).*

3. Urban Growth, National Scandal and Economic Panic: 1871–1873

THE HISTORICAL CONTEXT

During the early 1870s, a pattern of economic activity began to emerge. Industrial growth and urban development were aggressively pursued by the public and the private sectors, giving distinctive flavor to the American life-style, which had been primarily rural and agricultural before the Civil War. Periods of financial optimism, punctuated by episodes of economic instability, were a hallmark of the next 30 years. Nowhere was the uneven quality of national fiscal policy better illustrated than in Congress. Its profligate, yet ambivalent, attitude was mirrored in the so-called Salary Grab Act of 1873, which increased by 50% all congressional salaries—and which was later repealed. The continuing debate over protective tariffs would also point to the conflicting expectations of House and Senate members.

The country seemed to be on a seesaw. There was no way of predicting when, how, or even if order could be introduced to the national economy. Some acclaimed projects, like the completion of the transcontinental railroad, turned into nightmares of corruption and betrayal. As cities and towns grew, municipal governments often became little more than dens of public thieves. The basic problem seemed clear—there was a lack of leadership and minimal understanding of what the country needed in order to flourish as it became more heavily industrialized.

Urban growth offered some benefits, however. In 1873, population expansion led to U.S. Postal Service delivery for all communities of 20,000 or more. This enhanced federal service fueled a veritable explosion in the mail-order retail market, first established by Montgomery Ward in 1872 and followed a decade later by Sears, Roebuck & Company. In 1871, federal election supervision was mandated in cities with

29

Thomas Nast's view of "Boss" Tweed in Harper's Weekly. *Courtesy of the Library of Congress.*

populations over 20,000. This control became more significant as former slaves began to exercise their right to vote.

U.S. cities also experienced an architectural renaissance, spearheaded by the efforts of men like H.H. Richardson and Louis Sullivan. As the first skyscrapers were built, more ornamentation appeared in the design of important buildings. Neo-Gothic and Romanesque styles grew popular and the wealthy endowed cities with churches, museums, concert halls and railway terminals, and also subsidized construction of university buildings. The rich hired accomplished architects to design gifts of civic embellishment, among the more prominent of which were New York City's Grand Central Station and the First Baptist Church in Boston, Massachusetts. Also in New York, architect Richard Morris Hunt provided plans for the Lenox Library.

But cities well-known for impressive buildings and beautiful parks often became synonymous with graft and deceit. Headed by corrupt characters like William Marcy ("Boss") Tweed in New York, municipal officeholders appeared to operate in the interest of their constituents, instead pouring public funds into private coffers. In 1871, several members of New York City's Tweed Ring, as his group of close supporters was called, informed the *New York Times* about Tweed's illegal dealings. Although the party boss offered the newspaper $500,000 to cease an investigation of his actions, he was later found guilty of fraud and sentenced to prison. Boss Tweed was among the more colorful urban robbers, but political machines in smaller cities were similarly cursed by avarice and indifference to public interest. In each case, these corrupt urban leaders did their best to deny any ethical principles by which more honest politicians might have been propelled.

While graft enriched the dishonest, the energetic were rewarded for their entrepreneurial spirit. Retail sales expanded in the 1870s, since there was a market for virtually everything. Mail order, the newest idea in retailing, thrived as a wide circle of customers welcomed Montgomery Ward's scheme to sell merchandise by catalog. Purchases formerly made in person were available to anyone within the delivery route of the U.S. Postal Service. The success of this marketing strategy—and the prosperity of its promoters—was thus assured.

Despite the retail expansion represented by mail-order business, by 1873 the seemingly stable economy was balanced precariously between prosperity and ruin. Get-rich-quick schemes threatened to tip that balance, and even as honest investors placed their money in legitimate stocks, clever swindlers sought ways to defraud them.

One of the most elaborate hoaxes was the Credit Mobilier scandal. When uncovered, it implicated Representative Oakes Ames (R-Massachusetts), Vice President Schuyler Colfax and numerous others in illegal dealings during the completion of the nation's transcontinental railroad. The joining of the Union Pacific and Central Pacific lines had been the wonder of 1869. But an investigation revealed that the accomplishment had involved bribery, corruption and personal gain.

The railroad investment scandal was widely publicized. Because of this, many Americans grew skeptical of government, a reaction reported in most popular magazines and newspapers. Taking advantage of this cresting uncertainty about U.S. leadership, leading opinionmakers of the day, Charles Francis Adams, E.L. Godkin and Lyman Trumbull, organized other powerful and disgruntled Republicans and put forth a liberal (and, they felt, honest) candidate—Horace Greeley—for President in 1872. Supported by disillusioned G.O.P. members who believed their party had nothing to offer the nation, Greeley ran on the Democratic ticket. But despite this bipartisan effort, another decade would pass before a truly reform-minded President would be elected.

For many, the Credit Mobilier affair was proof that both elected and appointed officials often acted dishonestly and needed governmental control. By the end of 1872, confidence in the federal government was just as shaky as it had been during the 1868 Senate impeachment proceedings against President Andrew Johnson. Republicans were assailed by charges of corruption. Nevertheless, the president was reelected by a landslide in November 1872—largely due to the general unpopularity of Horace Greeley, whom critics labeled a crank and an idealist.

More Americans were crowding into what economist Thorstein Veblen would define later in the century as "the middle class." People wanted more, and were not ashamed to pursue wealth and social standing. The growth of educational opportunities was seductive, but the lure of get-rich-quick schemes was even more alluring. The national attitude was one that encouraged people to leave the ranks of farmers and day laborers and to seek more lucrative endeavors that would provide them with some leisure time.

Those who worked hard and hoped to make their fortune helped promote recreational activities that all Americans could take advantage of. A wide range of sports grew fashionable during the 1870s and Americans developed a passion for two games that soon would become major national pastimes—football and baseball. By 1871, the National Association of Professional Base-ball Players had been organized and more professional teams were touring the country. By 1873, four universities met in New York City to establish rules for varsity football.

The public's interest in sports was piqued by the growth of intercollegiate and professional teams, but this interest was rivaled by the intense scrutiny of business investments. A sudden flurry of activity on Wall Street in late 1873 caused Jay Cooke's brokerage house to fail. Thirty-seven banks and investment firms fell into ruin soon after Cooke's folded, and the New York Stock Exchange closed for 10 days. According to most experts, the Panic of 1873 stemmed from a dozen years of overspeculation and inflated stock prices. But whatever its cause, the crash crippled some of the nation's largest investment houses and banks. It destroyed dreams of riches and prosperity for thousands of Americans, plunging the nation into an economic depression that lasted for several years. It was also a forerunner of the cyclical periods of depression that would characterize the U.S. economy right through the end of the century.

CHRONICLE OF EVENTS

1871:

January 21: At a meeting secret labor assembly, labor leader Uriah Stephens urges the adoption of more equitable work hours and wage conditions.

February 21: The District of Columbia establishes a territorial government.

February 28: Congress passes a law requiring federal election supervision in cities with populations over 20,000.

March 3: The Indian Appropriation Act is passed by Congress. This reverses earlier policy and now all Native Americans are considered wards of the State rather than members of independent political entities. Native-American negotiating powers are severely curtailed with the passage of this act.

March 4: The Federal Civil Service Commission is established by President Grant. He appoints George W. Curtis to head the commission.

March 27: The Arkansas Industrial University is founded at Fayetteville. It is later to become the University of Arkansas.

May 1: The Legal Tender Act, passed in 1862, is declared constitutional by the U.S. Supreme Court decision in *Knox v. Lee.* The previous year, on February 7, the court had declared the act unconstitutional in *Hepburn v. Griswold.*

May 8: The United States and Great Britain sign the Treaty of Washington. This document guarantees arbitration for the *Alabama* claims and renews Canadian–American fishing agreements.

July 8: The *New York Times* exposes the corruption of William Marcy ("Boss") Tweed. Tweed is later brought to trial and charged with a variety of fraudulent activities. Railroad baron Jay Gould helps post the $1 million bail bond required of Tweed.

July 12: Protestants and Roman Catholics in New York City riot; there are 52 deaths and substantial numbers injured.

George William Curtis, first head of the Civil Service Commission. Courtesy of the Library of Congress.

July 30: A boiler explodes aboard the *Westfield,* a ferry traveling between Staten Island and Manhattan, killing over 100 people.

October 8: A fire in Chicago, Illinois, devastates 1,688 acres and destroys nearly $200 million in property, including 17,450 buildings. There are 250 known fatalities, and 98,000 people made homeless as a result of the fire. Among the artifacts destroyed when the Chicago Historical Society burns is the original draft of President Abraham Lincoln's Emancipation Proclamation.

October 24: Race riots aimed at Chinese immigrant labor erupt in Los Angeles, California.

1872:

February 2: Congress enacts legislation that provides for congressional elections to be held on the first Tuesday in November beginning in 1876.

February 22: The Prohibition party holds its national convention in Columbus, Ohio. James Black is nominated for the presidency.

March 23: The *Indianapolis Sentinel* first used the term "Mugwump." On this date, the term appears in the *New York Sun*, describing Republicans who do not support the policies of James G. Blaine. As the term gains broader usage, it grows to include any individual whose ideas are too lofty, too narrow, too intellectual to fit mainstream political positions.

April 10: Julius S. Morton proclaims this date as Arbor Day in Nebraska, a day on which trees should be planted to beautify and improve the landscape. Morton is named secretary of agriculture of the United States in 1885.

May 1: The Liberal Republican party nominates Horace Greeley for president of the United States. He will later be selected to run as a Democrat, retaining Liberal Republican support.

May 23: Ulysses S. Grant is nominated for president at the Workingmen's National Convention in New York City.

June 5: The Republican National Convention opens in Philadelphia, Pennsylvania, and President Grant is endorsed on the first ballot. His vice-presidential running mate is Henry Wilson. At this gathering, convention-goers hear speeches delivered by the first black Americans ever chosen as delegates to any major party convention. The three men are William E. Gray (Arkansas), B.B. Elliott (South Carolina), and John Roy Lynch (Mississippi).

July 9: Democrats gather in Baltimore, Maryland, for the beginning of their party convention. Horace Greeley receives the nomination for president.

September 4: The Credit Mobilier scandal is uncovered and made public in articles appearing in the *New York Sun*. The scandal involves high-level politicians who received substantial payments made by the federal government, funds dispersed during the building of the

transcontinental railroad which was completed in 1868. Massachusetts Representative Oakes Ames was chief among the organizers of Credit Mobilier of America, a company receiving construction contracts estimated at $73 million. Shares in the company went to numerous congressmen, and even to the vice president of the United States, Schuyler Colfax.

November 5: President Ulysses S. Grant wins re-election with 286 electoral votes. Horace Greeley receives only 66 electoral votes.

William Marcy ("Boss") Tweed is convicted of defrauding the New York City government of $200,000.

November 9: In Boston, Massachusetts, a fire destroys 800 buildings, kills 13 people, and causes $75 million in damage.

1873:

January 9: The *National Labor Tribune* begins publication in Pittsburgh, Pennsylvania. John M. Davis is the publisher, and circulation soon runs to 6,000. Readers are almost exclusively mine workers.

February 12: The Coinage Act is passed by Congress, removing silver coins from circulation and establishing a federal gold standard.

February 18: Despite being found guilty of bribery in the Credit Mobilier scandal, Representative Oakes Ames (R-Massachusetts) is not expelled from Congress but is merely officially censured.

March 3: Congress passes legislation known as the Salary Grab Act, in which it retroactively raises the salaries of most public officials including the President and members of the Supreme Court, whose pay is doubled. Members of the House and Senate are to receive 50% increases. Due to widespread popular outrage at this measure, the act is later repealed.

Congress passes the Timber Culture Act, which awards 160 acres of land to any individual who will plant 25% of the land with trees.

Congress passes the Coal Lands Act.

March 4: President Grant is inaugurated for a second term of office, with Henry Wilson replacing Schuyler Colfax as vice president.

March 8: George W. Curtis, head of the Civil Service Commission, resigns.

April 14: The U.S. Supreme Court rules 5–4 that the state of Louisiana has acted unconstitutionally in enforcing a law permitting only one slaughterhouse in the city of New Orleans.

May 1: The first penny postcards are made available by the U.S. Postal Service.

May 7: Chief Justice Salmon P. Chase dies of paralysis from a stroke suffered in 1870.

July: The Industrial Brotherhood is established to replace the National Labor Union, following the latter's fragmentation several years earlier.

August 18: The nation's highest peak, Mount Whitney, is conquered by three American climbers.

September 18: Jay Cooke and Co., a brokerage house in New York City, fails. This plunges the nation into an economic depression lasting five years. The Panic of 1873 was, according to most experts, the inevitable result of a dozen years of overspeculation and inflated prices. Cooke's firm had planned to underwrite the Northern Pacific Railroad, but due to difficulties could not handle the financing required.

The resulting crash also precipitates the closing of 37 other banking houses and brokerages.

September 20: The New York Stock Exchange closes for 10 days in the wake of the ruinous conditions among New York banks and other financial institutions caught up in the Panic. In response, the Treasury secretary issues greenbacks as a way of allaying the nationwide fiscal panic.

October 19: In New York City, four universities—Yale, Princeton, Columbia, and Rutgers—meet to draw up rules for playing football.

October 31: The steamer *Virginius* is captured by a Spanish gunboat in Cuban waters. Eight U.S. citizens are executed by authorities in Cuba.

November 19: William Marcy ("Boss") Tweed, former Democratic party machine leader, is sentenced to 12 years' imprisonment.

November 27: The Hoosac Tunnel, begun in 1858, is completed in western Massachusetts.

December 24: In Hillsboro, Ohio, Eliza Trimble Thompson leads a group of temperance-minded women through the town, stopping at the doors of saloons to pray and sing hymns. This event is the beginning of a temperance effort known as the Women's Crusade.

EYEWITNESS TESTIMONY

The great operations of war, the handling of large-scale masses of men, the influence of discipline, the lavish expenditure of unprecedented sums of money, the immense financial operations, the possibilities of effective cooperation, were lessons not likely to be lost on men quick to receive and apply all new ideas.
Charles F. Adams and Henry Adams, 1871, in
DeNovo's The Gilded Age and After *(1972).*

The system of corporate life and corporate power, as applied to industrial development, is yet in its infancy . . . It is a new power, for which our language contains no name. We know what aristocracy, autocracy, democracy are; but we have no word to express government by monied corporations . . . It remains to be seen what the next phase in this process of gradual development will be. History never quite repeats itself, and . . . the old familiar enemies may even now confront us, though arrayed in such a modern garb that no suspicion is excited.
Charles F. Adams and Henry Adams, 1871, in
DeNovo's Gilded Age *(1972).*

I don't care a straw for your newspaper articles, my constituents don't know how to read, but they can't help seeing them damned pictures.
Political boss William Marcy ("Boss") Tweed,
in the New York Times, *1871, in Callow's*
American Urban History (1973).

Well, I don't think I'll do it. I made up my mind not long ago to put some of those fellows behind bars, and I'm going to put them there.
Thomas Nast, Cartoonist for the New York
Tribune, *after being asked by Tweed Ring sup-*
porters to accept $500,000 to leave the country
to study art, 1871, in Callow's Urban History
(1973).

The Times has been saying all the time I have no brains. Well, I'll show Jones that I have brains . . . I tell you, sir, if this man Jones had said the things he has said about me, twenty-five years ago, he wouldn't be alive now. But, you see, when a man has a wife and children, he can't do such a thing (clenching his fists). I would have killed him.
Political boss William Marcy ("Boss") Tweed,
in the New York Times, *1871, in Callow's*
Urban History *(1973).*

Thomas Nast. Courtesy of the Library of Congress.

Tweed's impudent serenity is sublime. Were he not a supreme scoundrel, he would be a great man.
George Templeton Strong, lawyer and diarist,
1871, in Callow's Urban History *(1973).*

Boston is the only place in America where wealth and knowledge of how to use it are apt to coincide.
E.L. Godkin, journalist and editor of the At-
lantic Monthly, *1871, in Hoogenboom and*
Hoogenboom's The Gilded Age *(1967).*

I was at Washington last week and found anarchy ruling our nation. I don't know who has power or is responsible, but whoever it is, I cannot find him, and no one confesses to more knowledge.
Henry Adams, to E.L. Godkin, 1871, in Hoo-
genboom and Hoogenboom's Gilded Age
(1967).

There is something in the country which repels men. In the city alone can they nourish the juices of life.

It used to be a matter of pride with the better sort of our country people that they could raise on their own land or manufacture within their own households almost everything needed for domestic con-

William Marcy ("Boss") Tweed. Courtesy of the Library of Congress.

sumption. But if now you leave the rail, at whatever remote station, the very advertisements on its walls will manifest how greatly this is changed.

Frederick Law Olmsted, architect and landscape planner, 1871, Hoogenboom and Hoogenboom's Gilded Age *(1967).*

The hours of labor are too long and should be shortened. I recommend a universal movement to cease work at five o'clock on Saturday as a beginning. There should be greater participation in the profits of labor by the industrious and intelligent laborer. In the present arrangement of labor and capital the condition of the employee is simply that of wage-slavery; capital dictating, labor submitting; capital superior, labor inferior. This is an artificial and man-created condition, not God's arrangement and order, for it degrades man and ennobles mere pelf; it demeans those who live by useful labor, and in proportion exalts all those who eschew labor and live (no matter by what pretense or respectable cheat, for cheat it is) without productive work.

Uriah Stephens, labor leader, 1871, in Powderly'sf Thirty Years of Labor 1859–1889 *(1967).*

There can hardly be a more serious act than a change of country. To emigrate is to take a step, of which neither the most hopeful nor the most thoughtful can correctly foresee the full consequences, for good or for evil. It means nothing less than to part for years, if not forever, with home, relations, and friends; to break up old and dear habits; to live among strangers in a strange land; to recommence, often from the very beginning, the struggle of life.

American Social Science Association, Handbook for Immigrants to the United States, *1871, in Hoogenboom and Hoogenboom's* Gilded Age *(1967).*

Mr. Steadman, who sought for an introduction to me, told me that during the war I had been to him, and, he believed, to most people, the beau ideal of the Chevalier Bayard, "knight sans peur et sans reproche" and that I stood unrivaled as the "young American hero." I repeat this *to you alone*, as I know it will please you. Another said no officer holding a commission was so popular with the retired men.

General George A. Custer, to his wife, letter of 1871, in Slotkin's The Fatal Environment *(1985).*

When I am gone, think of our country . . . Always remember that your father never sold his country. You must stop your ears whenever you are asked to sign a treaty selling your home . . . Never sell the bones of your father and mother.

A Nez Perce Indian chief, to his son, about their lands in the Wallowa Valley in Washington Territory, 1871, in Lockwood and Harris's Reasoning with Democratic Values: Ethical Problems in United States History *(1985).*

I have an inalienable, constitutional, and natural right to love whom I may, to love as long or as short a period as I can, to change that love every day if I please! And with that right neither you nor any law you can frame have any right to interfere.

Victoria Woodhull, feminist and stockbroker, speaking in 1871, in Lockwood and Harris's Democratic Values *(1985).*

[Sheridan] has arranged with the genial and daring Buffalo Bill to be on hand and act as guide, and this renowned scout was promptly on hand in all his element. He was seated on a spanking charger, and with his long hair and spangled buckskin suit he appeared in his true character of the feared and beloved of all for miles around. White men and barbarous Indians are alike moved by his presence, and none of them dare do in word or deed contrary to the rules of law and civilization.

Victoria Woodhull. Courtesy of the New York Public Library Picture Collection.

New York Herald, *account of Buffalo Bill Cody's accompanying Russia's Grand Duke Alexis on a Great Plains buffalo hunt, 1871, in Slotkin's* Fatal Environment *(1985).*

Equality in rights is not only the first of rights, it is an axiom of political truth. But an axiom, whether of science or philosophy, is universal, and without exception or limitation; and this is according to the very law of its nature. Therefore, it is not stating an axiom to announce grandly that only white men are equal in rights; nor is it stating an axiom to announce with the same grandeur that all persons are equal in rights, but that colored persons have no rights except to testify and vote. Nor is it a self-evident truth, as declared; for no truth is self-evident which is not universal. The asserted limitation destroys the original Declaration, making it a ridiculous sham, instead of that sublime Magna Carta before which kings, nobles, and all inequalities of birth must disappear as ghosts of night at the dawn.

Senator Charles Sumner, Radical Republican leader (Massachusetts), January 15, 1872, in

Current and Garraty's Words that Made American History, Since the Civil War *(1965).*

The Southern communities will be a desolation until there is a thorough change of affairs in all the departments of the government. There is now no responsibility—and we are fast losing all of our ancient notions of what is becoming & fit in administration. The public are tolerant of corruption, maladministration, partiality in courts, worthlessness in juries, & regard government as only a means of exploitation. Indifference to anything wrong is the common Sentiment. Hope is disappearing from the motives to exertion.

John A. Campbell, former Supreme Court associate justice, to Justice Clifford, letter of 1871, in Fairman's Mr. Justice Miller and the Supreme Court *(1939).*

There will be an informal meeting of the Presidents of the National and International Trade Organizations of America in Cleveland, Ohio on the 19th of November, 1872, for the purpose of taking the initiative steps looking to the formation of an Industrial Congress of North America, to be composed of bona fide representatives of bona fide labor organizations.

Senator Charles Sumner. Courtesy of the Library of Congress.

It is to be hoped that there will be a representative from every National or International Trade Union in America present at the meeting . . .

M.A. Foran, in an 1872 advertisement in various trade society journals, in Powderly's Thirty Years *(1967).*

The subject of female labor is one that demands our attention and most earnest consideration . . . If they received the same wages that men do for similar work, this objection would in a great measure disappear . . . Woman was created and intended to be man's companion, not his slave.

William H. Sylvis, head of the National Labor Union, 1872, in Powderly's Thirty Years *(1967).*

I can give you some striking examples of the profit of raising corn and wheat in this vicinity, if you desire . . .

I knew [another] man who took a ton of corn to market for the purpose of buying coal. It purchased just a ton, and he spent a day with his team in hauling . . .

Wheat is so uncertain a crop, it has so many enemies from the time it is sown until it is threshed, and it is so exacting of the farmer who must attend to it at a certain time, or he will lose it, that we can't afford to raise it for less than ninety cents a bushel.

Now something is wrong in all this. With our productive soil, and facilities for reaching market, the farmers of Illinois ought to be forehanded, comfortably housed and clothed, and able to save a little every year, instead of getting deeper and deeper into debt. We are an intelligent, hard-working, economical people, and every one of us who owns his farm is to that extent a capitalist; and we ought to be able to do as well as the journeyman mechanic, with less education than we and no capital.

. . . It is not worth eleven cents a bushel to take our corn from here to Chicago, and the railroad that is charging it is robbing us of a part of the fruits of our labor.

S.M. Smith, secretary of the Illinois State Farmers' Association, 1873, in Hoogenboom and Hoogenboom's Gilded Age *(1967).*

For many years it has not been the American fashion for the owners of railroads to put their own money into their construction. If it had been it would have insured a more conservative and businesslike use of that species of property. The favorite plan has been to get grants of land, and loans of credit from the General Government; guarantees of interest from the State governments; subscriptions and donations from counties, cities and individuals; and upon the credit of all this, issue all bonds that can be put upon the market; make a close estimate as to how much less the road can be built for than the sum of these assets; form a ring . . . for the purpose of constructing the road, dividing the bonds that are left, owning the lands, owning and operating the road until the first mortgage becomes due and graciously allowing the Government to pay principal and interest upon the loan of her credit, while "every tie in the road is the grave of a small stockholder." Under this plan the only men in the community who are absolutely certain not to contribute any money are those who own and control it when it is finished. The method requires a certain kind of genius, political influence, and power of manipulation, and furnished one clew to the reason why railroads "interfere in politics." The personal profit upon this enterprise is not a profit upon capital investment, but the result of brain work—administrative talent they call it—in a particular direction.

Jay Cooke, Republican financier, 1873, in Ginger's People on the Move *(1975).*

This act [creating the Union Pacific] was not passed to further the personal interests of the corporators, nor for the advancement of commercial interests, nor for the convenience of the general public alone; but in addition to these the interests, present and future, of the Government, as such, were to be subserved. A great highway was to be created, the use of which for postal, military, and other purposes was to be secured to the Government "at all times," but particularly in time of war . . . To make such a highway . . . required a strong solvent corporation . . .

Your committee find themselves constrained to report that the moneys borrowed by the corporation, under a power given them, only to meet the necessities of the construction and endowment of the road, have been distributed in dividends among the corporators; that the stock was issued, not to men who paid for it at par in money, but who paid for it at not more than 30 cents on the dollar . . .

. . . at least one of the commissioners appointed by the President has been directly bribed to betray his trust by the gift of $25,000; that the chief engineer of the road was largely interested in the contracts for its construction; and that there has been an attempt to prevent the exercise of the reserved power in Congress by inducing influential members of Congress to become interested in the profits of the transaction.

Congressman Jeremiah M. Wilson, chair, Select Committee on the Credit Mobilier, "Affairs of the Union Pacific Railroad Company," House Report No. 78, 42nd Cong. 3d sess., 1873.

We need all the Jay Cookes we have and a thousand more.

Writer in Baptist Quarterly, *remarking on the significance of wealth as a sign of piety, 1873, in Baltzell's* The Protestant Establishment *(1966).*

Generally the proposition is true, that where you find the most religion there you find the most worldly parishioners.

Henry Ward Beecher, Congregational minister, sermon of 1873, in Baltzell's Protestant Establishment *(1966).*

The new Liberal Church has a consistent scheme of thought; it goes to the mind for its ideas; it admits the claim of spontaneity; its method of obtaining truth is rational; the harmony it demands is harmony of principles—the orderly sequence of laws.

Octavius Brooks Frothingham, Unitarian minister and first president of the Free Religious Association, on a free religion for all Americans, 1873, in Ahlstrom's A Religious History of the American People *(1972).*

[parks] in different parts of the future or present city . . . to be connected with a broad and well-made avenue . . .

. . . from all parts to all parts there would be direct and easy avenues of communication, and the main avenue or boulevard would thread . . . all the parks and public grounds and bring them into a common system . . .

An editorial attributed to Robert Morris Copeland, landscape planner and architect, in the Boston Advertiser, *1873, in Zaitzevsky's* Frederick Law Olmsted and the Boston Park System *(1982).*

Our modern frontiersman, who clings to the railroads out along the prairies, is a very different person. He insists on being followed up by all the modern conveniences. Not only must he have a church and school, but he must have the newspapers and magazines, and his wife and daughters must have a piano and silk dresses, and the new novels, and their minds, instead of being intent on the homely joys of the forest and the prairie, are vexed by the social and religious discussions of the far East. They want to hear Froude lecture, wonder what Plymouth Church is going to do with Bowen, would like a chance of listening to Lucca, are eager to try the newest thing in stoves, and wonder what the Emperor of Austria will think of the Illinois school-house at the Vienna Exhibition.

The Nation, editorial of 1873, in DeNovo's Gilded Age *(1972).*

4. The Consequences of Economic Instability: 1874–1875

THE HISTORICAL CONTEXT

As the effects of economic depression grew, congressional debate over monetary policy became more heated. As a reaction, and in hopes of relieving some of the problems, in early 1874 Congress approved the Legal Tender Act. This legislation promised to add nearly $20 million in greenbacks to the national economy, despite the fact that some economic forecasters were wary of the move and that President Grant had repeatedly voiced his opposition to it. Grant formally vetoed the Legal Tender Act because he thought the bill was inflationary, but Congress passed the measure on an override vote. It was just one more example of the extremely opposing views of the executive and legislative branches of government.

Hard money supporters were incensed at the legislation, and although the issue of paper versus coin was debated continually, many agreed with the greenback measure. Farmers especially favored it, as their debt load was enormous. They approved of any action that would alleviate the difficulties confronting American agriculture, even if the cure was short-lived. As public support grew, a political party devoted to the issue of paper currency sprang to life. It rallied, meeting in November 1874. The Greenback party held its convention in Indianapolis, Indiana, and there Peter Cooper—former New York governor—was named to run in the 1876 election as the party's candidate for president.

However, continuing concern for the economy prompted Congress to respond to inflation with yet another legislative solution. In January 1875, a move that acknowledged public pressure saw both houses of Congress pass the Resumption of Specie Payment Act. It called for gradual withdrawal of greenbacks from the economy and replacement of this paper currency with gold coin. Hard currency advocates were overjoyed; farmers and others hurt by the depression were dismayed.

41

The reputation of President Grant's administration was tarnished by his advisers' and associates' involvement in the Credit Mobilier affair and the Whisky Ring scandal. Courtesy of the Library of Congress.

These debates and disagreements continued for 20 years. In 1896, William Jennings Bryan would campaign for the presidency on a Democratic platform that featured free coinage of silver, as opposed to a single, gold, standard.

The nation had other problems, however. In addition to President Grant's unwillingness to support congressional monetary policies, continuing scandal in the Republican administration fueled public criticism and brought closer scrutiny of the activities of the president and his associates. The Whisky Ring scandal, which surfaced in May 1875, revealed that G.O.P. officials had accepted shakedown payments from midwestern distilleries. The chief clerk of the Treasury was named as one of those allegedly involved, as was Orville Babcock, President Grant's personal secretary. Following allegations in the Whisky Ring scandal, the House of Representatives passed legislation in December 1875 limiting a U.S. president to two consecutive terms of office.

These and other developments caused some observers to take a dim view of American culture and society. Among the more trenchant comments were those contained in a book coauthored by Mark Twain and Charles Dudley Warner, the novel *The Gilded Age*. The name of the book became synonymous with the era it so mercilessly described. Twain's insightful description of the fictional Colonel Beriah Sellers was a stereotype of the pompous, avaricious men of the post–Civil War era. Looking around him, Twain saw much to ridicule in the manners and morals of the newly rich. He and Warner underscored social problems by depicting them in a larger-than-life fashion in their book. This successful satire was similar in intent to Thomas Nast's caricatures which, when published in the newspapers, heightened read-ers' awareness of irresponsible civil servants, politicians and others who sought private gain at public expense.

While the Grant administration attempted to polish its somewhat tarnished image, labor organizations gained more support. Labor had a strong foothold in America by the time the second session of the In-dustrial Congress of the United States met in Rochester, New York, in April of 1874. Labor activity in this period increased, fueled by wage cuts in mining and manufacturing. In the Hocking Valley of Ohio, for example, cuts in miners' pay led to a strike. By midsummer of 1874, the Social Democratic Workingman's party of the U.S.—later the So-cialist Labor party—was established. The proliferation of labor unions, secret societies and similar groups that supported working persons' rights caused occasional ripples of concern among rich mine and fac-tory owners. But in general, there was little real alarm on the part of owners, nor did they feel any responsibility to respond immediately to laborers' demands.

Overall, the nation grew more intolerant of publicly immoral or unethical behavior due to the scandals of the Grant administration as well as other scandals that had been widely reported in the newspa-pers. The subsequent disclosure of graft and corruption at high levels of New York City government and the breakup of the Tweed Ring outraged many Americans and prompted demands for reform.

An increased awareness of the need for change led to the formation of organizations seeking to impose higher public and personal stan-dards. Groups like the Women's Christian Temperance Union (WCTU) attracted hundreds of members nationwide as the campaign to elimi-nate the consumption of alcoholic beverages increased.

As a means of controlling social behavior, or for the promotion of educational efforts, both the Chautauqua movement—rooted firmly in Christian tradition—and the Young Men's Hebrew Association exem-plified the public desire for more upright behavior. In 1875, Mary Baker Eddy, founder of the Christian Science Church, published *Sci-ence and Health*, a volume that combined Christian theology with a growing popular awareness of the benefits of healthy life-styles.

A breach of ethics was the focus of what may have been the nation's most titillating scandal of the decade. During this time, a well-known and respected Protestant minister was accused of adultery by a parish-ioner. Henry Ward Beecher (brother of novelist and abolitionist Harriet Beecher Stowe) was publicly charged by Theodore Tilton of having an affair with Mrs. Tilton. While a trial eventually found Beecher innocent of all charges, notoriety surrounding the revelations severely divided his New York City congregation and proved to be a frequent moral reference point for Sunday sermons in churches nationwide for years to come.

CHRONICLE OF EVENTS

1874:

January 20: Congress repeals the Salary Grab Act.

March 8: Former President Millard Fillmore dies.

March 22: The Young Men's Hebrew Association is founded in New York City.

April 1: A wage cut for miners is announced in the Hocking Valley of Ohio. This leads to labor strikes in the area.

April 14: The Legal Tender Act passes Congress, adding nearly $20 million in greenbacks to the money circulating.

The second annual session of the Industrial Congress of the United States convenes in Rochester, New York. Robert Schilling is elected president.

April 15: In Arkansas, Joseph Brooks lays claim to the state capitol, despite his loss in recent gubernatorial elections to Elijah Baxter.

April 22: President Grant vetoes the Legal Tender Act. Despite his opposition to the bill, which he considers inflationary, Congress passes the legislation on an override vote.

May 15: President Grant proclaims Elijah Baxter to be the legal governor of Arkansas.

May 16: Over 100 people lose their lives as the Ashfield Reservoir Dam in Williamsburg, Massachusetts, collapses.

June 20: The governmental structure of the District of Columbia is changed from a territorial jurisdiction to one governed by a commission.

The Treasury Department is to award a Life-saving Medal, as enacted by Congress, to those who perform rescues "from the perils of the sea within the United States or upon any American vessel." This award precedes formation of the U.S. Coast Guard.

July 4: A steel bridge across the Mississippi River is completed at St. Louis, Missouri. It is the first such access across the nation's widest waterway.

The Social Democratic Workingmen's party of the United States is founded. In 1877 it changes its name to the Socialist Labor party.

August 21: Henry Ward Beecher, well-known and respected Congregational minister and brother of novelist Harriet Beecher Stowe, is accused of adultery by parishioner Theodore Tilton. A trial finds Beecher innocent.

November 7: The magazine *Harper's Weekly* is the first to use an elephant to symbolize the Republican party. It appears in a cartoon drawn by Thomas Nast.

November 18: The Women's Christian Temperance Union (WCTU) is founded in Cleveland, Ohio. Annie Wittenmyer is elected the organization's first president, and the educator Frances Willard, corresponding secretary.

November 25: The Greenback party is formed during a convention in Indianapolis, Indiana. Peter Cooper is named the party's presidential candidate.

1875:

January: President Grant appoints a commission to arrange for negotiating purchase of the Black Hills from Indians in early summer.

January 7: The Resumption of Specie Payment Act is passed. Its purpose is to withdraw greenbacks from circulation gradually and replace them with hard money.

January 30: The United States signs a trade treaty with Hawaii, and provides protection for Hawaii against acquisition by a third power.

March 1: The Civil Rights Act passes Congress.

March 3: Congress passes the Tariff Act.

March 18: A reciprocity treaty with the Hawaiian Islands is ratified by Congress, permitting imports on a duty-free basis.

May 1: The Whisky Ring scandal is uncovered, further tarnishing President Grant's reputation. The scandal involves Republican officials, including the chief clerk of the Treasury, as well as President Grant's personal secretary, Orville Babcock. Allegations include acceptance of shakedown payments from at least 32 distillers in the Midwest, and use of blackmail and other threats.

July 31: Former President Andrew Johnson dies at age 66.

October 12: Rutherford B. Hayes is elected governor of Ohio.

November 3: President Grant meets with Gener- als Sherman and Sheridan to discuss Indian policy with respect to the Black Hills.

November 22: Vice President Henry Wilson dies.

December 4: "Boss" Tweed escapes from jail, fleeing to Cuba.

Eyewitness Testimony

No sooner does a depression in trade set in than all expressions of friendship to the toiler are forgotten.

David A. Harris, leader of the Sons of Vulcan, a national craft union for puddlers and boiler-makers, 1874, in Hoogenboom and Hoogenboom's The Gilded Age *(1967).*

The wealth producers of this nation are the men and women who dig, delve and spin. Upon their shoulders rests the burden of giving to all the people that which money merely represents—the wealth itself. Without toil there can be no wealth. He who toils is a wealthmaker.

A delegate to the second annual convention of the Industrial Congress of the United States, 1874, in Powderly's Thirty Years of Labor 1859–1889 *(1967).*

I have little hope of much success in elevating the Indians, until the Indian is made an individual, and worked upon as such, with a view toward incorporating him on our side.

Richard Henry Pratt, Indian educator, Carlisle, Pennsylvania, 1874, in Kelley's The Shaping of the American Past *(1978).*

[It is] neither right nor practicable for all the loss to be borne by the employers. Some of it must be shared by the workingmen . . . We must hereafter be contented with lower wages for our labor and be more thankful for the opportunity to labor at all.

James Swank, secretary, American Iron and Steel Association, 1874, in Hoogenboom and Hoogenboom's Gilded Age *(1967).*

I hope, however, that you will enlarge the sphere of your labors beyond this narrow field, and extend an invitation to the laborers and workers of all other cities and towns to form similar organizations, harmonizing in spirit and action with your own; more particularly with a view of joining hands with the farmers, the laborers of the country, your natural allies, in one common, united effort to free this country from the shackles of monopoly . . . extend a helping hand to the farmers, the laborers of the field. They are your vanguard . . . Aid them in their brave warfare with your common enemy, hydra-headed monopoly.

Workingmen, laborers, come in solid phalanx, unite with your brethren [*sic*] in the country . . .

Labor reformer Francis A. Hoffman Jr., to the Workingmen's party, Chicago, Illinois, address of January 25, 1874, in Roche's American Political Thought from Jefferson to Progressivism *(1967).*

Nature intended him for a savage state; every instinct, every impulse of his soul inclines him to it. The white race might fall into a barbarous state, and, afterwards, subjected to the influence of civilization, be reclaimed and prosper. Not so for the Indian. He cannot be himself and be civilized.

General George A. Custer, in an essay of 1874, in Slotkin's The Fatal Environment *(1985).*

The simple fact is that a great many laboring men are out of work. It is not the fault of merchants and manufacturers that they refuse to employ four men when they can pay but one, and decline to pay four dollars for work which they can buy for two and a half.

New York Graphic, editorial of 1874, in Hoogenboom and Hoogenboom's Gilded Age *(1967).*

We have got to go through hay-seed, possibly ignorance, most likely inexperience, to light. At any rate, the old must pass away and all things become new—through granges and young men's reform clubs and disgust, generally. Primary schools for political education are in order.

Samuel Bowles, editor of the Springfield Republican, *to economist David A. Wells, letter of 1874, in Morgan's* The Gilded Age *(1970).*

It is the center of all those trades which harden and brutalize the men who engage in them. Its gutters run with ordure and blood; its buildings reek with smells of slaughter and stenches abominable beyond description . . .

Narrow alleys, dark and filthy, bordered by sluggish black streams of stinking filth, traverse this quarter in every direction. Night-carts, which elsewhere leave far behind them a wake of stench suggestive of epidemics, here may pass through in broad daylight without betraying their presence. Amid these scenes and smells lives and labors a large and strangely healthy population of brawny butchers, sinewy coopers, muscular tanners—a foreign population, speaking a foreign tongue, and living the life of the Fatherland. The greater part of them labor in tanneries, slaughter-houses and soap factories, receiving small salaries upon which an American workman could not support his family, and doing work which Americans instinctively shrink from . . . The air they breathe is indeed foully odorous, but it is heavily rich with globules of fresh blood and tallow and reeking flesh—healthy for the lungs and veins of the breathers.

Lafcadio Hearn, reporter for the Cincinnati Enquirer, *describing an immigrant section of the city, 1874, in Hoogenboom and Hoogenboom's* Gilded Age *(1967).*

It should be our purpose to arrange a business system by which an exchange of products may be made direct between the producer and consumer without the intervention of an unnecessary number of middle men. It is of but little satisfaction to our brothers of the South to know that corn in Iowa is selling at thirty cents per bushel while they pay eighty, or that meat in Illinois is four cents per pound, while it costs them eight. It is a questionable consolation to the manufacturer of New England to know that in the valley of the Mississippi a yard of his cloth will buy three loaves of bread, when but one of them ever reaches his family.

Patrons of Husbandry, proceedings of their 7th Session, St. Louis, Missouri, 1874, In De-Novo's The Gilded Age and After *(1972).*

I think it is a great mistake to take from Joseph and his band of Nez Perce Indians that valley . . . possibly Congress can be induced to let these . . . peaceable Indians have this poor valley for their own.

General Oliver O. Howard, military commander of the Wallowa Valley area in Washington Territory, to the War Department, letter of 1875, in Lockwood and Harris's Democratic Values *(1985).*

If an Indian can be possessed of rights of country . . . this country [the Black Hills] belongs for occupation by the Sioux.

Commissioner of Indian Affairs, E.P. Smith, in his Annual Report, *1875, in Slotkin's* Fatal Environment *(1985).*

For years the ruling idea of the Western mind has been the bringing of remote acres . . . under cultivation. There was thought to be some occult virtue in expediting this process—a service to God and one's country. Every artificial appliance and inducement was thus set to work to force the population out in advance of the steady and healthy growth of civilization into regions beyond the reach of the world's centres and outside the pale of social influence . . .

The result brought about by the unnatural diffusion of population . . . was exactly what any thinking and observing man should have anticipated, overproduction at remote points. This difficulty no increased cheapness of transportation can alleviate; it can only transfer the locality of the difficulty to a point somewhat more remote. The darling vision of the Granger's dreams . . . is a double-track, steel-rail, government-built, exclusively freight railroad from every farmer's barn-door straight to the city of New York.

Charles Francis Adams Jr., historian and railroad expert, in the North American Review, *1875, in DeNovo's* Gilded Age *(1972).*

5. Compromise Politics and Labor Unrest: 1876–1877

THE HISTORICAL CONTEXT

A curious mix of issues dominated the national scene in the mid-1870s. Americans were proud of their many industrial and technological accomplishments, a fact made clear during the Centennial Exhibition in Philadelphia, Pennsylvania, in 1876. Demonstrated at the exhibition was one of the most tantalizing of these advances, Alexander Graham Bell's telephone.

Public attention continued to be absorbed with concern over ethics and morality. The Prohibition party met in the spring of 1876 and nominated as its presidential candidate General Green C. Smith, who ran on this single issue. Prohibition of alcohol was advocated by a small but vocal portion of the U.S. population; one representative from New Hampshire proposed a constitutional amendment banning the sale of liquor. It symbolized for many the inexorable changes overtaking American society—the influx of immigrants since the Civil War had forced the native-born to confront new ideas and new practices. For some, increased consumption of alcohol (and its concurrent problems) was a direct result of immigrant influence. For Prohibitionists it was a practice to be eliminated quickly and completely.

In June, Republicans and Democrats met at their parties' conventions. Since Grant was limited by tradition to two terms of office—and had served as president since 1868—he was out of the running. Instead, the G.O.P. nominated Rutherford B. Hayes, who ran against Democrat Samuel J. Tilden. Their close presidential race showed how nearly aligned both parties were ideologically. Tilden won the popular vote, but four states' votes were in dispute. Congress intervened and the resulting Joint Electoral Commission devised a compromise in early 1877—and delivered the presidency to Hayes. In return, he promised to remove federal troops from the South. This Compromise of 1877 meant the end of Reconstruction. It also marked a clean break with the wartime era and seemed to symbolize the start of a new, more progressive and optimistic age.

Continued labor organization and growing unrest among the ranks of the nation's workers proved to be a serious political force, underscoring a need for social and economic reforms. For example, the Workingmen's party, a socialist group, was formed in 1876, as was the secret fraternal society known as the Mystic Shrine. Boston area women established the Women's Educational and Industrial Union to help provide a wider outlet for women's abilities. Some individuals also hoped to improve the condition of working people and did so by independent efforts; many of these were missionaries who served the thousands of immigrants flocking to urban areas.

Workers' power grew stronger through organizing efforts aimed at seizing control from the wealthy few. By 1877 the Great Railroad Strike forced the federal government to call out troops to settle the disturbance and to control unruly mobs of striking workers. The strike, symbolic of the threat that continuing labor organization posed to management, was only the forerunner of violent activity that would break out time and again on behalf of workers' interests over the next 20 years. The Haymarket Riot, the Pullman strike and others would focus public attention on the need for improved working conditions, better wages and more realistic hours for laborers. Each time these riots or strikes occurred, they reminded onlookers of the real power behind the growth and expansion of the United States in the late 19th century—the power of the worker, without which industry and agriculture would remain immobile and unproductive.

Congress continued to wrestle with monetary policy. Farmers wanted the federal government to issue more money so prices would fail, while banking interests wanted money to remain relatively scarce. With the resumption of Specie Payment Act of 1875, the government had committed itself to removing greenbacks from circulation. The country would be back on a gold standard by the end of the decade. But settlement of the West meant that mining activities increased and the country's silver supply grew. While currency was now limited to gold coin, mining interests added their voices to the chorus of support for a return to silver coinage. Combined with tariff questions and discussion about trade regulation, this issue would grow to be the prevailing question under debate in the Congress throughout the next decade and into the new century.

The potential of the American West was on everyone's mind. One of the more compelling frontier figures in the popular press of 1876 was General George Armstrong Custer. The federal government's interest in opening up western regions to settlement was continually thwarted by Native-American resistance. With his brash, outspoken views about control of Native Americans, Custer was a hero in the eyes of the government. Canny federal officials saw in this vain, ambi-

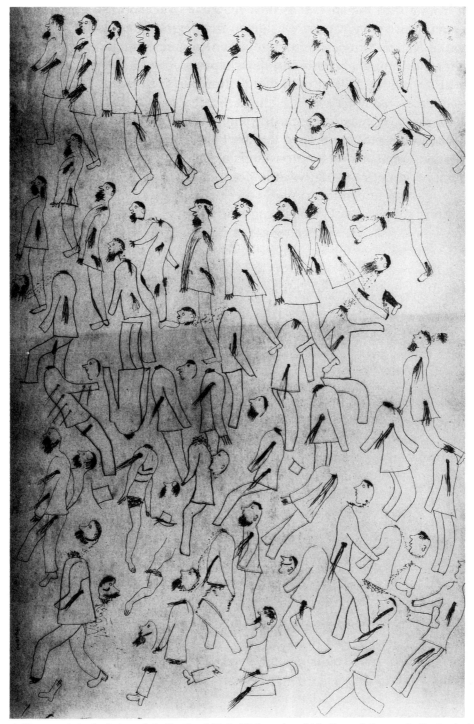

A Sioux artist's depiction of the Battle of Little Bighorn in which General George A. Custer lost his life. Courtesy of the Smithsonian Institution, Photo Number 47001.

tious young man the answer to their dilemma over land use and Native-American policy. Custer was given free reign to handle the removal of Native Americans from government land, and his actions were enthusiastically reported in newspapers across the nation. Custer's death in June 1876 at the Little Bighorn River in South Dakota caused a national outcry. When author Frederick Whittaker published the *Complete Life of George A. Custer*, shortly after the general's death, it was a best-seller. Many believe that because of Custer's flamboyance and broad popularity, the outcry over his death sped federal action that was destructive to Native-American life.

CHRONICLE OF EVENTS

1876:

February: A contractor, Caleb P. Marsh, reports that he has been offered control of trading posts at Fort Sill, in Indian Territory, by Secretary of War Belknap, in exchange for a payment of $12,000.

March 2: Secretary of War William W. Belknap, found to have been selling trading post privileges in Indian Territory, has impeachment proceedings brought against him. He resigns, however, and Congress is unable to carry out the resolution for impeachment.

March 7: Alexander Graham Bell is given a patent for the telephone.

March 10: Alexander Graham Bell talks for the first time on the telephone with his assistant, Thomas Watson.

April 1: The first game of baseball in the National League is played—Boston beats Philadelphia, 6–5.

May 10: The Centennial Exhibition opens in Philadelphia, Pennsylvania. The exhibition is designed to display America's triumphs in areas of science and technology.

May 17: The Prohibition party holds its national convention in Cleveland, Ohio, where General Green Clay Smith is nominated for the presidency of the United States; Gideon Stewart is nominated for vice president.

May 18: The Greenback party has its convention in Indianapolis, Indiana. Peter Cooper and Samuel Cary are nominated for president and vice president, respectively.

June 6: The Imperial Council of the Ancient Arabic Order of Nobles of the Mystic Shrine is organized in the United States. This group is connected to the Masonic Order.

Another depiction of Custer's last charge at the Battle of Little Bighorn. Courtesy of the Library of Congress.

June 14: Cincinnati, Ohio, is the site of the Republican National Convention, which opens today. Rutherford B. Hayes is nominated for president, and William A. Wheeler is selected as his running mate.

June 23: The telephone is demonstrated at Massachusetts Institute of Technology. Two days later, Alexander Graham Bell demonstrates the invention at the Philadelphia Centennial Exhibition.

June 25: General George A. Custer leads a surprise attack against Sioux Indian forces at Little Big Horn. Custer is outnumbered; he and virtually all of his federal troops are killed.

June 28: The Democrats open their national convention at St. Louis, Missouri. Samuel J. Tilden and Thomas H. Hendricks are nominated for president and vice president, respectively.

July 14: Despite widespread support for his candidacy, James G. Blaine is denied the Republican nomination for president, which goes instead to Rutherford B. Hayes.

July 25: Representative Richard P. Bland (D-Missouri) proposes legislation to issue unlimited silver coinage.

August 1: Colorado is the 38th state to enter the Union.

November 7: Samuel J. Tilden wins the presidential election with a total of 4,284,020 popular votes. Hayes amasses 4,036,572 popular votes. But the votes in four states—Oregon, South Carolina, Florida and Louisiana—are declared invalid.

November 23: William Marcy "Boss" Tweed is returned to New York, where he had escaped from jail nearly a year before.

December 5: A fire in a Brooklyn, New York, theater kills more than 300 people.

December 6: Republican voters in the four disputed states cast all their votes for Rutherford B. Hayes, which gives him the majority with one electoral college vote. Democrats in these states cast their votes for Tilden. The returns are sent to Congress.

December 12: Henry W. Blair, a representative

Rutherford B. Hayes served two terms as Ohio's governor before his nomination for U.S. president in 1876. Courtesy of the Library of Congress.

from New Hampshire, proposes a constitutional amendment prohibiting the production and sale of alcohol.

December 13: The House passes a bill permitting unlimited coinage of silver. The bill is sent to the Senate, where it languishes for over a year without action being taken on it.

1877:

January 9: Congress establishes the Joint Electoral Commission to clear up the dispute over the recent presidential election results.

January 30: Alexander Graham Bell obtains a second patent for an improved version of the telephone.

February 8: The Joint Electoral Commission, in ruling for Hayes, establishes the conditions necessary for federal troop withdrawal from the South.

March 1: The Supreme Court rules in favor of permitting individual states to regulate their own interstate and intrastate traffic as well as the charges for warehouse rates. The cases are *Peik v. Chicago & Northwestern Railroad Company* and *Munn v. Illinois.*

March 2: After President Hayes pledges to uphold certain compromise measures—chief among them is removal of federal troops from the three remaining Radical states (Louisiana, South Carolina and Florida)—electoral votes are counted and Hayes is named president of the United States.

March 3: The Desert Land Act passes Congress, offering 640 acres of land to anyone willing to irrigate a portion of the claim for a period of three years.

March 5: Rutherford B. Hayes is inaugurated as the nation's 19th president.

April 10: By federal decree, troops are officially withdrawn from South Carolina, ending Reconstruction.

April 24: President Hayes orders the last of the federal troops removed from New Orleans, Louisiana.

May 17: Former President Grant leaves for a round-the-world trip.

June 1: The Society of American Artists is established.

June 14: Flag Day is made a national holiday, commemorating the 100th anniversary of the United States' flag.

July 1: Workers at the Lackawanna Iron and Coal Company in Scranton, Pennsylvania, are notified that their wages are to be reduced. Within a month, they go out on strike.

July 14: The Great Railroad Strike begins in response to pay cuts of 35% over a three-year period.

July 16: Activities surrounding the Great Railroad Strike are interrupted by federal troops, called out for the first time since before the Civil War.

July 20: Nine striking railroad workers are shot and others are wounded in Baltimore, Maryland, where militia have fired into a crowd of demonstrators.

The Great Railroad Strike involved thousands of workers and resulted in extensive destruction of property. Courtesy of the Library of Congress.

July 21: In Pittsburgh, Pennsylvania, striking railroad workers are attacked by state troops.

July 26: Nineteen die in Chicago, Illinois, where police break up a gathering of strikers.

July 31: Despite the solidarity of thousands of striking railroad workers, the federal government is successful in bringing an end to the Great Railroad Strike. Few of the strikers' demands are met, but the labor movement has grown nationwide as a result of the summer's violent activities.

August 29: Mormon leader Brigham Young dies. His death will enable the Utah Territory to pass laws prohibiting polygamy and set the stage for Utah's entrance into the Union.

November 5: The Senate continues to avoid action on the proposed unlimited silver coinage bill.

November 23: The United States pays Great Britain $5.5 million for North Atlantic fishing privileges, under the terms of the Treaty of Washington.

EYEWITNESS TESTIMONY

At a mighty interval and with unequal steps we are the followers of Copernicus and Galileo and Bacon and Newton and Adam Smith and Bentham. How does it concern us that the mass—the mighty majority—of our fellow voters are ignorant and stupid and selfish and short-sighted? That's the practical statesman's affair . . . Don't you talk to me of popular acceptance. The moment you and I begin on that we are lost.

Charles Francis Adams, Jr. writing about policies regarding trade regulation, 1876, in Morgan's The Gilded Age *(1970).*

When one becomes a member of society, he necessarily parts with some rights or privileges which, as an individual not affected by his relations to others, he might retain . . .

Common carriers exercise a sort of public office, and have duties to perform in which the public is interested . . . Enough has already been said to show that, when private property is devoted to a public use, it is subject to public regulation . . .

We know that this is a power which may be abused; but that is no argument against its existence. For protection against abuses by legislatures the people must resort to the polls, not the courts.

Chief Justice Morrison R. Waite, in an opinion on Munn v. Illinois, *1876, in DeNovo's* The Gilded Age and After *(1972).*

Mr. Watson, come here. I want you.

Inventor Alexander Graham Bell, to his assistant Thomas A. Watson, via the first telephone, on March 10, 1876, in Schlesinger's Almanac of American History *(1983).*

The earth was my mother . . . I could not consent to sever my affections from the land which bore me. I ask nothing of the President. I am able to take care of myself. I do not desire the Wallowa Valley as a reservation, for that would subject me to the will of another and make me dependent on him and subject to laws not of our own making. I am disposed to live peaceably.

Chief Joseph of the Nez Perce tribe, commenting on the U.S. Army order to move to a reservation, 1876, in Lockwood and Harris's Reasoning with Democratic Values, *(1985).*

It has been estimated that the government pays $1,000,000 for every Indian slain in battle, squaws and papooses not counted. This is hardly true of the estimates upon a fair basis, but if the dead Indians cost Uncle Sam so much it would be interesting, and perhaps more to the point, to know how much the self-sacrificing old gentleman is called upon to pay yearly for each live Indian.

General George A. Custer, 1876, in Slotkin's The Fatal Environment *(1985).*

The experience of the past, particularly that of recent years, has shown too that no one measure so quickly and effectually frees a country from the horrors and devastations of Indian wars and Indian depredations generally as the building and successful operation of a railroad through the region overrun.

General George A. Custer, 1876, in Slotkin's Fatal Environment *(1985).*

It is really Custer's expedition, gotten up under his auspices and for his benefit, and that of his brother officer, if it be possible that any good can come of it . . . It is understood by many here that the object of the expedition is to succeed in driving the Indians from the Black Hills . . . so that white adventurers may seize their lands . . . in the wild and crazy search for gold . . . It will also give Custer an opportunity to distinguish himself . . . gratify his restless and rash ambition, and secure his further promotion.

New York Herald, article of 1876, in Slotkin's Fatal Environment *(1985).*

General George Armstrong Custer. Courtesy of the Library of Congress.

Only a small part of the throng can get within a range of the orator's voice, but the rest seem none the less happy, for it is the holiday diversion, the crowds, the bravery of the procession, the music, the fun of the occasion they came chiefly to enjoy . . . The speaker, Gen. Harrison, is a man of medium height . . . In conversation his manner is quiet . . . He talks for an hour and a half about the war and the record of the Democratic party, and even goes way back to the Fugitive Slave law in hunting out the bad points in the record. There is almost nothing in his speech, except a brief reference to the Presidential candidates, that might not have been said just as well four years ago, or eight years ago; but the people are pleased with it. Evidently in their minds the memories of the Rebellion have but to be roused to supplant all later issues.

New York Tribune, description of a Republican meeting and a speech by Harrison, gubernatorial nominee, in Cambridge City, Indiana, September 1876, in Hoogenboom and Hoogenboom's The Gilded Age *(1967).*

Would any gentleman stand up here and tell me that he is willing and ready to have his private correspondence scanned over and made public for the last eight or ten years? Does it imply guilt? Does it imply wrong-doing? Does it imply any sense of weakness that a man will protect his private correspondence? No, sir: it is the first instinct to do it, and it is the last outrage upon any man to violate it.

Senator James G. Blaine (R-Maine), to congressional committee investigating improper railroad investments, 1876, in Lockwood and Harris's Democratic Values *(1985).*

The Corliss engine does not lend itself to description . . . It rises loftily in the centre of the huge structure, an athlete of steel and iron with not a superfluous ounce of metal on it; the mighty walking beams plunge their pistons downward, the enormous flywheel revolves with hoarded power that makes all tremble, the hundred life-like details do their office with unerring intelligence.

William Dean Howells, novelist and critic, on the 2,500-horsepower Corliss engine at the Centennial Exhibition in Philadelphia, 1876, in Schlesinger's American History *(1983).*

I think all Chinamen come free [to the United States], except the women . . .

The women as a general thing are held as slaves. They are bought or stolen in China and brought here. They have a sort of agreement, to cover up the slavery business, but it is all a sham.

The Reverend Otis Gibson, missionary in the Methodist Episcopal Church, San Francisco, California, 1876, in Morgan's Gilded Age *(1970).*

These Chinawomen that you see on the streets here were brought for the accommodation of white people, not for the accommodation of Chinese; and if you pass along the streets where they are to be found, you will see that they are visited not so much by Chinese as by others—sailors and low people. The women are in a condition of servitude . . . They are sold here. Many women are taken from the Chinese owners, and are living as wives and as secondary wives. Some have children, and these children are legitimate.

The Reverend A.W. Loomis, Presbyterian minister, San Francisco, California, in testimony before a California State Senate Committee, 1876, in Morgan's Gilded Age *(1970).*

I send you by today's mail a copy of my dissenting opinion in the Chicago Elevator case and in the so-called Granger cases. I think that the doctrine announced by the majority of the Court practically destroys the guarantees of the Constitution intended for the protection of the rights of private property.

Supreme Court Associate Justice Stephen J. Field, to David A. Wells, letter of June 25, 1877, in Roche's American Political Thought from Jefferson to Progressivism *(1967).*

. . . these men have experience and command all the avenues to power, and every channel of communication with the heads of the government and the party is in their hands. All we want is a hearing.

H.A. Brown, to Carl Schurz, on the difficulty some Republican reformers face in becoming an effective influence on party decisions, 1877, in Hoogenboom and Hoogenboom's Gilded Age *(1967).*

They [strikes] ought not to occur here. The great problem of the [nation's] future is the equal distribution of wealth out of the profits of labor . . . I believe myself that, in general, the laboring classes do not receive their fair share. Strikes are one of their means of getting more . . .

Reverend Charles Loring Brace, New York reformer, on the effects of the Great Railroad Strike, 1877, in Degler's The Age of the Economic Revolution 1876–1900 *(1977).*

I have just witnessed a terrible exhibition of the power of machinery. Friends had advised me to visit the huge cotton press at the Cotton Landing, and I spent several hours in watching its operation. Excepting, perhaps some of the monster cotton presses of India, it is said to be the most powerful in the world; but the East Indian presses box the cotton instead of baling it, with enormous loss of time. This "Champion" press at the New Orleans Levee weighs, with all its attachments, upwards of three thousand tons, and exerts the enormous pressure of four million pounds upon the bales placed in it . . . The spectacle of this colossal press in motion is really terrific. It is like a nightmare of iron and brass . . . It is not a press as we understand the term generally, but an enormous mouth of metal which seizes the bale and crushes it in its teeth.

Lafcadio Hearn, reporter for the Cincinnati Enquirer, *1877, in Hoogenboom and Hoogenboom's* Gilded Age *(1967).*

The Great Spirit made the world as it is and as He wanted it . . . I do not see where you get your authority to say that we shall not live here as He placed us.

A Nez Perce chief, to General Oliver O. Howard, 1877, in Lockwood and Harris's Democratic Values *(1985).*

I stand here for the President, and there is no spirit good or bad that will hinder me. My orders are plain, and will be executed. I hoped that the Indians had good sense enough to make me their friend, and not their enemy.

General Oliver O. Howard, announcing the U.S. Army's intention of moving Nez Perce

Indians to reservation lands, 1877, in Lockwood and Harris's Democratic Values *(1985).*

That force of yours should pursue the Nez Perce to the death, lead where they may . . . If you are tired, give the command to some young energetic officer.

General William T. Sherman, commander of U.S. Army troops, to General Howard, 1877, in Lockwood and Harris's Democratic Values *(1985).*

I am tired of fighting. The old men are all dead. [My brother] who led the young men is dead. It is cold and we have no blankets. The little children are freezing to death. My people, some of them, have run away to the hills. No one knows where they are. I want to have some time to look for my children and see how many I can find. Maybe I shall find them among the dead.

Hear me, my chiefs. From where the sun now stands, I will fight no more forever.

Chief Joseph of the Nez Perce tribe, after surrendering to troops under the command of General Oliver O. Howard, 1877, in Weinstein and Wilson's Freedom and Crisis *(1860).*

You must not blame me. I have endeavored to keep my word, but the chief who is over me has given the order and I must obey it or resign. That would do you no good. Some officer would carry out the order.

Colonel Nelson Miles, to Nez Perce Chief Joseph, at the surrender of Nez Perce Indians, 1877, in Lockwood and Harris's Democratic Values *(1985).*

There is hardly a good thing in [the world] that is not the result of successful strife.

E.L. Godkin, the Nation's *editor, on the superiority of the white race, 1877, in Slotkin's* Fatal Environment *(1985).*

6. Monetary Policies Reviewed and Revised: 1878–1879

THE HISTORICAL CONTEXT

Although there had been attempts to settle it, most notably by printing paper "greenbacks," the currency question remained one of the most pressing issues debated in Congress. There were strong arguments made for, and against, silver coinage, bimetallism, and paper currency. Most Americans were hard-pressed by an economy spiraling downward, particularly farmers and others dependent on agricultural production or on meager hourly wages. Various measures had been discussed and proposed by Congress as it sought ways to alleviate inflation and stimulate the economy. In February 1878, the Bland-Allison Act was passed, permitting coinage of silver and increasing the value of paper money. This legislation had the support of midwestern congressmen whose constituents wanted relief from crushing debt loads on farm equipment and property. By the end of the year, paper currency would have a value equal to that of gold coin, but the debate over coinage and its effect on the economy continued to dominate politics through the end of the century.

In early 1878, the Greenback Labor party was formed by those determined to further influence the federal government's monetary policy. In November the Democratic party again took control of the House and Senate although a Republican—President Rutherford B. Hayes— sat in the White House. In part because of this Democratic control of Congress, Hayes's record of achievement would be limited and he was not nominated for re-election after his first term of office.

Women's rights were promoted heavily by advocates of gender equality. Among these advocates were Elizabeth Cady Stanton, Frances Willard, and Susan B. Anthony. In 1878, a women's suffrage amendment was proposed in Congress for the first time, although it would not be passed and ratified until 1920. In 1879, women achieved parity in another area when women lawyers finally were permitted to

Ellis Island, New York, the point of entry for European immigrants. Courtesy of the Library of Congress.

practice before the U.S. Supreme Court. Despite some gains, particularly in educational opportunity, women in the U.S. continued to struggle against social and cultural restrictions throughout the period.

Thomas A. Edison continued to amaze the nation with his technological abilities. He developed and perfected the phonograph, and established the first electric light company in New York City. His inventions greatly augmented and eased everyday life for thousands of Americans, and many of his ideas were widely implemented by the end of the 1880s.

Debate over the power of railroads continued, and causes of the Great Railroad Strike were investigated by Congress. Many officials and private citizens pressed for regulation of the growing railroad industry. And in 1878, with the case *Hall v. Cuir*, the U.S. Supreme Court ruled that protection of an individual's civil rights did not extend to racial integration in railroad accommodations.

Labor unions grew in number; in 1878, the Amalgamated Association of Iron, Steel, and Tin Workers was organized. It would later become one of the most powerful union organizations. Labor leaders debated the best ways to bring about an eight-hour workday, and questioned whether union membership should be denied on the basis of certain occupations.

Control and review of immigration policy were priority issues for the federal government and also took precedence during discourse among labor unions and private reformers. Partly due to workers' concern over unemployment related to inexpensive Chinese immigrant labor, Congress attempted to limit immigration of this group, although restrictive legislation was vetoed by President Hayes. Also, some labor leaders worried about the influence of the socialist ideas carried to this country by European immigrants. And there were increased investigations into the needs of the immigrant population in large cities where immigrant health and housing problems had become a political issue as well as a moral one.

CHRONICLE OF EVENTS

1878:

January 10: Senator A.A. Sargent introduces a women's suffrage amendment into the Congress. It will not be adopted until 1920.

January 14: The Supreme Court rules, in *Hall v. Cuir,* that the railroads are under no obligation to provide equal accommodations to rail passengers regardless of race.

January 17: As part of a growing interest in expansion, the Congress ratifies a treaty between the United States and Samoa, giving the U.S. jurisdiction over the harbor at Pago Pago, where the U.S. can refuel its naval fleet.

January 28: The nation's first commercial telephone switchboard is installed in New Haven, Connecticut.

The Yale Daily News begins publication as the country's first college daily paper.

February 11: In Boston, Massachusetts, the nation's first bicycle club is formed.

February 12: F.W. Thayer patents the first baseball catcher's mask.

February 19: Thomas A. Edison patents the first phonograph.

February 21: The first telephone directory is published in New Haven, Connecticut.

February 22: The Greenback Labor party is formed in Toledo, Ohio.

February 28: The Bland-Allison Act is passed by Congress. It requires the government to mint silver coin in amounts between $2 and $4 million per month.

April 2: The Women's Hotel is opened, the first to be run exclusively for women, in New York City.

April 18: Thomas Edison reveals his newly developed phonograph to the National Academy of Sciences in Washington, D.C.

April 21: In New York City, the first firehouse pole is installed. This innovation quickly becomes a symbol of the efficiency and speed with which fire fighters respond to alarms.

May 8: Paul Hines becomes the first professional baseball player to make an unassisted triple play.

June 3: Congress passes the Timber and Stone Act in order to make additional land available to farmers. The act permits the purchase of 160 acres of land at $2.50 per acre.

June 3: The American Laryngological Association is founded in Buffalo, New York, by physicians specializing in diseases of the throat.

June 11: The District of Columbia is permanently established as the nation's capital by act of Congress.

July 3: The first dirigible flight is scheduled.

July 9: Henry Tibbe patents the manufacture of corncob pipes.

July 11: President Hayes begins a series of much-needed civil service reforms by removing Chester A. Arthur from the post of customs collector for the Port of New York.

August 10: The nation's first home-study course is organized in Chautauqua, New York. Chautauqua will soon become synonymous with learning and the arts, and thousands will flock there during the summer months for institutes organized around a variety of subjects.

August 21: The American Bar Association is established in Saratoga, New York.

September 1: The first woman telephone operator is employed in Boston, Massachusetts.

October 4: The Chinese Embassy opens in Washington, D.C.

October 12: In Glasgow, Missouri, a contract for the construction of the first all-steel railroad bridge is signed.

October 15: Thomas Edison establishes the Edison Electric Light Company in New York City.

November 5: As an outcome of congressional elections nationwide, the Democratic party resumes control of both the House and the Senate.

November 14: The American Humane Association adopts its constitution in Baltimore, Maryland.

December 9: Today marks the first time, since the beginning of the Civil War, that greenbacks are equal to gold dollars and redeemable at face value on Wall Street.

December 26: The first retail store electric lighting is installed in Philadelphia, Pennsylvania.

1879:

January 23: In Crawfordsville, Indiana, the first national archery association is established. Archery rapidly becomes a favorite pastime of many Americans and the sport is among the first in which U.S. women will earn a medal in the 20th-century Olympic Games.

January 25: Congress passes the Arrears of Pension Act to authorize back-payment of military pensions.

February 15: Women lawyers can now bring cases before the U.S. Supreme Court.

B.K. Bruce of Mississippi is the first African-American senator to preside over the U.S. Senate.

February 22: The first five-cent store opens in Utica, New York. Its proprietor is F.W. Woolworth.

March 1: President Hayes vetoes passage of a rider to the Army Appropriations Act designed to weaken the Enforcement Acts of 1865 and 1874. The latter provide the president with the authority to use federal troops during elections as a means of protecting civil rights. As Hayes is successful in these attempts to usurp executive powers, he begins to build once again the power of the presidency that has been eroding since the Reconstruction era.

March 3: Belva Lockwood is the first woman to be admitted to law practice before the U.S. Supreme Court.

Congress authorizes issuance of the first postage-due stamps.

March 11: Congress attempts to restrict Chinese immigration; President Hayes vetoes the proposed legislation.

April 2: Toll-line commercial service for telephone customers begins in Springfield, Massachusetts.

April 29: Electric lights are first used to illuminate city streets in Cleveland, Ohio.

April 30: The nation's first factory inspection law is enacted in Massachusetts.

May 8: An automobile patent is filed by George Selden in Rochester, New York. He is the first to perfect the internal-combustion engine.

May 9: The first postage-due stamps are issued by the U.S. Postal Service.

May 10: The nation's first archeological society is founded in Boston, Massachusetts.

May 23: The first state school of veterinary medicine opens in Ames, Iowa.

May 28: The Mississippi River Commission is formed by Congress to help make better use of the river for commercial and other purposes.

July 1: The Illinois legislature passes a law prohibiting employment of women.

September 23: The first hearing aid is patented in River Park, Illinois. It is known as the audiophone.

September 27: The first amateur athletic competition is held in New York City.

November 1: An American-Indian school opens in Carlisle, Pennsylvania.

November 4: A patent is taken out for the manufacture of a cash register in Dayton, Ohio.

November 17: Thomas Edison's incandescent lamp burns for an unprecedented 16 hours. This development ushers in the era of electric lighting.

December: The first photograph to be taken using incandescent lighting is shot in Menlo Park, New Jersey.

December 5: The first automatic telephone is patented.

December 10: The American Library Association is incorporated.

EYEWITNESS TESTIMONY

A new power has entered into the industrial world, which must be recognized . . . It must be heard. Its just demands must be heeded . . . The great result achieved is that capital is ready to discuss. It is not to be disguised that till labor presented itself in such an attitude as to compel a hearing capital was unwilling to listen; but now it does listen. The results already attained are full of encouragement.

Representative Abram S. Hewitt (R-Pennsylvania), chairman of a congressional committee investigating the railroad strikes, in 1878, in Smith's The Rise of Industrial America *(1984).*

The railway exercises political power, firstly, by reason of its being a great employer—as a matter of *esprit de corps* the employees will follow the unconcealed inclination of the employer towards one or the other of the political parties or nominees; secondly, by the expenditure of money in elections.

As to the press, the railway is among the largest of advertisers, and it is an interest, therefore, not to be criticized with impunity; and perhaps finding that the press is not wholly under the influence of its advertising columns, railway kings have become large proprietors of stock in newspapers—investments which are supposed not to be made in the expectation of large dividends on such stock, nor for philanthropical and educational purposes . . .

Hence the railway is the real government—two removes behind a fluctuating, temporal government, as represented by our State and National officers. It has all the substantial elements of power, without the responsibility connected with the office.

Simon Sterne, a New York merchant, 1878, in Hoogenboom and Hoogenboom's The Gilded Age *(1967).*

My friend Brandeis is a character in his way—one of the most brilliant legal minds they have ever had here . . . Hails from Louisville, is not a college graduate, but has spent some years in Europe, has a rather foreign look and is currently believed to have some Jew blood in him, though you would not suppose it from his appearance—tall, well-made, dark, beardless, and with the brightest eyes I ever saw. Is supposed to know everything and to have it always in mind. The professors listen to his opinion with the greatest deference. And it is generally correct . . .

William E. Cushing, Harvard Law School student, to his mother, letter of 1878, in Baltzell's The Protestant Establishment *(1966).*

It does not appear that the friends of freedom should spend either time or talent in furtherance of this exodus [of former slaves out of the South] as a desirable measure, either for the North or the South. If the people of this country cannot be protected in every state of the Union, the government of the United States is shorn of its rightful dignity and power, the late rebellion has triumphed, the sovereignty of the nation is an empty name, and the power and authority in individual states is greater than the power and authority of the United States.

The colored people of the South, just beginning to accumulate a little property, and to lay the foundation of family, should not be in haste to sell that little and be off to the banks of the Mississippi. The habit of roaming from place to place in pursuit of better conditions of existence is never a good one. A man should never leave his home for a new one till he has earnestly endeavored to make his immediate surroundings accord with his wishes. The time and energy expended in wandering from place to place, if employed in making him a comfortable home where he is, will, in nine cases out of ten, prove the best investment. No people ever did much for themselves or for the world without the sense and inspiration of native land, of a fixed home, of familiar neighborhood, and common associations. The fact of being to the manor born has an elevating power upon the mind and heart of a man. It is a more cheerful thing to be able to say, I was born here and know all the people, than to say, I am a stranger here and know none of the people.

It cannot be doubted that, in so far as this exodus tends to promote restlessness in the colored people of the South, to unsettle their feeling of home, and to sacrifice positive advantages where they are or fancied ones in Kansas or elsewhere, it is an evil.

Frederick Douglass, black leader, 1879, in Kelley's The Shaping of the American Past *(1978).*

The best things come, as a general thing, from the talents that are members of a group; every man works better when he has companions working in the same line, and yielding the stimulus of suggestion, comparison, emulation. Great things, of course, have been done by solitary workers; but they have been done with double the pains they would have cost if they had been produced in more genial circumstances.

Writer Henry James, 1879, in Schlesinger's Almanac of American History *(1983).*

Here is the yard of No. 5 Jersey Street [New York City], on lines strung across, were thousands of rags hung up to dry; on the ground, piled against the board fences, rags mixed with bones, bottles, and papers; the middle of the yard covered with every imaginable variety of dirt . . . We then turned to go into the cellars, in which was a large and a small room (containing a cook-stove and sleeping-bunks). There was scarcely standing room for the heaps of bags and rags, and right opposite to them stood a large pile of bones, mostly having meat on them in various stages of decomposition . . . Notwithstanding the dense tobacco smoke, the smell could be likened only to that of an exhumed body.

Kate Holladay Claghorn, immigration specialist, in a report of 1878, in Hoogenboom and Hoogenboom's Gilded Age *(1967).*

Some misunderstanding exists as to the amount of rum a man has to sell to become a rum-seller. My idea is that no grander principle was ever ingrafted upon the laws of a labor organization than that law of ours which denies membership to the rum traffic. The two deadliest foes of labor are rum and ignorance. We should show no quarter to rum and its damning, blighting influence; but should rigidly prohibit membership to any one who sells *even a single glass.* Thus will this foe be conquered or made powerless.

Grand Secretary Lichtman, Knights of Labor, 1879, in Powderly's Thirty Years of Labor 1859–1889 *(1967).*

. . . I deem it highly necessary to call your attention to the ominous frequency of the attempts being made all over the country to break down the ten-hour standard and enforce longer hours. Whether these movements are preconcerted and form a part of an organized effort to offset and obstruct the eight-hour movement, time will tell.

. . . a plain demand upon employees for an increase of hours of labor show what may be expected in this country; and they give us timely warning of the struggle and fierce opposition to be encountered before eight hours can be firmly established by statute law in the various States, backed as such laws will have to be by penal enactments for infringements in order to make them efficient.

. . . Active exertion and agitation will be necessary to bring public sentiment up to a point that will successfully carry the principle through the ballot-box. Until that is done absolutely nothing valuable has been gained.

Uriah Stephens, Grand Master of the Knights of Labor, 1879, in Powderly's Thirty Years *(1967).*

I detest the name of socialism on account of the actions of the men who profess to believe in it. They rush to every gathering and attempt to man or officer it. Having done that, and having driven all decent men away, they are supremely happy in the delusion that they have spread their ideas still further.

. . . They tear down and very seldom ever attempt to build up. They do nothing for the cause of labor, save to do it harm. If the socialists ever gain control . . . they will kill off the work of years.

Uriah Stephens, Grand Master of the Knights of Labor, 1879, in Powderly's Thirty Years *(1967).*

7. Populism, Assassination and Material Culture: 1880–1881

THE HISTORICAL CONTEXT

The cultural change, economic instability and technological development that marked American life following Reconstruction continued unabated in the opening years of the 1880s. This relatively rapid transformation of the United States from a homogeneous, agrarian society to one that embraced international commerce and a multiplicity of ethnic groups grew in momentum during 1880 and 1881. But for sheer drama, the election of James A. Garfield to the presidency—and his assassination only months later—overshadowed Supreme Court decisions, congressional debate over monetary policy and anything Thomas A. Edison, Alexander Graham Bell and their counterparts could invent. Shocked by the president's death, the public thereafter focused its attention on issues of national political importance.

However, many were amazed at the singular innovations of 1880 and 1881, developments that would be accepted as unremarkable just a few years later. Among them were the process for manufacturing rolls of camera film (patented by George Eastman of Rochester, New York), the completion of an elevated railway system in Manhattan, the development of the incandescent lamp by Thomas A. Edison and the manufacture of house paint by the Sherwin-Williams Company in Cleveland, Ohio.

Too, the ever-growing popularity of team sports such as baseball, and more leisurely outdoor pursuits like croquet and bicycling proved that Americans continued to enjoy free time. This growing appreciation for recreation and pleasurable pastimes led to the greater regulation of some sports. New baseball rules, for example, were established, and the League of American Wheelmen was founded in Newport, Rhode Island, by bicycle enthusiasts hoping to gain national prominence for their sport.

Republican James A. Garfield, who would be elected president in 1880. Courtesy of the Library of Congress.

A series of Republican presidents with a relatively benign, predictable and lackluster style of leadership characterized the period from 1877 to 1901. When Garfield was elected in 1880, following Rutherford B. Hayes, few anticipated an appreciable difference in the White House. Even when Vice President Chester A. Arthur assumed office in 1881 following Garfield's tragic death, few expected that the presidency would change in quality of character. But while the executive branch receded in power and influence, merely carrying out the determinations of Congress and avoiding any executive initiatives, this was a time of considerable activity for the two major parties.

The Republicans, solidly in control of the presidency, seemed to dominate in other important areas of leadership. Maine's James G. Blaine and Connecticut's Orville H. Platt were two senators who dominated their party and helped to promote and sustain high tariffs and government interest in business. The Democrats found their ranks growing by leaps and bounds as immigration rapidly changed the urban electorate. Soon, nativism and outright xenophobia would merge with prohibitionism and anti-labor unionism to tax the strength of the Democratic party, which welcomed the Irish, Jews, French Canadians and other immigrant groups.

The desire among urban working people and farmers to organize had become very strong during the late 1870s. As fraternal and labor organizations multiplied, they provided an opportunity for outspoken, sometimes visionary, individuals to influence and lead large numbers of Americans for whom conventional political and social approaches to

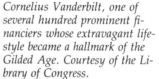

Cornelius Vanderbilt, one of several hundred prominent financiers whose extravagant lifestyle became a hallmark of the Gilded Age. Courtesy of the Library of Congress.

problem-solving appeared ineffective. The National Farmers' Alliance was formed in 1880 by disgruntled farmers and other citizens committed to the needs and interests of agriculture. This group would later be transformed into one of the nation's most viable third parties, the Populists. At this same time, a somewhat obscure labor activist named Eugene V. Debs was named the national secretary-treasurer of the Brotherhood of Locomotive Firemen. Years later, Debs would become head of the Socialist party and be jailed under the terms of the 1918 Sedition Act for his public statements against U.S. participation in World War I. The desire to congregate in groups defined by political ideology or cultural and ethnic lines continued right into the 20th century.

Materially, Americans were beginning to see the effects of an expanding business sector, which lined the pockets of shrewd, often ruthless, men for whom the making of millions became a game at which they grew more and more proficient. William Vanderbilt's mansion at Fifth Avenue and 52nd Street in New York City was completed in 1881, one of the nation's first opulent private homes in an urban setting. Vanderbilt set the style for the design and construction of hundreds of such homes for the rich and those with aspirations to wealth and social position in various locations throughout the country. That same year, President Eliot of Harvard University built a summer home at Northeast Harbor, Maine, becoming one of the dozens of notable individuals whose leisure retreats made areas like Newport, Rhode Island, and the Adirondacks in upstate New York, both fashionable and inaccessible to all but the very wealthy. In fact, the trend toward this rather conspicuous enjoyment of leisure time was specific to the Gilded Age.

Henry James's novel *The Portrait of a Lady*, Mark Twain's *A Tramp Abroad* and even Lew Wallace's *Ben Hur* revealed a growing predilection for writing that was peculiarly American in appeal. Magazines grew in popularity and circulation, and new ones appeared. *Century Magazine* for example, was founded in 1881. Formerly known as *Scribner's Monthly*, its editor, Richard Watson Gilder, was recognized for his interest in social issues. *Century* would publish a range of material during its lifetime, written by political leaders such as President McKinley and Theodore Roosevelt, as well as by professional journalists.

Finally, the 1880s ushered in a decade in which the public further refined its interest in art and architecture. The building of magnificent private homes paralleled the construction of commercial and municipal structures. Architects like H.H. Richardson and Louis Sullivan were widely employed, exercising their creativity and building a following in many cities and towns. Among Richardson's projects was the Metropolitan Museum of Art, which opened in New York City in 1880. It would eventually house the paintings of Mary Cassatt and John Singer Sargent, both of whom critics hailed in 1881 as original, innovative contributors to the American art scene.

CHRONICLE OF EVENTS

1880:

January 21: Memphis, Tennessee, becomes the first city in the nation to establish a separate system of sewage disposal.

January 27: Thomas A. Edison patents the incandescent lamp.

February 12: President Hayes warns settlers on Indian lands west of the Mississippi that their illegal presence may further damage government relations with Native-American tribes. Within a decade, however, the land will be taken from the Indians and made available to white settlers.

The first croquet league is founded.

February 16: The American Society of Mechnical Engineers is formed in New York City.

February 21: The first freight service on municipal railroads begins.

March: The U.S. branch of the Salvation Army is formed in Philadelphia, Pennsylvania. Commissioner George Railton and seven women

Another of Edison's inventions. Courtesy of the Library of Congress.

Inventor Thomas Alva Edison can be credited with helping to usher in a new technological age in the United States. Courtesy of the Library of Congress.

are among these first U.S. members. Commander Evangeline Booth, daughter of Salvation Army founder William Booth, will later assume command of the American branch.

March 1: The U.S. Supreme Court rules that it is unconstitutional to deny black Americans participation in jury duty. The case is *Strauder v. West Virginia.*

March 4: The first halftone engraving is done at the *Daily Graphic*, a New York city newspaper.

March 18: A House committee hears testimony from Ferdinand de Lesseps, builder of the Suez Canal. Congress is anxious to confirm U.S. authority over the canal being built across the isthmus of Panama by de Lesseps's company.

March 22: In Grand Rapids, Michigan, the nation's first hydroelectric commercial power plant is organized. It is named the Grand Rapids Electric Light and Power Company.

March 23: The first flour rolling mill is patented by John Stevens.

April: The National Farmers' Alliance is formed; it is later to become the Populist party.

The first facility for occupational therapeutic treatment opens in Boston, Massachusetts. It is known as the Adams Nervine Asylum.

April 27: The first bone-conduction hearing aid device is patented.

May 15: The Archeological Institute of America holds its annual meeting in Boston, Massachusetts.

June: The four-masted schooner *William J. White* is launched in Bath, Maine.

June 1: Paddy Ryan wins the world heavyweight bare-knuckles championship at Colliers, West Virginia.

The first pay telephone goes into service in New Haven, Connecticut.

June 2: Chicago, Illinois, is the site of the Republican National Convention, which opens today.

June 8: James A. Garfield wins the Republican nomination for president after 36 ballots, during which General Grant is also put forth as a candidate. Chester A. Arthur is nominated as the vice-presidential candidate.

June 9: James B. Weaver is nominated for president of the United States by the Greenback Labor party.

June 17: The Prohibition party nominates Neal Dow for U.S. president.

June 23: Democrats open their national convention in Cincinnati, Ohio. General Winfield Scott Hancock receives the nomination for president; William H. English is his vice-presidential running mate.

September: The nation's first Italian-language

The Republican National Convention in Chicago, 1880. Courtesy of the Library of Congress.

newspaper is published in New York City.

September 1: In Staten Island, New York, the first lawn tennis tournament of national importance is held.

September 7: The clay pigeon target is patented for trapshooting enthusiasts by G. Ligowsky in Cincinnati, Ohio.

October 1: In Menlo Park, New Jersey, the first incandescent light bulb factory opens.

October 4: The University of Southern California is founded in Los Angeles.

November 2: James A. Garfield defeats the Democratic candidate for president, Winfield S. Hancock, by a 214–155 electoral college vote. This is the first time that a U.S. representative in office is elected president.

November 8: Actress Sarah Bernhardt makes her American stage debut.

November 17: A treaty with China allows the U.S. to regulate the number of, but not exclude, Chinese immigrants.

December 17: The Edison Electric Illuminating Company is incorporated.

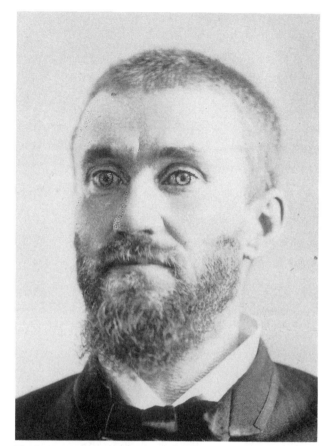

Charles J. Guiteau, assassin of President Garfield. Courtesy of the Library of Congress.

1881:

January 24: The federal Income Tax Law of 1862 is declared constitutional by the U.S. Supreme Court, in *Springer v. U.S.*

February 19: Kansas passes a law to prohibit liquor sales.

February 22: According to President Hayes, no alcohol will be available for sale at U.S. military posts.

March 3: Congress establishes a national registration agency to protect company trademarks.

March 4: President James A. Garfield is inaugurated.

March 5: Garfield appoints James G. Blaine secretary of state, which draws some G.O.P. criticism.

May 16: Two New York senators, Roscoe Conkling and Thomas Platt, refuse to endorse James G. Blaine as secretary of state. They resign their seats, and are not re-elected; Blaine's appointment is approved.

May 21: Clara Barton founds the American Red Cross in Washington, D.C.

July 2: While waiting for a train in Washington, D.C., President Garfield is shot. His assassin, Charles J. Guiteau, a fanatic with a history of mental instability, had sought an appointment in the new Republican administration.

July 4: Booker T. Washington, founder of the Tuskegee Institute in Atlanta, Georgia, convenes his first class there.

August 8: The Brotherhood of Carpenters and Joiners of America is founded in Chicago, Illinois. In 1886 it will be combined with the American Federation of Labor.

August 24: A naval observatory is set up in Greenland by a group under the direction of Lieutenant Adolphus W. Greeley. They remain there for two years preparing for an international scientific expedition.

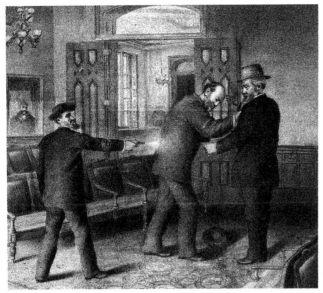

The assassination of President James A. Garfield, 1881. Courtesy of the Library of Congress.

Secretary of State James G. Blaine.

September 6: The General Assembly of the Knights of Labor agree that after January 1, 1882, the name of their fraternal order should be used publicly on letterhead and other printed materials. They had operated as a secret organization until this time.

September 19: President Garfield succumbs to the wounds he received in July. His body is brought to the Capitol rotunda to lie in state, and two days later he is carried by train to Cleveland, Ohio, for burial.

September 20: Garfield's vice president, Chester A. Arthur, is sworn in as the nation's 21st President.

October 15: American Angler, the first U.S. fishing journal, is published in Philadelphia, Pennsylvania, by William C. Harris.

October 22: The Boston Symphony Orchestra performs its inaugural concert under the direction of Georg Henschel. The orchestra is

founded by the philanthropist and Civil War veteran Henry Lee Higginson.

November 17: Secretary of State James G. Blaine invites Latin American nations to a Pan-American meeting in Washington, D.C., in 1882. No meeting takes place, however, since Blaine will resign his cabinet position because of the death of President Garfield.

December 1: Secretary of State Blaine announces that the Hawaiian Islands are to be protected under the terms of the Monroe Doctrine.

Eyewitness Testimony

I do not allow myself to anticipate any very decided measure of success possibly because we live here so completely under the domination of a perfectly organized and vigorously managed machine that one grows hopeless of any permanent change for the better.

Henry C. Lea, scholar and publisher from Philadelphia, to Harvard professor Charles Eliot Norton, on the ability of reformers to effect change in the Republican party, 1880, in Hoogenboom and Hoogenboom's The Gilded Age *(1967).*

I believe in a country where every man has an equal chance. That's the reason why I work for the Republican party . . .

This is a Government of liberty regulated by law. This is a Government founded on reason. This is a Government where the people have honest thought on every subject. The man who has these privileges himself and is not willing to accord them to others is a barbarian . . . Is there a Democrat who denies the common right of free speech? He dare not say it! Is there a Democrat who denies the right to talk and breathe in one common air? He dare not say it.

Now, if that liberty is to be preserved, whom will you have preserve it? . . . I'm going further off, and the longer the lever the more I can lift! Maine is a good place in which to begin. Let a Republican try it in Alabama and see how soon he'll get Ku-Kluxed. Let a Greenbacker try it, and see how soon he'll get mobbed for attempting to draw voters away from the Democratic party!

. . . Are you going to have the South protect your ballot-box for you? In the South elections are a farce. It is there that Bulldozing holds the election, Dishonesty counts their votes, and Fraud declares the result! Now it is a fact, my friends, that since the Rebellion, the South has killed more men, in a time of profound peace, that our country lost in the two wars with Great Britain! Are they the men you will have protect your ballot-box? Do you want to leave it with the masked man who shoots fathers, mothers, and children? Oh, Mr. Honest Greenbacker and Democrat! 'Way down in your soul I know you say "No"! no matter what you say outside.

Robert G. Ingersoll, Radical Republican lawyer and orator, during a rally in Lewiston, Maine, 1880, in Garraty's Labor and Capital in the Gilded Age *(1968).*

We must without delay begin to build a navy which will at least equal that of England when the canal shall have become a fact . . . That this will be done I don't for a moment hope but unless it is we may as well shut up about the Monroe Doctrine at once.

Alfred Thayer Mahan, naval historian, 1880, in Tuchman's The Proud Tower *(1966).*

I knew the wild riders and the vacant land were about to vanish forever and the more I considered the subject, the bigger *forever* loomed . . . I began to record some facts around me.

Frederick Remington, sculptor and painter of the American West, recalling his view from a train crossing the prairie in 1880, in Ginger's People on the Move *(1975).*

Organization once perfected, what must we do? In answer, study the best means of putting your organization to some practical use by embarking in a system of cooperation, which will eventually make every man his own master—every man his own employer; a system which will give the laborer a fair proportion of the products of his toils. It is to cooperation, then, as the lever of labor's emancipation that the eyes of the workingmen and women of the world are directed, upon cooperation their hopes are centered, and to it do I now direct your attention.

Terence V. Powderly, Grand Master Workman, Knights of Labor, speech in Pittsburgh, Pennsylvania, September 1880, in Powderly's Thirty Years of Labor 1859–1889 *(1967).*

As a result of labors of the eight-hour delegation, resolutions passed the House calling for a strict enforcement of the eight-hour law according to the spirit and intent of those by whose labors the law was originally adopted . . .

The delegation has the assurance from prominent members and friends of the measure that it shall be called up and pressed to a vote early in the session when Congress convenes in December. It will be necessary for someone there to look after and remind the Senators of the former promises. I would strongly urge upon the General Assembly the necessity of having someone in Washington at the opening of the

Senate to take such measures in the name of the united labor in America as shall convince the Senators that workingmen are in earnest in this matter.
Grand Secretary Lichtman, Knights of Labor, in a speech in Pittsburgh, Pennsylvania, September 1880, in Powderly's Thirty Years *(1967).*

[A salt marsh] would be novel, certainly, in labored urban grounds, and there may be a momentary question of its dignity and appropriateness . . . but [it] is a direct development of the original conditions of the locality in adaptation to the needs of a dense community. So regarded, it will be found to be, in the artistic sense of the word, natural, and possibly to suggest a modest poetic sentiment more grateful to town-weary minds than an elaborate and elegant garden-like work would have yielded.
Frederick Law Olmsted, architect and landscape planner, report to the city of Boston concerning his plan for the improvement of Back Bay, 1880, in Zaitzevsky's Frederick Law Olmsted and the Boston Park System *(1982).*

They fell upon an ungenial climate, where there were nine months of winter and three months of cold weather and that called out the best energies of the men, and of the women, too, to get a mere subsistence out of the soil, with such a climate. In their efforts to do that they cultivated industry and frugality at the same time—which is the real foundation of the greatness of the Pilgrims.
Former President Ulysses S. Grant, speech at a New England Society dinner, December 1880, in Smith's The Rise of Industrial America *(1984).*

. . . the railroads do not make the discriminations or differences themselves and . . . The Creator instituted them when He determined not to make his creation a dead level of mud and water, and all other material elements stirred up together in uniform collusion, inhabited, perhaps, by a single variety of queer fish which would enjoy that sort of premises . . . He laid the foundation of every so-called discrimination in freight rates which exists in the United States to-day. *Every one of them is simply a railroad trying to compete with a water-route.* On the water the Creator gives free right-of-way, and maintains the road-bed and furnishes the motive power, if man is not too much hurried to wait on sailing vessels.

. . . So far as any discriminations exist simply against individuals . . . I condemn them utterly; and I am sure no railroad manager can attempt to justify them. But circumstances, I think, will often justify cases of apparent discrimination which would be pronounced unjust where the circumstances are not understood.
Edward Porter Alexander, vice president of the Louisville & Nashville Railroad, 1881, in Hoogenboom and Hoogenboom's Gilded Age *(1967).*

Let us think that his dying eyes read a mystic meaning which only the rapt and parting soul may know. Let us believe that in the silence of the receding world he heard the great waves breaking on the farther shore, and felt already upon his wasted brow the breath of eternal morning.
Secretary of State, James G. Blaine, giving the eulogy at the funeral of President Garfield, 1881, in DeNovo's The Gilded Age and After *(1972).*

Kerosene has become, by its cheapness, the people's light the world over. In the United States we used 220,000,000 gallons of petroleum last year. It has come into such demand abroad that our exports of it increased from 79,458,888 gallons in 1868 to 417,648,544 in 1879. It goes all over Europe, and to the far East. The Oriental demand for it is increasing faster than any other . . . Very few of the forty millions of people in the United States who burn kerosene know that its production, manufacture, and export, its price at home and abroad, have been controlled for years by a single corporation, the Standard Oil Company. The company began in a partnership, in the early years of the civil war, between Samuel Andrews and John Rockefeller in Cleveland. Rockefeller had been a bookkeeper in some interior town in Ohio, and had afterwards made a few thousand dollars by keeping a flour store in Cleveland. Andrews had been a day laborer in refineries, and so poor that his wife took in sewing . . .
The contract is in print by which the Pennsylvania Railroad agreed with the Standard, under the name of the South Improvement Company, to double the freights on oil to everybody but to repay the Standard one dollar for every barrel of oil it shipped, and one dollar for every barrel of any its competitor's shipped . . . Ostensibly this contract was given up, in def-

erence to the whirlwind of indignation it excited. But Rockefeller, the manager of the Standard, was a man who could learn from defeat. He made no more tell-tale contracts that could be printed . . .

Henry Demarest Lloyd, reformer and journalist, in Story of a Great Monopoly, *published in 1881, in Ginger's* People *(1975).*

8. The Impact of Education: 1882–1883

The Historical Context

There were innovations in every field, from science and agriculture to sports and home management, during the early 1880s. It grew increasingly important to most Americans that they be well-informed about the way these new developments could help change—and improve—their lives. Therefore, the next few years saw an expansion of communications technology in the United States and a corresponding willingness to pay for the means to convey ideas.

Entrepreneurs, publishers and editors seized the opportunity to define what the public wanted and to determine how to make a profit at the same time. In 1882 the *New York Morning Journal*, published by Albert Pulitzer, was founded and quickly became notorious for its lurid headlines and sensational reporting. The *Journal*'s circulation grew rapidly; in 1895 it would be renamed the *New York Journal*. To cater to and to cash in on the American woman's growing interest in improving herself and her family life, *Ladies' Home Journal* magazine was founded in 1883 by Cyrus H.K. Curtis, a publisher in Philadelphia, Pennsylvania. Many other publications appeared during the 1880s and by the end of the decade specialty journals and self-help or literary magazines were read nationwide.

The importance and availability of education grew in significance during the 1880s. Helen Hunt Jackson, a popular writer, published *The Training of Children* in 1882, in which she outlined various ways to help young children learn. Both public and private schools proliferated and public school populations changed as immigration brought more and more non-English-speaking children into urban areas. These children would need to learn the language and customs of their families' adopted nation in order to flourish there.

The wealthy sought exclusive educational opportunities for their children and founded numerous independent schools. In 1882, the Browne and Nichols School was founded in Cambridge, Massachusetts, for the children of rich, socially correct Bostonians. In nearby Groton, Massachusetts, the exclusive Groton School was established

By the 1880s, many found opportunity in homesteads on the western frontier, such as this one in South Dakota. Courtesy of the Library of Congress.

for young men by Endicott Peabody, the moving force behind this and several other schools. It was believed that educating young men according to the English public-school tradition would help prepare politically and socially correct leaders for the next century.

In higher education there were similar patterns of growth and development. The Morrill Land Grant Act of 1862 continued to influence the growth of public higher education. In 1883 the University of North Dakota opened its doors, as did the University of Texas at Austin. In 1882, the University of Dakota was chartered under the terms of the Morrill Act and would, in 1891, become the University of South Dakota. Cornell University offered the nation's first college-level electrical engineering course.

Education of women at separately established institutions also continued during the 1880s. In Massachusetts in 1883, Radcliffe College was chartered separately from Harvard University. It joined Smith College (founded in 1872) and Wellesley College (founded in 1875), both also in Massachusetts, to become one of the country's top women's colleges. These and other schools would have a growing impact on the number of women entering society as social workers, educators, librarians, doctors and other professionals.

Hostility toward immigrants continued in the United States, an enmity that focused sharply on Asians in 1882 with passage of the Chinese Exclusion Act. There was recognition, however, that an influx of new workers could be helpful to national economic growth. As a means of promoting fiscal stability, the Southern Immigration Association was founded to encourage European settlement in the South. The region was still experiencing a stalled economy that followed the Civil War and Reconstruction.

The never-ending stream of immigrants into the country sparked some concern for their health and welfare. As they crowded into city tenements, living conditions declined to the point that many municipalities established boards of inquiry or public health commissions to investigate ways in which the immigrant families could be helped. Some citizens who served on these commissions became leaders in the settlement-house movement, which grew in influence and strength throughout the 1880s and 1890s.

CHRONICLE OF EVENTS

1882:

January 2: The Standard Oil Trust is formed under the leadership of John D. Rockefeller.

January 15: The U.S. Postal Service is charged with fraud in the Star Route frauds. During a two-year trial, it is revealed that bogus delivery routes generated hundreds of thousands of dollars in illegal budget requests. Several U.S. senators are indicted in the course of investigations, and Second Assistant Postmaster General Thomas J. Brady resigns under pressure.

February 28: In Cambridge, Massachusetts, the first cooperative college store in the nation opens for business.

March 11: The U.S. Intercollegiate Lacrosse Association is organized in Princeton, New Jersey. The first member institutions are Harvard, Princeton, and Columbia universities.

March 22: Congress enacts the Edmunds Law, aimed at further strengthening prohibitions against polygamy in the Utah Territory. Under this law, polygamists are denied voting privileges.

March 29: The Knights of Columbus, a Roman Catholic fraternal order, is chartered in Connecticut.

March 31: Congress passes a law that will provide an annual pension for the wives of U.S. presidents.

April 4: President Arthur uses his power to veto the Chinese Exclusion Act, which seeks to limit Asian immigration. There is a strong labor lobby against permitting Asian workers to enter the country.

April 28: The country's first newspaper room in a public library is dedicated in Newburyport, Massachusetts.

May 6: Congress passes the Chinese Exclusion Act on an override. The act seeks to prevent Chinese laborers from entering the U.S.

May 15: Congress establishes a tariff commission to protect U.S. business interests.

May 22: The United States recognizes Korea's independence and signs a commercial treaty with the Asian nation.

June 6: The electric iron is patented in New York City.

June 29: The American Forestry Congress merges with the American Forestry Association.

June 30: Congress authorizes establishment of the nation's first hospital for the military.

July 26: Congress votes to accept the Geneva Convention of 1864.

July 28: The country's first accounting society is established in New York City.

August 2: Congress votes to fund public works projects totaling $18 million under the terms of the Rivers and Harbors Bill.

August 7: The Senate Committee on Education and Labor adopts a resolution that will enable it to study and report on the causes and effects of the divisions existing between labor and capital.

August 16: Radcliffe College is chartered as a separate institution from Harvard University to educate young women.

September 4: By way of demonstrating its utility and potential for widespread business and industrial use, the electric light is turned on in several strategic buildings in New York City, including the Stock Exchange, the *New York Times* building and the *New York Herald* building.

September 5: The first Labor Day parade is held in New York City in honor of all working men and women.

September 13: The Country Club is founded in Brookline, Massachusetts, the first of exclusive country clubs established by and for the wealthy.

November 6: Actress Lily Langtry appears in New York City in a production of *As You Like It*.

December 11: The Bijou Theater in Boston, Massachusetts, uses incandescent lighting for the first time at a Gilbert and Sullivan performance.

1883:

January 10: The nation's most devastating hotel fire ever occurs in Milwaukee, Wisconsin, where 71 people die at the Newhall House.

January 16: Congress passes the Pendleton Act, which authorizes a bipartisan commission to administer civil service exams, eliminating a number of political appointment positions.

February 12: King Kalakaua and Queen Kapiolani are crowned in Honolulu in the Hawaiian Islands, a territory of the United States.

February 14: The first state to legalize labor unions is New Jersey.

February 23: The Anti-Vivisection Society is organized in Philadelphia, Pennsylvania.

The University of North Dakota is founded.

Alabama becomes the first state to enact a state anti-trust law.

February 27: The first cigar-rolling machine is patented by Oscar Hammerstein. His nephew and namesake will later become a famous songwriter.

March 2: Illinois becomes the first state to provide funding to railroad lines.

March 3: Congress reduces the cost of first-class postage to one-half cent from two cents.

The U.S. Navy is authorized to contract for the construction of steel vessels.

March 16: In Philadelphia, Pennsylvania, Susan Hayhurst becomes the nation's first woman graduate of a pharmacy college.

March 24: New York and Chicago are connected for the first time by telephone lines.

March 28: In New York City, the nation's first cooperative apartment house is incorporated.

April 30: In Sunbury, Pennsylvania, the Edison Electric Illuminating Company incorporates the nation's first three-wire central-station lighting plant.

May 1: The first National League baseball game is played, with Philadelphia beating Providence, 4–3.

May 24: The Brooklyn Bridge, construction of which began in 1869, opens, connecting Manhattan to Brooklyn. The bridge spans 1,595 feet and has two stone towers.

The Brooklyn Bridge, completed in 1883, helped promote commercial growth in New York City. Courtesy of The Museum of the City of New York.

June: The first intercollegiate lawn tennis match is held in Hartford, Connecticut.

June 2: In Fort Wayne, Indiana, the first baseball game is held under electric lights.

June 16: The first Ladies' Day is held by the New York Giants baseball team. Women are admitted to the park free of charge.

July 4: William F. "Buffalo Bill" Cody organizes his Wild West show along with E.Z.C. Judson. It has its premier at the Omaha fairgrounds and draws an audience of 25,000.

September 6: T.E. Burns becomes the first baseball player to hit a home run and a double in one inning.

September 11: A mail chute is patented by J.G. Cutler in Rochester, New York.

September 15: The first classes are held at the University of Texas at Austin.

September 21: The United States is connected by telegraph to Brazil.

Cornell University in Ithaca, New York, establishes the first college electrical engineering course.

October 15: The U.S. Supreme Court states that the Civil Rights Act of 1875 is unconstitutional, except if it pertains to jury duty and interstate travel.

October 22: The first national horse show is held in New York City.

November 6: The New York Athletic Club hosts the nation's first cross-country championship meet.

November 18: Four time zones are established by Congress via the Interstate Commerce Commission. This action is taken as a way of helping to regularize railroad services nationwide.

December 4: The patriotic organization Sons of the American Revolution is organized in New York. Membership is limited to male descendants of those who participated in the War of Independence.

EYEWITNESS TESTIMONY

Public officers are the servants and agents of the people, to execute the laws which the people have made.

Grover Cleveland, in his speech accepting the Democratic nomination for New York governor, 1882, in Bartlett's Familiar Quotations *(1951).*

No man in this country is so high that he is above the law. No officer of the law may set that law at defiance with impunity. All the officers of the government, from the highest to the lowest, are creatures of the law, and are bound to obey it.

It is the only supreme power in our system of government, and every man who by accepting office participates in its functions is only the more strongly bound to submit to that supremacy, and to observe the limitations which it imposes upon the exercise of the authority which it gives.

Samuel Freeman Miller, Supreme Court associate justice concerning United States v. Lee, *which dealt with sovereign immunity, 1882, in Fairman's* Mr. Justice Miller and the Supreme Court *(1939).*

. . . if we ever expect to obtain commercial supremacy, if we ever expect to have our proper rank among the nations of the earth, we must have a navy.

Representative E. John Ellis (R-Louisiana), 1882, in Paterson's American Imperialism and Anti-Imperialism *(1973).*

Mexico is now undergoing a physical conquest by our people. Our railroads and other enterprises are permeating her territory. Before long Mexico will wake up to the fact that she is gradually being subjugated by the United States; and then will come the recoil and the revolt, and the United States may be called upon to conserve the interests and property of her citizens there.

Representative E. John Ellis (R-Louisiana), 1882, in Paterson's American Imperialism *(1973).*

I think that there is no disagreement between the great mass of the employees and their employers. These societies [labor unions] that are gotten up

Railroad magnate Jay Gould. Courtesy of the Library of Congress.

magnify these things and create evils which do not exist—create trouble which ought not to exist.

Jay Gould, prominent New York financier and former head of the Erie Railroad, to the Senate, 1883, in Garraty's Labor and Capital in the Gilded Age *(1968).*

[The tenements of Manchester] are too small . . . they do not repair them at all for many years; and all around those tenements in the back streets all kinds of dirty things are allowed to stand. In many cases I have seen that myself. When they have good houses they live well, and their health is good; but in many places they get sick on account of the bad condition of the houses.

I think that tenement houses ought to be kept in better condition.

Father Joseph A. Chevalier, priest in Manchester, New Hampshire, testifying before a Senate committee, 1883, in Garraty's Labor and Capital *(1968).*

I believe in general that that government is best which governs least, and that interference with trade or manufactures is very undesirable. Yet I recognize the fact that evils may and do exist which require correction by the force of law. I think government will reduce its function to the desired minimum best by diffusing information and spreading light, rather than by interfering positively by commands and prohibitions. Therefore I believe in governmental collection and diffusion of information in the highest degree, mainly because in that way I believe government may reduce to the lowest terms its own active interference with trade and industry.

Economist Francis A. Walker, superintendent of the U.S. Census of 1870 and 1880, and president of Massachusetts Institute of Technology, testifying before a Senate committee, 1883, in Garraty's Labor and Capital *(1968).*

A department of health has two objects in view, one entirely of a public character, and another of a humanitarian character. The lives of laboring men are supposed to have a public or a business value . . . it is to the public interest that the lives of laboring men should be preserved, and also that their health be preserved, in order that they may settle their families and keep them from being subjects of charity.

Colonel Emmons Clark, secretary of the New York Board of Health, speaking before a Senate committee, 1883, in Garraty's Labor and Capital *(1968).*

This is certainly a glorious country for opportunity. A man has no stone upon his head here unless he carries it voluntarily. He has a clear road if he wants to go up.

John W. Britton, president of a New York bank, testifying before the Senate Committee on Education and Labor, 1883, in Garraty's Labor and Capital *(1968).*

That the rapid changes now going on are bringing up problems that demand the most earnest attention may be seen on every hand. Symptoms of danger, premonitions of violence, are appearing all over the civilized world. Creeds are dying, beliefs are changing, the old forces of conservatism are melting away.

Roscoe Conkling, who opposed Garfield's attempts at civil service reform. Courtesy of the Library of Congress.

Political institutions are failing, as clearly in democratic America as in monarchical Europe. There is a growing unrest and bitterness among the masses, whatever be the form of government, a blind groping for escape from conditions becoming intolerable. To attribute all this to the teachings of demagogues is like attributing the fever to the quickened pulse. It is the new wine beginning to ferment in old bottles. To put into a sailing-ship the powerful engines of a first-class ocean steamer would be to tear her to pieces with their play. So the new powers rapidly changing all the relations of society must shatter social and political organizations not adapted to meet their strain.

Economic reformer Henry George, in his book Social Problems, *1883.*

Those who devised the Fourteenth Amendment wrought to grave sincerity. They may have builded better than they knew.

They vitalized and energized a principle, as old and as everlasting as human rights. To some of them, the sunset of life may have given mystical lore.

They builded, not for a day, but for all time; not for a few, or for a race; but for man. They planted in the Constitution a monumental truth, to stand four-square whatever wind might blow.

Roscoe Conkling, former Republican congress-man from New York, 1883, in Fairman's Mr. Justice Miller *(1939).*

9. Third-Party Politics and Labor Unrest: 1884–1885

THE HISTORICAL CONTEXT

Americans in the mid-Gilded Age eagerly embraced new ideas. And just as magazines and daily newspapers grew in popularity in the 1880s, so did books—both those written for leisure-time reading and those meant to educate or improve the reader. In 1884, author Sarah Orne Jewett, a Maine native, published *A Country Doctor*, the first of many well-received and authentic volumes about life in New England. Historian Francis Parkman continued writing up his research findings of the French and British generals who were so crucial to the settlement of North America, and published his splendid study—*Montcalm and Wolfe*—that same year.

One of the most popular novels of all time, however, was among the top sellers following its publication in 1884: Mark Twain's *The Adventures of Huckleberry Finn*. This book enjoyed a wide readership for decades, remaining the top favorite among Twain's many readers. In 1885, the minister Josiah Strong published *Our Country*, a book that outlined the need for a sober, well-educated Anglo-Saxon leadership in America, one that would preserve the nation's future against what Strong saw as the tainting force of immigration and internationalism.

But the printed word was representative of a somewhat tamer and more conservative period. Perhaps the most daring, even desperate, new initiative during the mid-1880s was launched when disgruntled Republicans formed a third political party. For some time many G.O.P. faithfuls had been frustrated with the slavish adherence to conservative issues espoused by their party. Instead of looking for party affiliates, they sought elected leadership that would be more responsive to a larger population, one that would take social needs into consideration when introducing and supporting legislation. Soon, these dissatisfied Republicans came to represent a strong force against the traditional Republican position of support where big business was con-

Samuel Clemens, known by his pen name of Mark Twain, was among the most popular writers of his day. Courtesy of the Library of Congress.

cerned. It was a force that ultimately helped put a Democrat in the White House for the first time in over two decades. It was also the beginning of over a decade of more frenetic, unpredictable activity by the two major political parties.

In 1884, a group of Republicans broke away from the G.O.P. after the party nominated James G. Blaine for president. This splinter group called itself the Liberal Republican party and its members were nicknamed "Mugwumps," a term that denoted the party members' tendency to express opinions on popular issues of the day in an overly intellectual manner.

Republican party members ridiculed the Mugwumps' statements, but while it may have chosen cumbersome prose to explain its position, the group demanded reform and sought responsible answers to many of the nation's social and economic difficulties. And they expected that leaders, once elected, would live up to their demands for a responsive government.

The Liberal Republicans convened for the first time in June 1884, and agreed to support a Democratic presidential candidate. The one condition of the support was that the man to be approved would have acceptable liberal leanings and be a person who was likely, through combined Democratic and third-party support, to beat Blaine.

This was accomplished through the shrewd choice of Grover Cleveland as the Democratic nominee. Cleveland had been governor of New York from 1882 to 1884 and was a former mayor of Buffalo. He was a

Cyrus Hall McCormick invented the reaping machine, which enabled farmers in the late 19th century to transform American agriculture. Courtesy of the Library of Congress.

man who steadfastly refused to act in the interest of big business, a dedicated and proven reformer whose support of a federal civil service made him the symbol of a new type of party leader.

While the politicians wrangled, the economy continued to be a major concern of private citizens and companies as well as at all levels of government. The desire for economic stability, federal intervention on behalf of business interests, better wages and salaries, more profits and increased productivity clashed time and again and underscored the division between management and labor.

Strikes, work stoppages and walk-outs grew more common in the mid-1880s as organized workers protested wage cuts. Union Pacific Railroad workers were hit with one such wage cut in 1885 and promptly went on strike. A year earlier, Knights of Labor head Terence Powderly had begun to make increasingly inflammatory statements about the need for a strong labor attitude against "the existing industrial system." And by the end of 1885, striking laborers at the McCormick Works threatened unprecedented violence and disruption if their wage and hour demands went unmet.

At the same time, grass-roots activity and mutual concern over economic issues brought greater attention to the needs of American workers. Those involved in the study of the nation's economy founded the American Economic Association as a way of effecting lasting change in the structure of commerce, manufacture and government. The association's leaders, such as economist Richard T. Ely, of Johns Hopkins University, his colleagues Simon Patten, Washington Gladden and other reform-minded individuals, were concerned with more than the mere study of economics, however. Through their organization, they hoped to apply economic theory to real problems. Since there was a growing degree of unrest among workers and factory owners, and heightened concern among bankers about pressure on the national economic system, members of the association felt they could ease tensions by a systematic, scientific analysis of the fiscal problems that created them.

In order to solve a problem, reformers knew that they first needed to define it clearly. The nation's top policymakers therefore established the Federal Bureau of Labor in 1884 as a way of quantifying the array of products, activities and people contributing to the U.S. economy. Carroll D. Wright, formerly chief of the Massachusetts State Labor Statistics Bureau—the first of its kind in the country—was named the first commissioner of the new federal bureau.

CHRONICLE OF EVENTS

1884:

January 8: The chrome process for tanning leather is patented by Augustus Schultz in New York City.

January 30: The Anti-Vivisection Society, which was founded the previous year, holds its annual meeting in Philadelphia, Pennsylvania.

February 7: The New York Cancer Hospital is organized in New York City.

February 9: Seven hundred people are killed by tornadoes in the South.

February 14: Flooding of the Ohio River causes widespread damage. The river crests at 71 feet, the highest flooding ever recorded.

March 3: The U.S. Supreme Court states that Congress is able to order Treasury notes printed for use as legal tender.

March 4: Iowa prohibits the sale of alcohol.

March 12: Mississippi Industrial Institute and College receives its charter at Columbus, Mississippi. The institute is the first among state-supported schools for women.

March 17: In Otay, California, the nation's first glider flight is completed.

April 22: The first bicycle rider to plan a round-the-world trip begins the first leg of his journey in San Francisco, California.

April 24: The Medico-Chirurgical Society is organized in Washington, D.C. It is the first medical society for African-Americans.

May 14: A political party, the Anti-Monopoly Organization of the U.S. is founded by Benjamin F. Butler of Massachusetts. A former general in the Union army, Butler is nominated for the presidency at the Anti-Monopoly party convention in Chicago.

May 16: The Tenth Annual Kentucky Derby is won by Buchanan in Churchill Downs, Kentucky. The purse is $3,990 and the winning jockey is an African-American, Isaac Murphy, one of the finest American jockeys of his era.

May 28: The Greenback party holds its national convention at Indianapolis, Indiana.

During the 1884 presidential election, liberal Republicans broke with the G.O.P. and supported Democratic nominee Grover Cleveland, who was a strong proponent of civil service reform. Courtesy of the Library of Congress.

May 29: Congress establishes the Bureau of Animal Industry as a branch of the Department of Agriculture.

June 3: The Republican National Convention opens in Chicago, Illinois. James G. Blaine receives the nomination for president three days later; General John A. Logan is chosen as his running mate.

June 16: The Liberal Republicans—the Mugwumps—hold a convention in New York City.

June 27: The U.S. Bureau of Labor is established by Congress; it will be part of the Department of the Interior.

July 11: In Chicago, Illinois, the Democrats hold their national party convention. The governor of New York, Grover Cleveland, is nominated for president, with Thomas A. Hendricks as his running mate.

July 23: The Prohibition party convenes in Pittsburgh, Pennsylvania, where it nominates John P. St. John and William Daniel for president and vice president, respectively.

July 30: The Labor party holds its national convention in Chicago, Illinois, and votes to support the Democratic ticket in the upcoming presidential election.

August 5: On Bedloe's Island in New York Harbor, the cornerstone of the Statue of Liberty is laid in place.

August 26: Ottmar Mergenthaler patents the linotype machine, which will revolutionize the publishing industry.

September 10: The American Historical Association is founded in Saratoga, New York.

November 4: Grover Cleveland, a Democrat, defeats Republican James G. Blaine in the presidential election, garnering 219 electoral votes to Blaine's 182 votes.

November 8: The first news syndicate is established by Samuel McClure.

December 16: The World's Industrial and Cotton Centennial Exposition opens in New Orleans, Louisiana.

1885:

January 4: The nation's first appendectomy is performed in Davenport, Iowa.

February: Rail workers on the Union Pacific Railroad strike after owner Jay Gould cuts wages by 10%. Through the efforts of the Knights of Labor, the wage cut is later rescinded.

February 1: The first modern tuberculosis sanatorium in the U.S. opens in Saranac Lake, New York.

February 21: In the nation's capital, the Washington Monument is completed. It was begun in 1848, and cost $1.3 million to construct.

March 3: The first special delivery service is authorized by the U.S. Postal Service.

California establishes the first state forest service.

March 4: Grover Cleveland is inaugurated. He is the first Democrat elected to the country's highest office in 24 years.

March 12: the University of Arizona is chartered.

March 26: The first commercial motion picture film is manufactured in Rochester, New York.

April 15: McCormick Harvester Works laborers go out on strike to protest a wage cut.

June 5: General William Tecumseh Sherman refuses to be considered for the Republican party's possible nomination as the next U.S. president.

June 24: S.D. Ferguson, the nation's first African-American bishop, is consecrated in the Protestant Episcopal Church.

July 1: The U.S. Navigation Bureau is organized.

The Economic Ornithology Division is established by the federal government as a bird protection agency.

July 23: Former President Ulysses S. Grant dies. He is buried in Riverside Park, New York, after lying in state at City Hall.

July 28: The first coin-operated scale is patented.

August 10: The first commercially operated electric streetcars appear in Baltimore, Maryland.

September 3: The nation's first naval war college opens.

September 4: The first self-service restaurant in the nation opens in New York City.

September 9: The American Economic Association is founded in Saratoga, New York.

October 1: The first daily newspaper delivery by railroad is established by the *Daily News* out of Dallas, Texas.

October 23: Bryn Mawr College opens the nation's first graduate school for women.

November 11: Stanford University is founded in Palo Alto, California.

November 24: The first nursing society in the country, the Philomena Society, is organized in New York City.

December 8: President Cleveland delivers his first annual message to the American people.

EYEWITNESS TESTIMONY

A man's first duty is to his own conscience & honor—the party & the country come second to that, & never first . . . the only necessary thing to do, as I understand it, is that a man shall keep *himself* clean, (by witholding his vote for an improper man), even though the party & the country go to destruction in consequence.

Author Mark Twain, to William Dean Howells, 1884, in Paterson's American Imperialism and Anti-Imperialism *(1973).*

No, thank you, I don't engage in criminal practice.

Republican Roscoe Conkling, when asked to support Blaine's candidacy for U.S. president, 1884, in Lockwood and Harris's Reasoning with Democratic Values *(1985).*

[He] wallowed in spoils like a rhinoceros in an African pool.

E.L. Godkin, journalist, describing politician James G. Blaine, 1884, in Paterson's American Imperialism *(1973).*

According to Mr. Spencer, the divine energy which is mandated throughout the knowable universe is the same energy that wells up in us as consciousness. Speaking for myself, I can see no insuperable difficulty in the notion that at some period in the evolution of Humanity this divine spark may have acquired sufficient concentration and steadiness to survive the wreck of material forms and endure forever.

John Fiske, in Cosmic Philosophy, *1884.*

[A ton of goods] can now be carried on the best managed railroads for a distance of a mile, for a sum so small that outside of China it would be difficult to find a coin of equivalent value to give a boy as a reward for carrying an ounce package across the street.

David A. Wells, economist, 1884, in Degler's The Age of the Economic Revolution 1876–1900 *(1977).*

Perhaps you would like to know what became of my presidential Boom. Well as I wrote you last spring I never permitted it to rise to the dignity of a boom. It was however the nicest and quietest little scheme and well arranged that you ever saw.

. . . I have thought ever since the reassembling of Congress last winter that Blaine would be nominated. I do not think this was very much due to active exertion of his own. But effort to elect Arthur and Edmunds necessarily brought Blaine's name to the front. The overthrow of the Cameron dynasty in Pennsylvania gave him that state. The northwest remained true to him and his nomination came spontaneously.

I had no reason to be dissatisfied with his course toward me. If he had failed he would have been for me and I should have been nominated, though my name was not put before the convention at all. This was my express instruction to many men who were there for that purpose. My name had but that one chance and it was not to be frittered away. No one can say now that I have ever sought the place or brought reproach or folly to the judicial ermine. I am fully content. I believe Blaine will be elected and I feel sure he ought to be. He is a friend and admirer of mine as I am of him.

Supreme Court Associate Justice Samuel Freeman Miller, to William Ballinger, letter of 1884, in Fairman's Mr. Justice Miller and the Supreme Court *(1939).*

They love him most for the enemies he has made.

Governor Edward S. Bragg, in a speech seconding Grover Cleveland's nomination at the Democratic National Convention in Chicago, Illinois, July 9, 1884, in Bartlett's Familiar Quotations *(1951).*

The great work of the present and future is not to justify ourselves, to free ourselves from unjust aspersion but to bring the first promise of this election to realization. Do you think this work can be done best by our standing outside as critics . . . ? I don't.

G.F. Williams, a Mugwump lawyer, to Carl Schurz, commenting on Grover Cleveland's recent election, letter of 1884, in Degler's Economic Revolution *(1977).*

In Jersey Street exist two courtyards . . . Six three-story houses are in each. These houses are old, and long ago worn out. They are packed with tenants, rotten with age and decay, and so constructed as to have made them very undesirable for dwelling purposes in their earliest infancy. The Italians who chiefly inhabit them are the scum of New York chiffoniers, and as such, saturated with the filth inseparable from their business . . . The courtyard swarms with, in

daytime, females in the picturesque attire of Genoa and Piedmont, moving between the dirty children. The abundant rags, paper, sacks, barrows, barrels, wash-tubs, dogs, and cats, are all festooned overhead by clothes-lines weighted with such garments as are only known in Italy.
Kate Holladay Claghorn, immigration specialist, 1884, in Hoogenboom and Hoogenboom's The Gilded Age *(1967).*

Our order contemplates a radical change in the existing industrial system, and labors to bring about that change. The attitude of our order to the existing industrial system is necessarily one of war.
Terence V. Powderly, leader of the Knights of Labor, to the group's 1884 general assembly in Dubofsky's Industrialism and the American Worker, 1865–1920 *(1975).*

It is perhaps the highest distinction of the Greeks that they recognized the indissoluble connection of beauty and goodness.
Charles Eliot Norton, scholar and editor, in a report of the executive committee of the Archeological Institute of America, 1884, in Bartlett's Familiar Quotations *(1951).*

New England has a harsh climate, a barren soil, a rough and stormy coast, and yet we love it, even with a love passing that of dwellers of more favored regions.
Of "Americanism" of the right sort we cannot have too much. Mere vaporing and boasting become a nation as little as a man. But honest, outspoken pride and faith in our country are infinitely better and more to be respected than the cultivated reserve which sets it down as ill-bred and in bad taste ever to refer to our country except by way of deprecation, criticism, or general negation.
Henry Cabot Lodge, Massachusetts' opinion leader, to the New England Society of New York, address, of 1884, in Bartlett's Familiar Quotations *(1951).*

It cannot be permitted that, when the Constitution of a State, the fundamental law of the land, has imposed upon its legislature the duty of guarding, by suitable laws, the health of its citizens, especially in crowded cities, and the protection of their person and property by suppressing and preventing crime, that the power which enables it to perform this duty can be sold, bargained away, under any circum-

stances, as if it were a mere privilege which the legislator could dispose of at his pleasure.
Supreme Court Associate Justice Samuel Freeman Miller, on upholding the principles set forth in the Slaughterhouse decision under the terms of the Fourteenth Amendment, 1884, in Fairman's Mr. Justice Miller *(1939).*

I look upon the four years next to come as a dreadful self-inflicted penance for the good of my country. I can see no pleasure in it and no satisfaction, only a hope that I may be of service to my people.
President Grover Cleveland, in a private conversation prior to his inauguration, 1885, in Morgan's The Gilded Age *(1970).*

Your every voter, as surely as your chief magistrate, exercises a public trust.
President Cleveland, to the nation, inaugural speech, 1885, in Bartlett's Familiar Quotations *(1951).*

. . . The people demand reform in the administration of the Government and the application of business principles to public affairs.
President Cleveland, to the nation, inaugural speech, 1885, in Morgan's Gilded Age *(1970).*

[There is] a feeling here to-night stronger than I ever saw it before, that the war is over.
Atlanta Constitution, report on Inauguration Day, 1885, in Morgan's Gilded Age *(1970).*

This whole question of the farming interest is a very important one, and to show you another of the evils that grow out of these railroad grants and that are incident to them, I will refer to the fact that there is a very rapid change of ownership being made in the farming lands; that the small farmer as the owner of his farm is rapidly disappearing. Our whole northern country is filled with loan agents. In every considerable town and city you find often where they make a sole business of lending money upon farm lands and taking mortgages, and a large proportion of the money so loaned is foreign capital—a very large proportion.
William Godwin Moody, farm and labor supporter, 1885, in Hoogenboom and Hoogenboom's Gilded Age *(1967).*

The average wages of a farm laborer in the South is nearer fifty than seventy-five cents, out of which the laborer must feed and clothe his family. He seldom ever pays rent and he seldom ever sees a cent of currency. He is paid in "orders" on some storekeeper friendly to the planter. He cannot negotiate these precious "orders" to any other than the store indicated. Hence a system of fraud is connived at and practiced, to the utter demoralization and impoverishment of the ignorant, helpless laborer.

T. Thomas Fortune, editor of the New York Globe, speaking before the Senate Committee on Education and Labor, 1885, in Hoogenboom and Hoogenboom's Gilded Age (1967).

Your question, therefore, reduces itself to, What is the condition of the negroes? I should say good, as compared with a few years ago, and improving. You must recollect that it has only been 18 years since the negroes emerged from slavery without a dollar and with no education, and that for generations they had been taught to rely entirely upon others for guidance and support . . .

Where a laborer owns his own teams, gears, and implements necessary for making a crop, he gets two-thirds or three-fourths of the crop, according to the quality and location of the land.

Under the rental system proper, where a laborer is responsible and owns his team, &c., first-class land is rented to him for $8 or $10 per acre. With the land go certain privileges, such as those heretofore enumerated.

John C. Calhoun, grandson of the statesman, speaking before the Senate Committee on Education and Labor, 1885, in Hoogenboom and Hoogenboom's Gilded Age (1967).

It should be constantly borne in mind that all investments and outlays in Pullman [Illinois] are intended to yield financial returns satisfactory from a purely business point of view. The minimum return expected is six per centum on expenditure, and the town appears to have yielded a far higher percentage on cost up to the present time. Much of the land was bought at less than $200 per acre, and it is likely that the average price paid did not exceed that . . . there seems to be no reason to doubt the emphatic assertion that the whole establishment pays handsomely . . .

It pays also in another way. The wholesome, cheerful surroundings enable the men to work more constantly and more efficiently. The healthy condition of the residents is a matter of general comment. The number of deaths has been about seven in a thousand per annum, whereas it has been about fifteen in a thousand in the rest of Hyde Park.

It is maintained that Pullman is truly a philanthropic undertaking, although it is intended that it should be a profitable investment, and this is the argument used: If it can be shown that it does pay to provide beautiful homes for laborers, accompanied with all the conditions requisite for wholesome living both for the body and the mind, the example set by Mr. Pullman will find wide imitation.

Economist Richard T. Ely, referring to the company town of the Pullman Palace Car Company, 1885, in Hoogenboom and Hoogenboom's Gilded Age (1967).

As a rule we do not employ a child under ten years.

Every fall, especially when there have been poor crops, we have a number of country people who have been broken up on their farms and who come into Graniteville with their families to put them in the mill, and in many cases the children have to support the parents. Some of those people, of course, are old and in bad health, and they come there and locate and the children often support the family. A great many of those are very good people.

Hamilton H. Hickman, president, Graniteville Manufacturing Company, South Carolina, 1885, in Hoogenboom and Hoogenboom's Gilded Age (1967).

The whole question of these labor troubles is vast and important and throws more new light on a department of our manufacturing interests which we have not hitherto studied with sufficient depth and understanding.

Cyrus McCormick, to his mother, Nettie Fowler McCormick, the summer before the Haymarket riot, letter of 1885, in Weinstein and Wilson's Freedom and Crisis (1978).

We have had a week of trial and anxiety on the great subject of disturbances in our main factory—the serious labor troubles we have encountered—a great "strike," and all the resulting derangement of our relations—old and pleasant as they were—with our workmen.

Trouble has come to hundreds of families in consequence; hatred and fierce passions have been aroused; and an injury has resulted to our good name.

It began with a few molders and went on, one force operating on another, until 1,200 men went out, part of them by intimidation and part of them led by ignorant and blind passion. It ended by our conceding the terms demanded.

What sore heart I have carried these days!

Nettie Fowler McCormick, widow of the inventor of the reaping machine, to her daughter Virginia, letter of April 1885, in Weinstein and Wilson's Freedom and Crisis *(1978).*

The rural journals of the South, which are usually ignorant of the first principles of political economy, object to popular education, on the ground that the blacks pay no taxes, supremely oblivious that the laboring classes of every country always create capital, and pay in rental the taxes of the land-owner, who has no more inherent right in owner-ship of the soil than the laborer. What the State refuses to pay for education it gladly pays for penitentiaries, preferring a pound of remedy to an ounce of cure.

T. Thomas Fortune, editor of the New York Globe, *speaking before the Senate Committee on Education and Labor, 1885, in Hoogenboom and Hoogenboom's* Gilded Age *(1967).*

We hold that the conflict of labor and capital has brought into prominence a vast number of social problems, whose solution requires the united efforts, each in its own sphere, of the church, of the state, and of science.

Economist Richard T. Ely, author of the original platform of the American Economic Association, 1885, in Baltzell's The Protestant Establishment *(1966).*

If nominated, I will not accept. If elected, I will not serve.

General William T. Sherman, in reply to a request that he consider running for U.S. president, 1885, in Carruth's The Encyclopedia of American Facts and Dates *(1979).*

10. Reform Impulses and Labor Difficulties: 1886–1887

THE HISTORICAL CONTEXT

In 1886, the first settlement in the United States, the Neighborhood Guild, was founded in New York City by Stanton Coit. This simple effort was patterned after similar settlements in England—namely London's Toynbee Hall. It was among the first of many such attempts by a growing number of college-educated individuals to help the urban poor. Vida Scudder, a Smith College alumna, founded the College Settlement Association in 1887 along with several other young women who had also visited London to view Toynbee Hall. Among other well-known groups doing settlement work was that headed by Jane Addams at Hull House in Chicago, Illinois. Addams had graduated from Rockford Female Seminary in Illinois—after her father firmly discouraged her from attending her first choice, Smith College in Northampton, Massachusetts. While Rockford did not have the prestigious reputation of Smith, it permitted Addams the opportunity to do college work among young women similarly inclined to an academic life.

A college education was fast becoming the passport to a certain type of life—for young men as well as women—almost unimaginable earlier. During the post–Civil War years, hundreds of students entered the many institutions being founded by public mandate and through private efforts. In 1886, Bryn Mawr College was founded in Pennsylvania and in 1887, Clark University was founded in Worcester, Massachusetts.

But the social and political activism of the upper-middle class in the mid-1880s did not occur quickly enough to forestall some of the most violent labor agitation the nation was to experience in the late 19th century. The Haymarket Square riot, in May of 1886, was the culmination of months of unsatisfactory dealings between labor leaders and management at the McCormick Reaper Manufacturing Company in Chicago, Illinois.

Chicago's Haymarket Square riot of May 4, 1886, drew national attention to increasing demands by American laborers for better working conditions and more adequate pay. Courtesy of the Library of Congress.

Several days prior to the actual riot, President Cleveland sensed the mood of the situation there and worried about impending disaster. Cleveland had tried to find an avenue of peaceful escape for angry negotiators in the labor dispute, and made a national appeal to the leaders of business and labor to settle their differences peaceably. Cleveland hoped that some means could be found to allow the federal government to act as an arbitrator, but was unfortunately unsuccessful.

Leaving destruction and death in its wake, the unrest that erupted in the violent Haymarket riot was far more interesting to the public than Stanton Coit's settlement work. And the message that this violence sent to the federal government perhaps brought the plight of the poor and laboring classes into better focus, more quickly, than any amount of social work ever could have done.

Following the Haymarket riot, the Church Association for the Advancement of the Interests of Labor (CAIL) was founded by Father James Otis Sargent Huntington, a labor activist and founder of the Order of the Holy Cross. This group was only one of many similar efforts that sought to determine reasons for—and thereby prevent in future—labor unrest and violence.

But despite their fine intentions, these well-meaning attempts could do little to change the living and working conditions of the poor. And it had virtually no effect on labor activism, which continued to find a variety of aggressive ways to make itself heard. In 1886, for example,

Samuel Gompers, head of the American Federation of Labor. Courtesy of the Library of Congress.

the American Federation of Labor (AFL) was founded, and Samuel Gompers was elected its president. The AF of L would remain the leading labor organization throughout the 19th and 20th centuries.

For those fortunate enough to have been born into families of wealth and position, published evidence of their class came in 1887 in the form of the *Social Register*. This book detailed for the first time an index of aristocratic family associations among the wealthy in the United States. Inclusion in the *Social Register* was much sought after, sometimes discreetly, sometimes not, by hundreds whose connections suggested social influence.

While an individual's social status was determined by birth, the circumstances that affected the nation's monetary system were less immovable. The issue of silver coinage versus the minting of gold coin was loudly debated, particularly by those seeking to influence voters. The avalanche of advice and opinion during the period on the subject of money flow and its effect on the economy led to publication of many books and pamphlets on the topic. Among the most vociferous were the Populists, who believed the nation's future stability depended on free silver coinage. A guide to bimetallism, *Seven Financial Conspiracies which have Enslaved the American People*, published in 1886 by Mrs. S. E. V. Emery, a Populist, was just one of many books on coinage read by thousands of Americans, no matter what their social class or political affiliation.

Finally, the Interstate Commerce Commission, signed into existence by President Cleveland in February 1887, meant that at last there would be careful federal scrutiny of certain aspects of private business. The ICC revolutionized the way that the government treated private businesses that conducted transactions across state lines. Its existence was long a symbol of the power that various federal regulatory commissions wielded during the 1880s and 1890s.

CHRONICLE OF EVENTS

1886:

January 1: The Valley Hunt Club in Pasadena, California, holds its first Tournament of Roses.

January 19: The Presidential Succession Act passes Congress. It allows for the heads of executive departments of government to succeed to the presidency in the event of an emergency—such as death, removal, resignation—wherein the president and vice president are unable to serve.

January 19: In Red Wing, Minnesota, the nation's first local ski club is formed.

February 7: Rioting erupts in Seattle, Washington, where white residents protest the presence of Chinese immigrant workers. Federal troops are called in to restore order after more than 400 Chinese are driven from their homes.

February 9: Civil War hero General Winfield Scott Hancock dies.

February 14: The first railroad shipment of California oranges leaves the West Coast bound for markets in the eastern U.S.

February 23: The process for manufacturing aluminum out of bauxite ore is perfected.

March 4: The University of Wyoming receives its charter in Laramie.

March 6: In Great Barrington, Massachusetts, the nation's first alternating-current power plant begins operation.

Over 9,000 members of the Knights of Labor go on strike against the Missouri-Pacific Railroad.

In New York City, the first national nursing magazine—entitled *Nightingale*—is published.

April 8: Representative Richard P. Bland (D-Missouri) introduces a free coinage of silver bill into the House of Representatives.

April 22: President Cleveland, in a message to the nation concerning labor unrest, suggests that the federal government act as arbitrator between workers and management.

April 24: Augustus Tolton, the nation's first black Roman Catholic priest, is ordained.

May 1: Workers in Chicago, Illinois, begin a nationwide strike on behalf of an eight-hour workday. Between 40,000 and 60,000 strikers participate in the demonstration.

May 4: Strikers in Chicago's Haymarket Square riot as dynamite is thrown into the crowd. Police open fire on rioters; 10 people are killed and many—strikers, police and some bystanders—are wounded. Months later, eight are jailed; four are convicted of murder and hanged for their alleged role in the rioting.

May 10: The U.S. Supreme Court rules that a corporation is protected under the Fourteenth Amendment in the same way that an individual is. Thus, a corporation cannot lawfully be deprived of profits or other rights without due process. The case is *Santa Clara County v. Southern Pacific Railroad.*

May 30: Specially scheduled trains carry hundreds of guests to Tuxedo Park, New York, where Pierre Lorillard unveils his exclusive residential community.

June 1: In New York State the first State Board of Mediation and Arbitration is organized. The intention is that this body will help lessen the tension between management and labor during the numerous disputes cropping up between owners and workers.

June 2: President Grover Cleveland marries Frances Folsom at the White House in Washington, D.C. It is the first wedding of a U.S. president to take place in the executive mansion.

June 19: The trial of accused Haymarket riot assassins begins. The men—August Spies, Albert Parsons, Samuel Fielden and Michael Schwab, and four others—are charged with conspiracy to kill.

June 29: In a move that illustrates the power of organized labor in pressing for demands from the federal government, Congress decrees that trade unions may be incorporated.

June 30: Congress forms the Division of Forestry, formerly part of the Department of Agriculture.

July 3: The *New York Daily Tribune* becomes the

first newspaper in the country to be set by linotype machine.

July 7: Evangelist Dwight L. Moody organizes the first summer conference for Bible students in Northfield, Massachusetts, on the site of what will become the Northfield-Mt. Hermon School.

August 3: Congress gives authorization for construction of several vessels that will help modernize the U.S. Navy. Two of the ships are ironclads and one is a torpedo boat.

August 4: The U.S. Postal Service announces that it will offer special delivery service, and issues stamps for this purpose.

August 10: An electric welding process is patented by Elihu Thompson in Lynn, Massachusetts.

August 20: Four anarchists are sentenced to be hanged for their activities during the Haymarket riot in Chicago in May.

September 4: Apache leader Geronimo is captured by General Nelson A. Miles and sent to a Florida reservation.

September 16: The Anti-Saloon Republicans hold their national convention.

October: The Quarterly Journal of Economics begins publication in Boston, Massachusetts.

October 10: A type of formal evening wear for men is introduced at Tuxedo Park, New York, and soon becomes known as the "tuxedo."

October 12: A flood along Texas's Gulf Coast leaves 250 dead.

October 28: President Grover Cleveland dedicates the statue, *Liberty Enlightening the World* (known as the Statue of Liberty), a gift from the people of France. It is unveiled at Bedloe's Island (later known as Liberty Island) in New York Harbor.

November 2: For the first time in the nation's history, two brothers, R.L. Taylor and A.A. Taylor of Tennessee, run against each other in a gubernatorial race.

An endless-chain tread tractor design is patented by Charles Dinsmoor of Warren, Pennsylvania.

November 17: The American Newspaper Publishers Association is organized.

November 18: Former President Chester A. Arthur dies at age 56. He is buried in Albany, New York.

December: The Hawaiian League forms, an organization of planters and businessmen dedicated to improving the island government and promoting the overthrow of the monarchy there.

December 8: The American Federation of Labor is organized in Columbus, Ohio. It is an outgrowth of the Federation of Organized Trades and Labor Unions established in 1881.

December 22: The American Association of Public Accountants is formed in New York City.

1887:

January 20: The United States leases Pearl Harbor in the Hawaiian Islands as a naval station.

February 3: The Electoral Count Act is passed by Congress. It decrees that each state is to determine its own electoral returns and submit them to the federal government for acceptance by Congress.

February 4: The Interstate Commerce Act is passed by Congress, giving the federal government the right to regulate business that passes over state boundaries. The law provides also for the establishment of a regulatory body, the Interstate Commerce Commission, the first of such powerful federal commissions.

February 8: The Dawes Severalty Act passes Congress, providing for division of Native-American lands among Indian families.

February 21: In Oregon, the state legislature declares Labor Day a legal holiday. It announces that the first Saturday in June will be the observance date. This is later changed to the first Monday in September.

March 2: The Hatch Act passes Congress. It provides for an agricultural experiment station to be part of each state's land-grant college.

March 3: The American Protective Association, a nativist, anti-immigrant society, is established in Clinton, Iowa.

April 19: The Catholic University of America is founded in the nation's capital.

June: The Hawaiian League demands governmental reform of King Kalakaua. It succeeds in forcing many of its demands to be met and the monarchy's powers are reduced.

August 10: In Chatsworth, Illinois, a train derailment occurs when a bridge collapses. Over 100 people die in the accident.

September 5: The first Labor Day is celebrated as a legal holiday in New York State.

November 11: August Spies and four other anarchists are hanged for their role in the Haymarket riot of May 1886.

December 6: In his annual message to the country, President Cleveland announces his support of tariff reform. By lowering the tariff, Cleveland hopes to expand the power base of the Democrats and to appeal to those in favor of lower costs for raw materials and consumer goods. Most specifically, Cleveland anticipates that this position will provide his party with the unifying element, a common issue, it needs in order to face Republican opposition in the upcoming election year.

EYEWITNESS TESTIMONY

. . . On the labor question My position is:

1. The previous question always must be in any popular excitement the supremacy of law. All lawless violence must be suppressed instantly, with overwhelming force and at all hazards. To hesitate or tamper with it is a fatal mistake. Justice, humanity, and safety all require this.

2. I agree that Labor does not get its fair share of the wealth it creates. The Sermon on the Mount, the golden rule, the Declaration of Independence all require extensive reforms to the end that labor may be so rewarded that the working man can with temperance, industry & thrift own a home, educate his children, & lay up a support for old age.

3. The United States must begin to deal with the whole subject.

President Rutherford B. Hayes, to Guy M.
Bryan, letter of 1886, in DeNovo's The Gilded
Age and After *(1972).*

1. Labor, like flour or cotton cloth, should always be bought in the cheapest market and sold in the dearest.

2. The sole legitimate condition that regulates wages is the demand for service and the supply of workers. If the demand diminishes, wages decrease; if the supply diminishes, wages increase.

3. The wage ordinarily paid is not determined by the automatic division of the whole amount which a community is willing to pay for the specified sort of work, but the whole number of persons willing and able to do it.

William A. Croffut, in an article in The
Forum, *May 1886.*

The protectionists, in advocating their system, always spend a great deal of effort and eloquence on appeals to patriotism, and to international jealousies. These are all entirely aside from the point. The protective system is a domestic system, for domestic purposes, and it is sought by domestic means. The one who pays, and the one who gets, are both Americans. The victim and the beneficiary are amongst ourselves. It is just as unpatriotic to oppress one American as it is patriotic to favor another. If we make one American pay taxes to another American, it will neither vex nor please any foreign nation.

. . . Free trade means antagonism to this whole policy and theory at every point. The free trader regards it all as false, meretricious, and delusive. He considers it an invasion of private rights. In the best case, if all that the protectionist claims were true, he would be taking it upon himself to decide how his neighbor should spend his earnings, and—more than that—that his neighbor shall spend his earning for the advantage of the men who make the decision. This is plainly immoral and corrupting; nothing could be more so. The free trader also denies that the government either can, or ought to regulate the way in which a man shall employ his earnings. He sees that the government is nothing but a clique of the parties of interest.

. . . The free trader further holds that protection is all a mistake and a delusion to those who think that they win by it, in that it lessens their self-reliance and energy and exposes their business to vicissitudes which, not being incident to a natural order of things, cannot be foreseen and guarded against by business skill.

Economist and philosopher William Graham
Sumner, speaking in 1886, in Hoogenboom and
Hoogenboom's The Gilded Age *(1967).*

William Graham Sumner, economist and philosopher. Courtesy of the Library of Congress.

Andrew Carnegie, a Scottish immigrant who became an American millionaire. Courtesy of the Library of Congress.

The American . . . need not fear the unhealthy or abnormal growth of cities . . . The free play of economic laws is keeping all quite right . . . Oh, these grand, immutable, all-wise laws of natural forces, how perfectly they work if human legislators would only let them alone.

Industrialist Andrew Carnegie, in Triumphant Democracy, *1886.*

It is evident that our members are not properly instructed, else we would not find them passing resolutions "approving of the action of our executive officers in fixing the 1st of May as the day to strike for eight hours." The executive officers of the Knights of Labor have never fixed upon the 1st of May for a strike of any kind, and they will not do so until the proper time arrives and the word goes forth from the General Assembly.

No Assembly of the Knights of Labor must strike for the eight-hour system on May 1 under the impression that they are obeying orders from headquarters, for such an order was not and will not be given. Neither employer nor employee are educated to the needs and necessities for the short-hour plan. If one branch of trade or one Assembly is in such a condition, remember that there are many who are in total ignorance of the movement. Out of the sixty millions of people in the United States and Canada, our Order has possibly three hundred thousand. Can we mould the sentiment of millions in favor of the short-hour plan before May 1? It is nonsense to think of it. Let us learn why our hours of labor should be reduced, and then teach others.

Terence V. Powderly, leader of the Knights of Labor, statement of 1886, in Powderly's Thirty Years of Labor 1859–1889 *(1967).*

Police and militias, the bloodhounds of capitalism, are ready to murder!

Anarchist and Haymarket riot leader August Spies, editor of the anarchist newspaper Die Arbeiter-Zeitung, *1886, in Tuchman's* The Proud Tower *(1966).*

I am not here for the purpose of inciting anybody, but to spell out, to tell the facts as they exist, even though it shall cost me my life before morning. It behooves you, as you love your wife and children— if you don't want to see them perish with hunger, killed or cut down like dogs in the street—Americans, in the interest of your liberty and independence, to *arm*, to *arm* yourselves!

Albert Parsons, socialist agitator and journalist, at the Haymarket rally in May 1886, in Weinstein and Wilson's Freedom and Crisis: An American History *(1978).*

When more of the people's sustenance is exacted through the form of taxation than is necessary to meet the just obligations of Government and expenses of its economical administration, such exaction becomes ruthless extortion and a violation of the fundamental principles of a free Government.

President Grover Cleveland, to the nation, his second Annual Message, December 1886, in Bartlett's Familiar Quotations *(1951).*

The American people are far in advance of Congress in respect to an American navy . . . We have no fear of any of the nations on this continent. Whenever the attack may come, it will come from across the seas. The American people almost unitedly are at the door of Congress today asking for something with which we may meet the foe away from our coast when he comes.

Representative Charles B. Lore (R-Delaware), 1887, in Campbell's Expansionism and Imperialism *(1970).*

They are running their business at a loss; they are making articles to which this bill refers; and this bill says that if those eight men should combine to get a fair, living profit upon their manufacture, that contract, that agreement is against public policy, unlawful and void.

Senator Orville Platt (R-Connecticut), on the unconstitutionality of the Sherman Anti-Trust bill, 1887, in Ginger's People on the Move *(1975).*

As I approach the end, I am more than a little puzzled to account for the instances I have seen of business success—money-getting. It comes from a rather low instinct. Certainly, so far as my observation goes, it is rarely met with in combination with the finer or more interesting traits of character. I have known, and known tolerably well, a good many "successful" men—"big" financially—men famous during the last half-century; and a less interesting crowd I do not care to encounter. Not one that I have ever known would I care to meet again, either in this world or the next; nor is one of them associated in my mind with the idea of humor, thought or refinement. A set of mere money-getters and traders, they were essentially unattractive and uninteresting.

Charles Francis Adams Jr., historian and railroad expert, 1887, in Paterson's American Imperialism and Anti-Imperialism *(1973).*

It has always been difficult for well-to-do people of the upper and middle classes to sympathize with and to understand the needs of their poorer neighbors.

Samuel Lane Loomis, Protestant minister, 1887, in Degler's The Age of the Economic Revolution 1876–1900 *(1977).*

The danger of alienating large bodies of workmen, whose ignorance is crass, who are thoroughly organized, and whose employers are extremely jealous of any danger of loss of profits, is to my mind the danger of the situation.

George Hoadley, to President Cleveland, cautioning against protective tariff reform, letter of 1887, in Morgan's The Gilded Age *(1970).*

Murder, insanity, suicide, divorce, drunkenness and all forms of immorality and crime have increased from that day [Panic of 1873] to this in the most appalling ratio.

Mrs. S.E.V. Emery, economics writer, observing that the nation's fiscal, social and cultural problems have been fueled by federal monetary policies, 1887, in Davis and Woodman's Conflict or Consensus in American History *(1966).*

11. A Changing American Landscape: 1888–1889

THE HISTORICAL CONTEXT

While many Americans agreed that the nation's economy demanded intervention by the government, by private reform groups or by individuals, no one was certain how best to relieve the monotonous cycle of recession and inflation. One man, however, had an answer to the widening gulf that separated the very rich and the very poor. Henry George, an economist, devised a simple strategy that he felt could solve the country's fiscal difficulties: the single tax.

The concept was simple—to eliminate all taxes except those on the value of land. George proposed that landowners be assessed for the value of their land as that value increased or decreased and that the tax be applied to the public good. In his book *Progress and Poverty*, George explained the nuances of his single-tax idea, and in numerous speaking engagements he was able to generate widespread support for its adoption. His reform impulses would perhaps have been translated into action if the most wealthy capitalists of the era, who wielded considerable influence, had not so vehemently opposed him.

By the late 1880s, industrial America was ascendant and the needs and interests of its most powerful and prominent citizens were well-served. The continued agitation by labor leaders was insufficient to convince the voters that they might benefit from reform of corporate structures. In fact, the reverse was true. The louder the noise from striking workers, the more entrenched *against* changes in the workplace or the length of the workday the average voter became.

But gradually, as they learned about the many needs for social and economic reform in the United States, more people began to seek change. Education played a role in this, as did a greater number of publications dedicated to new reform approaches and unique ways of implementing change. In early 1888, Edward Bellamy's novel of socialist utopia, *Looking Backward*, was published. This book was one of

A family sod house in Custer County, Nebraska, 1886. Courtesy of the Solomon D. Butcher Collection. Nebraska State Historical Society.

many efforts to outline the way in which social, economic or cultural reforms could improve human civilization. *Looking Backward* would sell over 200,000 copies within a few years of its publication. It was widely read even outside the U.S., as was the writing of social critic Henry George.

Although they were not new, fraternal organizations continued to grow in popularity and broadened their membership base. Many were religious or political in connection, ideology or form. The Southern Alliance was one of the more prominent political organizations of the late 1880s. Formed when the National Farmers' Alliance (founded in 1880) joined with the Agricultural Wheel, it became one of the most powerful special interest groups in the nation. Aimed at improving the farmer's situation, it was particularly vehement in its opposition to railroad interests, which Alliance members claimed had taken precedence over the needs of agriculture in the United States.

Also in 1888, the Student Volunteer Movement was established. It sought to put to use the evangelistic, social-activist fervor affecting hundreds of young men and women, many of whom were among a new group of college-educated Americans. The movement encouraged missionary work and was led by John R. Mott. He would later become national secretary of the YMCA. This effort was closely allied with the settlement house movement, the flagship of which—Hull House, in Chicago—opened in September 1889.

While the reform impulse began to change people's response to society, changes in the way buildings were designed and constructed transformed the urban landscape. In 1888, architect Louis Sullivan designed the Schlesinger Building in Chicago. It later became the department store Carson, Pirie, Scott, and its elegant facade quickly made it a well-recognized Chicago landmark. In Pittsburgh, Pennsylvania, the first Bessemer steel beams were produced, enabling construction of many skyscrapers nationwide. One of these, the 11-story Tower Building in New York City, was erected in 1888, the same year that the steel beams first became available. Among the first steel skeleton skyscrapers, the Tower Building was designed by architect Bradford Gilbert. Only three years later, Louis Sullivan—often referred to as the "father" of the skyscraper—completed the Wainwright Building in St. Louis, Missouri, another such steel-frame building.

Certain technological breakthroughs of the 1880s ushered in an entirely new world of leisure pursuits. Thomas A. Edison produced the first moving picture film in 1888, using technology developed by George Eastman of Rochester, New York. Within several decades, silent moving pictures would become popular wherever they were shown.

Bicycling grew more popular in 1889, especially with the advent of the safety bicycle, which had two equal-sized wheels. It replaced older-style bicycles with one large and one small wheel, which were much more difficult to maneuver. Also in 1889, the U.S. Lawn Tennis Association announced that its champion players were Henry Slocum and Bertha Townsend, indicating the public's growing interest in tennis as a spectator sport. That year too, the first All-American football team was chosen and appeared in a feature in *Collier's Weekly*.

Some Americans found less active, though no less absorbing, ways to spend their leisure time. American theatergoers were entranced with David Belasco and Henry De Mille's play, *The Charity Ball*, which debuted in 1889. In September, Bronson Howard's play about the Civil War, *Shenandoah*, was produced in New York City by Charles Frohman and became a theater classic. Elsewhere, in 1889, Henry James's short story, "The Liar," was published. Mark Twain's popular novel, *A Connecticut Yankee in King Arthur's Court*, appeared that year and poet Emma Lazarus, who became famous for her verse inscribed at the base of the Statue of Liberty in New York Harbor, published *The Poems of Emma Lazarus*.

As part of the continuing trend of establishing separate postsecondary institutions for women, Barnard College was founded in 1889 as part of Columbia University. And another land-grant university, the University of New Mexico, was established in Albuquerque. Although initially founded as a way of promoting the most effective agricultural practices among those homesteading or farming previously unsettled areas, by the mid-1900s these schools would be among the most respected in the nation.

One of the most interesting phenomena of these years was the opening up of land in Oklahoma territory, previously Indian territory, to homesteading settlers. Within several hours of the starting gun at midday on April 22, thousands of settlers had staked claims and established themselves as "Sooners." This land rush resulted in a popula-

While the Gilded Age was a time of urban growth, westward expansion was also crucial to national economic expansion. Homesteading families like this one, traveling in a covered wagon, made such expansion possible. Courtesy of the New York Public Library Picture Collection.

tion in the Territory of over 60,000 residents by the time the census was taken in 1890.

The close of the 1880s marked the end of a period in which most Americans focused on domestic concerns. The new decade would usher in challenges with foreign nations, and would increasingly demand that presidents and Congress alike make shrewd judgments about the role the United States played in a world economy. The election of Benjamin Harrison in 1888 forecast a trend: with one exception, Harrison's G.O.P. would maintain control of the executive branch until well into the 20th century. This fact, almost more than any other single detail, predicted the continuing favor that big business would enjoy. It also was a good predictor of the direction that American foreign policy would take for the next several decades.

CHRONICLE OF EVENTS

1888:

January 1: The nation's first municipally supported health laboratory is opened in Providence, Rhode Island.

January 3: Drinking straws are patented by M.C. Stone.

January 21: The Amateur Athletic Union of the U.S. is established.

January 24: The first typewriter ribbon is patented by J.L. Wortman in Philadelphia, Pennsylvania.

February 19: A cyclone in Mount Vernon, Illinois, kills 35 people.

February 22: The Industrial Reform party meets in Washington, D.C. Delegates to the convention nominate Albert E. Redstone for president.

February 24: In a change in the election laws in the state of Kentucky, the Australian ballot system is used for the first time in Louisville in local elections. This system requires a secret ballot; the last state to adopt it will be South Carolina in 1950.

March 2: In Richmond, Virginia, the nation's first bank owned and operated by and for black Americans is chartered.

March 12: A blizzard strikes New York City, lasting for 36 hours and isolating its inhabitants.

April: The first woman mayor and all-woman town council are elected in Oskaloosa, Kansas.

April 4: The first holding company laws in the nation are passed in New Jersey.

May: In New York City, actor DeWolf Hopper

Pioneers in Colorado, ca. 1885. Courtesy of the New York Public Library Picture Collection.

The Oklahoma land rush in 1889 provided land for over 50,000 settlers in the former Indian Territory. Courtesy of the New York Public Library Picture Collection.

recites "Casey at the Bat" for the first time, at Wallacks Theater.

May 1: The first electric freight engine is built and tested in Pullman, Illinois.

May 15: The Equal Rights party holds its second national convention in Des Moines, Iowa, and again nominates Belva P. Lockwood for president of the United States.

May 17: The Union Labor party holds its first national convention in Cincinnati, Ohio. Robert H. Cowdrey is nominated for president.

May 21: In New York State, the nation's first authorized crematory is opened.

May 31: The Prohibition party holds a national convention in Indianapolis, Indiana. General Clinton B. Fisk is nominated for the presidency.

June 1: The first seismograph is shown at the Lick Observatory at Mount Hamilton, California.

June 4: In New York State, Governor Hill signs legislation authorizing electrocution to be used in sentences of capital punishment. The law will take effect in 1889.

June 6: The Democrats hold their national convention in St. Louis, Missouri.

June 13: An act of Congress establishes a Department of Labor as separate from the Department of the Interior. It will not be given cabinet status until 1913.

June 19: Once again, the Republicans gather in Chicago, Illinois, for their national party convention.

June 25: On the eight ballot, the Republican party nominates Benjamin Harrison and Levi P. Morton for president and vice president, respectively.

July 4: The nation's first rodeo competition is held in Prescott Arizona.

July 27: Phillip Pratt demonstrates the first electric automobile, driven on storage batteries, in Boston, Massachusetts.

July 29: In Jacksonville, Florida, a yellow fever epidemic breaks out and lasts until December, killing over 400 people.

August 7: The first revolving door is patented by T. Van Kannel of Philadelphia, Pennsylvania.

August 14: An electric meter is patented in Rochester, New York, by O.B. Shallenberger.

August 15: The American party holds its convention in Philadelphia, Pennsylvania. The delegates nominate James L. Curtis for president.

August 21: A patent is taken out for the first adding machine.

September 1: In Worthington, Ohio, Pontifical College Josephinum is established.

October 1: The Scott Act is passed, which prevents Chinese immigrants from returning to the U.S. if they leave, even for a brief visit to their ancestral homeland.

   The nation's first interstate carrier arbitration law is enacted.

October 9: The Washington Monument is opened to the public.

October 14: Jane Addams, soon to be known for her social reform work in urban slums, is baptized at the age of 28 at the Presbyterian Church in Cedarville, Illinois. This acknowledgment of her personal faith acts as an initial public commitment in her lifetime of service and dedication to others.

October 17: The keel of the battleship *Maine* is laid in the first stage of its construction.

October 25: In Newburgh, New York, the first double-decker ferryboat is launched.

October 30: A patent is taken out for the first ballpoint pen, by J. Loud of Weymouth, Massachusetts.

November 6: Republican Benjamin Harrison defeats Grover Cleveland in the presidential elections with an electoral vote of 233–168.

November 20: The first employee time clock is patented in Auburn, New York.

December 24: On the Mississippi River, fires on two separate steamboats cause 55 fatalities.

1889:

January 19: The state of Georgia declares this date a legal holiday in observance of General Robert E. Lee's birthday.

January 28: Striking transit workers cause New York City's transportation system to come to a halt.

January 30: The University of Idaho is chartered.

February 9: With the increasing visibility and influence of farm interests in the U.S., the Department of Agriculture is raised to a cabinet-level agency.

February 11: Norman J. Colman is named the first secretary of agriculture by President Cleveland.

February 20: Congress incorporates the Maritime Canal Company of Nicaragua. Its purpose is to contruct a canal across the Central American isthmus, work on which is set to begin in October of this year.

February 22: President Cleveland signs an Omnibus bill which grants North and South Dakota, Montana and Washington statehood.

March 2: The state of Kansas passes an antitrust law.

March 4: Benjamin Harrison is inaugurated as the nation's 23rd president.

March 15: On Samoa, a civil war continues, with the U.S. backing the forces of King Malietoa. The Samoan Islands have provided a fueling station for American naval vessels since 1878. Germany supports the rebel cause on Samoa, and although Great Britain remains neutral it is prepared to aid U.S. interests at any time. Warships from the three nations cruise Samoan waters, but all but one are destroyed during a hurricane.

April 22: Despite a previous agreement that gives possession of large land areas in Oklahoma to Native Americans, the area opens to white settlement. Over 50,000 "Sooners" prepare to rush for the 2 million acres of land, and by the end of the day the entire area is claimed by white settlers.

Wheat harvesting in Kansas. Courtesy of The Kansas State Historical Society.

April 29: Great Britain, Germany and the United States meet and arrange to restore King Malietoa to his throne in Samoa. As a way of maintaining power over the island nation, however, the three countries hold the right to appoint the Supreme Court justice on the islands.

Theodore Roosevelt, who rose quickly in public life, was appointed head of the Civil Service Commission in 1889. He was known for his passion for reform and his aggressive, take-charge approach to any task.

May 9: New Jersey permits holding companies to be chartered in that state.

May 13: Theodore Roosevelt is named to head the federal Civil Service Commission.

May 16: Helen Culver, owner of a large Chicago building, signs a rental agreement with Jane Addams. The building, known as Hull House, is soon transformed into one of the nation's earliest settlement houses.

May 31: Nearly 5,000 people die in a flood in Johnstown, Pennsylvania, after a dam at Conemaugh Lake collapses. Although the lake was 18 miles away, the break allows a 40-foot-high wall of water to reach the city in eight minutes.

June 5: Boxer James J. Corbett knocks out Joe Choyinski with a left hook.

June 10: The United Confederate Veterans meet in New Orleans and elect Governor John B. Gordon the first general of the organization.

June 14: The U.S., Germany and Great Britain agree to establish a three-nation protectorate on Samoa.

July 8: The final bare-knuckles boxing match is held at Richburg, Mississippi, between John L. Sullivan and Jake Kilrain. Following this match, all boxing is conducted with gloves under rules introduced by the Marquess of Queensbury.

July 12: A concert of music by American composers is given at the Paris Exhibition. It marks the first time that works from the U.S. are so acknowledged.

September 18: Jane Addams and Ellan Gates Starr move into the former Charles J. Hull mansion in Chicago, Illinois. It will soon become world-famous as an urban settlement.

October 2: In Washington, D.C., the first International Conference of American States meets in an attempt to control trade issues in the Americas.

October 7: Columbia College announces that Seth Low is to be president of the institution. He later is elected mayor of New York City.

November 11: The first Congress of Roman Catholic laypersons meets in Baltimore, Maryland.

November 14: Journalist Elizabeth Cochrane, known by her pen name of Nelly Bly, begins a trip around the world that takes 72 days. She does this to challenge British author Jules Verne, whose book, *Around the World in Eighty Days*, set a standard she was determined to beat.

December 6: Former Confederate President Jefferson Davis dies in New Orleans, Louisiana. He is buried there but is later re-interred in Richmond, Virginia.

December 14: The American Academy of Political and Social Science is founded in Philadelphia, Pennsylvania.

EYEWITNESS TESTIMONY

They are great prison-like structures of brick, with narrow doors and windows, cramped passages and steep rickety stairs. They are built through from one street to the other with a somewhat narrower building connecting them . . . The narrow court-yard . . . in the middle is a damp foul-smelling place, supposed to do duty as an airshaft; had the foul fiend designed these great barracks they could not have been more villainously arranged to avoid any chance of ventilation.

The drainage is horrible, and even the Croton as it flows from a tap in the noisome courtyard, seemed to be contaminated by its surroundings and have a fetid smell.

Allan Forman, reform journalist, in the American Magazine, *describing "dumbbell" tenement apartments, November 1888, in Callow's* American Urban History *(1973).*

I am simply reminding our members of what the practical results of a strike are to our side of the house. A defeat is not the worst thing that can happen to men on strike; they lose hope, they abandon organization . . . What combination of hungry men could fight a battle against a combination of dollars? I believe that strikes are weakening the labor movement in America.

Terence V. Powderly, leader of the Knights of Labor, 1888, in Dubofsky's Industrialism and the American Worker, 1865–1920 *(1975).*

These heroes are dead. They died for liberty—they died for us. They are at rest. They sleep in the land they made free, under the flag they rendered stainless, under the solemn pines, the sad hemlocks, the tearful willows, the embracing vines. They sleep beneath the shadows of the clouds, careless alike of sunshine or storm, each in the windowless palace of rest. Earth may run red with other wars—they are at peace. In the midst of battles, in the roar of conflict, they found the serenity of death.

Robert G. Ingersoll, lawyer and former Radical Republican well-known for anti-Southern oratory, repeating a speech he first gave in Indianapolis, Indiana, in 1876.

Let every man honor and love the land of his birth and the race from which he springs and keep their memory green. It is a pious and honorable duty. But let us have done with British-Americans and Irish-Americans and German-Americans, and so on, and all be Americans . . . If a man is going to be an American at all let him be so without any qualifying adjectives; and if he is going to be something else, let him drop the word American from his personal description.

Henry Cabot Lodge of Massachusetts, shortly before he won a Congressional seat, speaking to the New England Society of Brooklyn, December 1888, in Bartlett's Familiar Quotations *(1951).*

The people admire old Grover's [Cleveland] strength so much, he is a positive man and an honest man, and when the people see these two exceptional virtues mixed happily in a candidate they grow to love and admire him out of the very idealism of their natures.

Franklin K. Lane, California journalist, to a friend, letter of 1888, in Morgan's The Gilded Age *(1970).*

. . . Is it reasonable to expect that Mr. Harrison, if elected, would oppose such a "clean sweep" with

Carl Schurz, civil service reform advocate. Courtesy of the Library of Congress.

greater courage and firmness than was shown by Mr. Cleveland? Mr. Harrison is, in point of personal character, no doubt vastly preferable to Mr. Blaine. But neither his professions nor his antecedents stamp him as a man who would resist the demands of the influential politicians of his party. He would on the contrary, to the extent of his power, meet them, as he asked his demands to be met under a previous Republican Administration. The cause of civil service reform would, therefore, have to hope rather less from Mr. Harrison than from Mr. Cleveland.

Carl Schurz, liberal Republican, and Secretary of the Interior under President Hayes, to Thaddeus C. Pound, letter of September 1888, in DeNovo's The Gilded Age and After *(1972).*

. . . the work of creating new gigantic and dangerous "trusts" or combinations, seems to be increasing and going steadily on. The plain truth is that these gigantic corporations . . . are beyond and above the control of municipal ordinances or State laws. It is even doubted by many whether the vast powers of the General Government will prove to be sufficiently potential [*sic*] against such an aggregation of capital and brains. Exercising functions that are largely public in their character they nevertheless enjoy all the rights and all the advantages of private enterprises. As absolutely essential agencies for the transaction of business they are protected by the business interests of the country from the operation of laws enacted for the purpose of bringing them into subjection to authority.

There is nothing democratic about such vast monopolies for controlling those channels through which intelligence and traffic are effected. Competition is crushed by its very weight, holding business men by the throat, and forcing them to deliver. They are despotic in spirit, tyrannical in method, openly hostile to liberty and free institutions, and threatening menaces to the pursuit of happiness, and to equality and equal opportunities under the law. When the people of this country once get their eyes wide open they will hardly permit such dangerous excrescences to fasten their deathlike grip upon our liberties and our laws . . .

W.A. Rapsher, journalist, in an article in North American Review, *May 1888.*

The tone of public life is lower than one expects to find in so great a nation. Just as we assume that an

individual man will at any supreme moment in his own life rise to a higher level than that on which he usually moves, so we look to find those who conduct the affairs of a great state inspired by a sense of the magnitude of the interests entrusted to them. Their horizon ought to be expanded, their feeling of duty quickened, their dignity of attitude enhanced . . .

Such a sentiment is comparatively weak in America. A cabinet minister, or senator, or governor of a State, sometimes even a President, hardly feels himself more bound by it than the director of a railway company or the mayor of a town does in Europe. Not assuming himself to be individually wiser, stronger, or better than his fellow-citizens, he acts and speaks as though he were still simply one of them, and so far from magnifying his office and making it honourable, seems anxious to show that he is the mere creature of the popular vote, so filled by the sense that it is the people and not he who governs as to fear that he should be deemed to have forgotten his personal insignificance. There is in the United States abundance of patriotism, that is to say, or a passion for the greatness and happiness of the Republic, and a readiness to make sacrifices for it . . . But these sentiments do not bear their appropriate fruit in raising the conception of public office, or its worth and its dignity.

James Bryce, British diplomat, in The American Commonwealth, *1888.*

It is a community for University men who live here, have their recreation and clubs and society all among the poor people, yet in the same style they would live in their own circle. It is so free from 'professional doing good,' so unaffectedly sincere and so productive of good results in its classes and libraries so that it seems perfectly ideal.

Jane Addams, founder of Hull House, to a friend, describing the English settlement Toynbee Hull, letter of 1888, in Davis's American Heroine *(1973).*

. . . I can find no warrant for such an appropriation in the Constitution, and I do not believe that the power and duty of the General Government ought to be extended to the relief of individual suffering which is in no manner properly related to the public service or benefit. A prevalent tendency to disregard the limited mission of this power and duty should, I think, be steadfastly resisted, to the end that the

Jane Addams, founder of the Chicago settlement known as Hull House. Courtesy of the National Portrait Gallery, Smithsonian Institution.

lesson should be constantly enforced that though the people support the Government the Government should not support the people.

President Grover Cleveland, articulating laissez-faire policy in vetoing federal aid to drought-stricken farmers in Texas, 1889, in Ginger's People on the Move *(1975).*

The "single tax will ruin the farmers" is shouted across the prairies and over the plains. If lifting a part of the burden from the back of the farmer, and placing it on the shoulders of the man who holds more acres than the farmer without the payment of a hundredth part of the taxes which the farmer is obliged to pay, is ruin, then indeed will the farmers be ruined . . . If there is a class of men on the soil of America who are directly interested in securing the passage of a single-tax law that class is to be found where farmers are numerous.

Previous to the birth of the land speculator in the West, the farmer was not troubled with such an encumbrance as a mortgage on his land, now he has an abundance of them. It was not to fight off the single tax that the farmers of the United States met in national convention in Georgetown, D.C. in January 1873, for the purpose of organizing the National Grange. They met because they were being gathered into the net of mortgage holder, because of excessive taxation, and because of discrimination in freights.

Terence V. Powderly, leader of the Knights of Labor, 1889, in Powderly's Thirty Years of Labor 1859–1889 *(1967).*

Frankly I don't know that I should be sorry to see a bit of a spar with Germany. The burning of New York and a few other sea coast cities would be a good object lesson in the need of an adequate system of coast defenses and I think it would have a good effect on our large German population to force them to an ostentatiously patriotic display of anger against Germany . . . It is very difficult for me not to wish a war with Spain, for such a war would result at once in getting a proper Navy.

Civil Service Commissioner Theodore Roosevelt, to a friend, 1889, in Paterson's American Imperialism and Anti-Imperialism *(1973).*

The artistic temperament is not a national trait of the English race. Our complex and exciting civilization has, indeed, developed, especially in America, a sensitiveness of nervous organization which often wears the semblance of the artistic temperament, and shows itself in manual dexterity and refined technical skill. And this tends to make mere workmanship, mere excellence of execution, the common test of merit in a work of the fine arts.

Charles Eliot Norton, Scholar and editor, in The Forum, *March 1889.*

We have exchanged the Washingtonian dignity for the Jeffersonian simplicity, which was in truth only another name for the Jacksonian vulgarity.

Henry Codman Potter, Protestant Episcopal Bishop of New York, Washington Centennial address at St. Paul's Chapel, New York City, April 30, 1889, in Bartlett's Familiar Quotations *(1951).*

12. Reform, Anti-Trust Legislation and Expansionism: 1890–1891

THE HISTORICAL CONTEXT

The Republican administration gave only lip service to the needs of the poor in America—it was the friend of trusts, of big business, of the railroads. Nevertheless, there were individuals and groups in the United States whose concern was put into action on behalf of the silent millions who slept in overcrowded tenements, put in long hours in factories, mills and mines and who were either too young—or too poorly educated—to vote.

As the plight of immigrants and the urban poor became more widely apparent, journalists actively promoted recognition of these problems. Among the more aggressive of these journalists was Jacob A. Riis. In 1890, he published *How the Other Half Lives*, a book that graphically depicted life in urban slums. He added his voice to the growing choir of reform journalists, like Henry Demarest Lloyd, Edward Bellamy and Robert Blatchford, that spoke for the poor.

Although the many problems facing laborers, immigrants and the indigent were being publicized, there remained a complexity of issues crippling the nation's cities. Social workers tried their best to address these issues and to effect change by hands-on efforts and by promoting reform legislation. During this time, too, there was an upsurge in the formation of groups dedicated to changing urban conditions. In 1891, the Christian Social Union was founded in the United States, an organization that was the American branch of a British group. It was dedicated to reforming society for the general good. The young Johns Hopkins economist Richard T. Ely was among its first members.

Ely, and others who considered the effect of national economic development on individuals' problems, knew that the solution to poverty

Expansion of the steel industry enriched a few, provided work for hundreds of thousands of laborers and made the United States an industrial giant among the world's nations. Shown here is an Alabama blast furnace. Courtesy of the Library of Congress.

was not simple. Before the country could expect to change labor and living conditions among the poor, it needed to confront the stalemate in the nation's monetary policy. Lobbyists for the Sherman Silver Purchase Act were overjoyed when the act was passed in 1890, requiring the Treasury Department to buy 4.5 million ounces of silver each month. It was hoped that this would prevent a further decline in the value of money and shore up the flagging economy.

Fiscal issues and city slums were not the only targets of reform efforts. Education also became the focus of reform. Sometimes, the result was schooling for the privileged, as in the case of the Taft School. Founded in 1890, in Watertown, Connecticut, it was a private boarding school for wealthy young men. But educators also recognized the need to provide schooling for those who might otherwise never have the opportunity for advancement. The nation's first correspondence school was opened in 1891 by Thomas Jefferson Foster as a way of making education available to miners, many of whom were immigrant workers and most of whom were virtually illiterate. In the arena of public education, the Committee of Ten on Secondary Schools was formed in 1891 to examine the preparation of students nationwide. And colleges and universities continued to be founded all over the country. The University of Chicago was chartered in 1891; Rice University and Throop Polytechnic (later Cal Tech) were also founded that year. An interest in athletics was growing on college campuses, and several new sports were introduced. In 1890, Dr. James A. Naismith invented the game of basketball at the YMCA Training College in Springfield, Massachusetts.

Fraternal and social organizations were founded in growing numbers as people's cultural interests and political affiliations became bet-

President Benjamin Harrison.

ter articulated. The Daughters of the American Revolution was founded in 1891, as was the Colonial Dames. Both groups, exclusive in their membership requirements, were the virtual opposites of the reform-oriented settlement organizations that attracted the attention of upper-middle class women at the end of the 19th century. Within the next several years, more of these exclusive clubs would be founded. In 1893, the Daughters of the Cincinnati was founded for descendants of those who had fought in the Civil War, and the Society of Mayflower Descendants was also established. Its membership became one of the nation's most respected and prestigious.

These and other social activities remained on the periphery of the nation's consciousness in the last decade, however. As far as the most powerful opinion-makers, or the federal government, was concerned, big business demanded a majority of attention and scrutiny. More companies' holdings included both the supply of raw materials and the manufacture of finished goods. Because these large companies were economically powerful, they edged out smaller, less profitable efforts and thereby reduced competition, particularly in the largest manufacturing areas, such as steel production. Concerned, Congress passed the Sherman Anti-Trust Act in 1890 to penalize companies that formed combinations "in restraint of trade." The act's intention was to limit the financial power of giants such as Carnegie Steel, but however well-placed this intent, the government could not prevail over the power of big business. The act would be rendered ineffective in 1895 by the U.S. Supreme Court ruling *U.S. v. Knight*. It stated that monopolies were not inherently illegal, a ruling that would set the stage for years of continuing profit for the nation's largest industries—at the expense of farmers and the small business community.

Because of the growing influence of reformers, and the dissatisfaction that many in the United States felt toward Harrison's Republican administration, there were Democrats who believed that Cleveland could be elected in 1892. An increasing number of Americans who were completely disillusioned with the two-party system founded the People's party in 1891, a clear sign that the G.O.P. was losing ground with large numbers of voters. It would be two more years, however, before the U.S. would be tested at the polls and Harrison had the opportunity to address the wider interests of the nation. The fact that he failed to do so made even more clear the path that the Democrats—and the Populists—would take in 1892.

CHRONICLE OF EVENTS

1890:

January 1: The first "Tournament of Roses" parade is held in Pasadena, California.

January 3: The University of Wisconsin begins offering the nation's first collegiate course in dairy farming.

January 7: The naval vessel *Baltimore* is commissioned.

January 23: The Atchison, Topeka & Santa Fe railroad achieves the fastest speed ever recorded—78.1 miles per hour.

January 25: The United Mine Workers is formed.

Journalist Nellie Bly returns form her round-the-world tour, the first to be made by a woman traveling alone.

February 4: The U.S. Senate ratifies a treaty with Great Britain and Germany that sets up a Samoan protectorate.

February 10: The federal government releases 11 million acres of former Sioux territory to settlement by whites.

February 18: The National American Women's Suffrage Association is established when two formerly opposing groups—the American Woman Suffrage Association and the National Woman Suffrage Association—combine. Among the speakers at the convention is Carrie Chapman.

February 24: The U.S. House of Representatives selects Chicago, Illinois, as the location for the World's Columbian Exposition in commemoration of the 400th anniversary of the discovery of the New World in 1492.

March 18: In Massachusetts, the nation's first state naval militia is formed.

March 20: The General Federation of Women's Clubs meets for the first time in New York City.

March 24: The U.S. Supreme Court, reversing a decision made in 1877 in the Granger cases, rules that a state cannot set fees so as to deprive an individual of the right of "reasonable profit." In deciding the case, *Chicago, Milwaukee, & St. Paul Railroad v. Minnesota*, the Supreme Court offers unprecedented protection to railroad corporations under the Fourteenth Amendment.

April 4: New York State passes legislation aimed at stopping corrupt election practices.

April 14: The Pan-American Union is established with passage of a resolution at the Pan-American Conference, which has been meeting since October of the previous year.

April 22: The *Cushing*, a torpedo boat, is commissioned at Bristol, Pennsylvania.

April 28: In *Leisy v. Hardin*, the U.S. Supreme Court strikes down state laws prohibiting liquor from being transported across state lines. The court rules that such restriction would interfere with gainful profits.

In Ohio, the first state employment service in the nation opens.

May 1: Philadelphia's Bank of America fails, provoking the collapse of several other financial institutions.

Members of the American Federation of Labor have chosen this as the date on which an eight-hour day should be established.

May 2: The Oklahoma Territory is created by Congress, further reducing the size of Indian territory.

May 24: George Francis Train bests Nellie Bly's record of around-the-world travel, completing his journey in 67 days, 13 hours and 3 seconds.

May 30: Construction of the Washington Square Memorial Arch begins in New York City.

June 1: The nation's first census to be compiled by machine begins.

June 6: The U.S. Polo Association is formed in New York City.

June 9: The comic opera *Robin Hood* is performed in New York City. Author Reginald De Koven achieves lasting fame for two songs in this production, "Brown October Ale" and "Oh, Promise Me."

June 10: Feminist Carrie Chapman marries George Catt.

June 27: James Tanner is appointed commissioner of pensions by President Harrison. Under Tanner's direction, federal pensions increase from 676,000 to 970,000 between 1891 and 1895.

June 29: The Federal Elections Bill, or "Force Bill," of 1890 is introduced by Massachusetts Senator Henry Cabot Lodge to help guarantee federal supervision of elections. The Force Bill meets with House approval but fails to pass the Senate.

June 30: Congress passes legislation that authorizes three new steel-clad ships to replace those lost in the storm in Samoan waters in the spring of 1889.

July 2: The Sherman Anti-Trust Act, introduced to the Senate by John Sherman (D-Ohio), is passed. It renders illegal "every contract, combination in the form of trust or otherwise, or conspiracy, in restraint of trade or commerce among the several States, or with foreign nations."

July 3: Idaho becomes the nation's 43rd state.

July 10: Wyoming is admitted to statehood. It is the first state to grant women the right to vote, having approved women's suffrage in 1869 while it was still a territory.

July 14: Congress passes the Sherman Silver Purchase Act, which obligates the federal government to purchase 4 million ounces of silver each month and issue paper currency simultaneously.

August 6: Auburn Prison in New York is the site of the nation's first death by electrocution.

August 8: The Knights of Labor go out on strike against the New York Central and Hudson River Railroad.

August 30: Congress votes to permit the Department of Agriculture to inspect pork slated for foreign export.

September 1: New York City is the site of a conference on the single-tax issue.

September 3: The Single Tax League of the U.S., established by Henry George, meets at Cooper Union, New York, and adopts a single-tax platform.

September 15: The first woman is elected to membership in the American Institute of Architects.

September 22: The nation's first high school for business is opened in Washington, D.C.

September 25: Congress establishes Yosemite National Park.

September 29: As a way to prompt railroads to continue expansion, Congress passes a bill requiring railroads to forfeit unused land.

October 1: The McKinley Tariff Act is passed, raising tariffs to their highest ever.

For the first time in U.S. history, federal regulations are passed dealing with narcotics.

The National Weather Bureau is made a part of the Department of Agriculture by Congress.

October 4: Ground is broken for a hydroelectric power facility to be built in Niagara Falls, New York.

October 6: The Mormon Church prohibits polygamy.

November 1: Mississippi accepts a new state constitution that limits voting rights of African-Americans.

November 4: A working-class Democrat, Benjamin Tillman, is elected governor of South Carolina.

November 18: The battleship *Maine* is launched.

November 29: The first Army–Navy football game is played in West Point, New York, with a score of Navy 24, Army 0.

December 15: In South Dakota, Sioux Chief Sitting Bull is killed in a clash with federal troops.

1891:

January: Hawaii's King Kalakaua dies and his sister Liliuokalani becomes queen.

Two new trade magazines are published—the first journal dealing with the phonograph industry, the *Phonogram,* and an optometry magazine, the *Optician.* Each points to greater professionalization of various fields, and a

Queen Liliuokalani of the Hawaiian Islands. Courtesy of the Library of Congress.

greater emphasis on the business aspects of each area.

March 1: The U.S. Supreme Court invalidates the income tax, which it had imposed during the Civil War.

March 3: Congress establishes the Circuit Court of Appeals.

Congress passes the Forest Reserve Act, which will enable President Harrison to set aside 13 million acres of public land for national forests.

The superintendent of immigration office is established by Congress.

March 4: The International Copyright Act is passed, initially protecting British, French, Belgian and Swiss authors.

Kittel Halvorson, the first Prohibition candidate to be elected to the U.S. House of Representatives, begins his term of service.

March 14: In New Orleans, Louisiana, 14 Sicil-ian immigrants are lynched by an angry mob in retaliation for the death of a police officer there.

March 30: The Shoshone National Forest is established in Wyoming, and Yellowstone Park Timberland Reserve is made a federal park.

April: The first pneumatic bicycle tire is manufactured in New York City.

April 1: Augustus Thomas produces his play *Alabama*, describing the newly united nation after the Civil War.

April 7: Nebraska passes a law establishing an eight-hour day.

April 14: The president begins a tour of the southern states.

May 4: The nation's first integrated hospital, Provident Hospital, opens in Chicago, Illinois.

May 5: Carnegie Hall, built by philanthropic millionaire Andrew Carnegie, opens in New York City.

May 6: The Amateur Fencers League of America is organized in New York City.

May 13: The Kentucky Derby is won by Kingman. The jockey, Isaac Murphy, is the first in history to have ridden a derby winner three times.

May 19: The Populist party is formed in Cincinnati, Ohio, by farmers and others convinced that government ownership of railroads, among other things, is a way to guarantee economic stability.

Rice Institute in Houston, Texas, is chartered.

July 20: Miners who have walked off their jobs in Briceville, Tennessee, return to work as state troops bring in convict labor to break the strike.

The Wistar Institute of Anatomy and Biology is established in Philadelphia, Pennsylvania.

August 24: The first movie camera is patented by Thomas A. Edison. He dubs it the "kinetoscope."

September 22: Another 900,000 acres of land owned by Indians in Oklahoma are taken by the federal government and opened up for white settlement.

October 16: In Chile, American sailors from the U.S.S. *Baltimore* are attacked by a mob; two are killed.

October 18: The first international six-day bicycle race is held in Madison Square Garden, New York City.

November 3: William McKinley is elected governor of Ohio.

November 10: The Women's Christian Temperance Union, known as the WCTU, holds its first worldwide convention.

November 21: Yale defeats Harvard to win the Intercollegiate Football Championship.

November 28: At the annual Army-Navy game, Army wins, 32–16.

December 29: Thomas A. Edison is granted a radio patent.

EYEWITNESS TESTIMONY

The state [South Dakota] contains thousands of women farmers, young women, spinsters, and widows who came here a few years ago, took up claims, improved them and are now full-fledged agriculturalists. In one county I found one hundred of these independent women farmers, yet it was not the county which contained the largest number by any means.

Carrie Chapman Catt, reformer, suffragist and temperance advocate, writing in 1890, in Van Voris's Carrie Chapman Catt: A Public Life *(1987).*

I went around town and begged money to keep [her] working and then she went off and got married. The loss . . . is very discouraging.

Women's rights advocate Margaret Campbell, to friend and long-time feminist campaigner Lucy Stone, concerning the marriage of the feminist activist Carrie Chapman Catt, letter of 1890, in Van Voris's Carrie Chapman Catt *(1987).*

The necessity of a navy, in the restricted sense of the word, springs . . . from the existence of a peaceful shipping, and disappears with it, except in the case of a nation which has aggressive tendencies, and keeping up a navy merely as a branch of the military establishment. As the United States has at present no aggressive purposes, and as its merchant service has disappeared, the dwindling of the armed fleet and general lack of interest in it are strictly logical consequences. When for any reason sea trade is again found to pay, a large enough shipping interest will reappear to compel the revival of the war fleet. It is possible that when a canal route through the Central-American Isthmus is seen to be a near certainty, the aggressive impulse may be strong enough to lead to the same result. This is doubtful, however, because a peaceful, gain-loving nation is not far-sighted, and far-sightedness is needed for adequate military preparation, especially in these days.

As a nation, with its unarmed and armed shipping, launched forth from its own shores, the need is soon felt of points upon which the ships can rely for peaceful trading, for refuge and supplies. In the present day friendly, though foreign, ports are to be found all over the world; and their shelter is enough while peace prevails. It was not always so, nor does peace always endure, though the United States have been favored by so long a continuing of it . . .

Alfred Thayer Mahan, in The Influence of Sea Power upon History, 1660–1783, *published in 1890.*

. . . our greatest need is the need of a fighting-fleet. Forts alone could not prevent the occupation of any town or territory outside the range of their guns, or the general wasting of the seaboard; while a squadron of heavy battle-ships, able to sail out and attack the enemy's vessels as they approached, and possessing the great advantage of being near their own base of supplies, would effectually guard a thousand miles of coast. Passive defense, giving the assailant complete choice of the time and place for attack, is always the most dangerous expedient. Our ships should be the best of their kind,—this is the first desideratum; but, in addition, there should be plenty of them. We need a large navy, composed not merely of cruisers, but containing also a full proportion of powerful battle-ships, able to meet those of any other nation.

Theodore Roosevelt, in his review of Alfred Thayer Mahan's book on sea power, in Atlantic Monthly, *October 1890.*

. . . this bill proceeds upon the false assumption that all competition is beneficent to the country, and that every advance of price is an injury to the country. That is the assumption upon which this bill proceeds. There never was a greater fallacy in the world. Competition, which this bill provides for as between any two persons, must be full and free. Unrestricted competition is brutal warfare, and injurious to the whole country, the great corporations of this country, the great monopolies of this country are every one of them built upon the graves of weaker competitors that have been forced to their death by remorseless competition. I am entirely sick of this idea that the lower the prices are the better for the country, and that any effort to advance prices, no matter how low they may be, and that any arrangement between persons engaged in business to advance prices, no matter how low they may be, is a wrong and ought to be repressed and punished.

Senator Orville H. Platt (R-Connecticut), to Congress, speech of March 27, 1890, in Ginger's People on the Move *(1975).*

Is it not better . . . that the income of the government shall be secured by putting a tax or a duty upon foreign products, and at the same time carefully providing that such duties shall be on products of foreign growth and manufacture which compete with like products of home growth and manufacture, so that, while we are raising all the revenues needed by the government, we shall do it with a discriminating regard for our own people, their products, and their employments? . . .

The Free-Trader wants the world to enjoy with our own citizens equal benefits of trade in the United States. The Republican Protectionist would give the first chance to our people, and would so levy duties upon the products of other nations as to discriminate in favor of our own. The Democratic party would make no distinction; it would serve the alien and the stranger; the Republican party would serve the State and our own fellow-citizens.

Representative William McKinley (R-Ohio), 1890, in Hoogenboom and Hoogenboom's The Gilded Age *(1967).*

What you farmers need to do is raise less corn and more Hell!

Agrarian orator Mary Elizabeth Lease, to an early gathering of Populists at Topeka, Kansas, 1890, in The Almanac of American History *(1983).*

The Farmer's Alliance is in itself more the product of social hunger than political thought or action. The farm neighborhood has little social life, has none of the secret societies, nothing of clubs, scarcely a church sociable [sic]. We propose to put a Republican club into every farm neighborhood possible, as soon as we can, and make it a social and literary as well as political force.

James S. Clarkson, editor of the Des Moines Register, *to President Harrison, letter of May 5, 1891, in Morgan's* Gilded Age *(1970).*

I can still shut my eyes and see the stately procession of majestic vessels, freighted with the native products of the vast Mid-west, moving noiselessly along the pathway of beneficent exchanges. What a lesson is here against government interference! How wisely the well-instructed spirit of self-interest works in self-directed channels, and is developed by natural competition without fear of contact with malificient [sic] statutes.

Senator Thomas F. Bayard (D-Delaware), letter of July 11, 1891, in Morgan's The Gilded Age *(1970).*

Mary Elizabeth Lease. Courtesy of the Kansas State Historical Society, Topeka, Kansas.

The American farmer of to-day is altogether a different sort of man from his ancestor of fifty or a hundred years ago. A great many men and women now living remember when farmers were largely manufacturers; that is to say, they made a great many implements for their own use. Every farmer had an assortment of tools with which he made wooden implements, as forks and rakes, handles for his hoes and plows, spokes for his wagon, and various other implements made wholly of wood. Then the farmer produced flax and hemp and wool and cotton. These fibers were prepared upon the farm, they were spun into yarn, woven into cloth, made into garments, and worn at home . . .

Coming from that time to the present, we find that everything nearly has been changed. All over the West particularly, the farmer threshes his wheat all at one time, he disposes of it all at one time, and in a great many instances the straw is wasted. He sells his hogs, and buys bacon and pork, he sells his cattle, and buys fresh beef and canned beef or corned beef, as the case may be; he sells his fruit, and buys it back in cans . . .

Besides all this, and what seems stranger than anything else, whereas in the earlier time the Amer-

The character of U.S. urbanization begins to develop. Shown here is Rockford, Illinois. Courtesy of the Library of Congress.

ican home was a free home, unincumbered, not one case in a thousand where a home was mortgaged to secure the payment of borrowed money, and whereas but a small amount of money was then needed for actual use in conducting the business of farming, there was always enough of it among the farmers to supply the demand, now, when at least ten times as much is needed, there is little or none to be obtained, nearly half the farms are mortgaged for as much as they are worth, and interest rates are exorbitant . . .
Senator William A. Peffer, Kansas Populist,
1891, in Ginger's People *(1975).*

Humanity demands that men should have sunlight, fresh air, the sight of grass and trees. It demands these things for the man himself, and it demands them still more urgently for his wife and children. No child has a fair chance in the world who is condemned to grow up in the dirt and confinement, the dreariness, ugliness and vice of the poorer quarters of a great city . . . There is, then, a per-

manent conflict between the needs of industry and the needs of humanity. Industry says men must aggregate. Humanity says they must not, or if they must, let it be only during working hours and let the necessity not extend to their wives and children. It is the office of the city railways to reconcile these conflicting requirements.
Charles Horton Cooley, sociologist, 1891, in
Callow's American Urban History *(1973).*

It is here, indeed, that the American 'go ahead,' the idea of always going forward . . . attains its maximum intensity.
Paul de Rousiers, writing about the city of Chicago, 1891, in Callow's Urban History *(1973).*

[The nation's alternatives are a] French Revolution . . . [or] an Anglo-Saxon revolution of peace, compromise and progress.
Henry Demarest Lloyd, reformer and writer, at
a union rally in Chicago, 1891, in Smith's The
Rise of Industrial America *(1984).*

It was great. In logic & law it cannot be disputed. It made me feel that I am a hypocrite & a slave and added to my resolution to make my term of servitude short.

Clarence Darrow, lawyer, writing in his journal after hearing Henry Demarest Lloyd speak at a union rally in Chicago, 1891, in Smith's Industrial American *(1984).*

. . . national unity is the determining force in the development of the modern constitutional states. The prime policy, therefore, of each of these states should be to attain proper physical boundaries and to render its population ethnically homogeneous. In other words, the policy in modern political organization should be to follow the indications of nature and aid the ethical impulse to conscious development.

. . . The morality of a policy which insists upon the use of a common language and upon the establishment of homogeneous institutions and laws cannot be successfully disputed. Under certain circumstances the exercise of force to secure these ends is not only justifiable, but commendable, and not only commendable, but morally obligatory.

John W. Burgess, in Political Science and Comparative Constitutional Law, *(1891).*

13. Strikes, Imperialist Policy and the Populist Voice: 1892–1893

THE HISTORICAL CONTEXT

Acting as the voice of the people, the Populist party gathered political momentum—and voter support—as the presidential elections of 1892 grew near. Some of that force was weakened by the Democrats, who nominated Grover Cleveland as the answer to the problematic incumbent, President Benjamin Harrison. Cleveland's election by a wide electoral margin indicated the mood of the country: the U.S. hoped that a Democrat could do what the Republicans had been powerless to effect: bring balance to the industrial and business monopolies that threatened to eliminate opportunity for individual Americans and those working for hourly wages. Cleveland also promised civil service reform and did so convincingly. He was, however, to be the last Democrat in the White House until 1913, as his promised reforms were ineffectual.

Despite the attentive concern of many union leaders and intervention by federal officials, labor disputes continued to disrupt production in many areas of the nation right through the 1890s. Calls for an eight-hour workday and demands for safer, healthier working conditions, adequate housing and fairer pay resulted in a volatile environment at numerous work sites. Among the most desperate was the situation of workers at the Homestead Steel Mill in Pennsylvania. This enormous operation had made the immigrant Andrew Carnegie a millionaire. His wealth permitted him to live a life of ease and luxury away from the mill and he had hired Henry Clay Frick to manage the huge plant in his absence so as to continue to ensure its profitability—and Carnegie's wealthy status.

When their old contract expired, workers in the Homestead Mill who belonged to the Amalgamated Association of Iron and Steel Workers demanded fairer contract terms. When Frick refused to deal with union members they went out on strike, in July 1892. Frick's response was to hire several hundred Pinkerton police to protect strikebreakers brought in to maintain the steel operation. Infuriated workers attacked the incoming Pinkerton men as they arrived by barge on the Monongahela River.

The strikebreaking move was an enormous public relations error on Frick's part. President Cleveland had openly stated the fitness of meeting the needs of the steelworkers and Frick's action was an invitation to disaster. He was adamant, however, and Carnegie—who was vacationing in Scotland, allowed Frick to keep the plant closed. An angry worker attacked Frick, nearly killing him. The Homestead Steel Mill remained closed, but the strike was broken in November, when workers gave up the struggle and returned to their jobs.

The Homestead strike and the ill-will and conflict it generated between labor and management was more publicized than many labor clashes. It illustrated clearly the need for federal intervention in assessing and responding to the changing balance of power between workers and their employers.

In addition to trying to meet the challenge of complex domestic issues, the U.S. was wielding greater influence in the political affairs of other nations. In 1892 Alfred Thayer Mahan had published a second book, *The Influence of Sea Power on the French Revolution*. Again, Mahan underscored the desirability of taking an active role in global issues. He had attracted the attention of many government officials with his earlier book, *The Influence of Sea Power upon History, 1660–1783*, published in 1890. Now, the general public expressed interest in a strong U.S. Navy and sufficient bases from which to launch and maintain this fleet. It was an interest that was seized by imperialists and expansionists like Theodore Roosevelt, Henry Cabot Lodge and Richard Olney and used to further the cause of making the U.S. a true world power by the turn of the century.

The interest in U.S. expansion outside its continental limits was fueled further in 1893 when historian Frederick Jackson Turner published his essay "The Significance of the Frontier in American History." This treatise described the positive effect on the development of the American nation of sufficient land for settlement. In Turner's view, the nation required a frontier in order to thrive and prosper; expansionists seized on this position to advance their own interests.

An example of the force with which those interests could affect other nations came early in 1893. The monarchy in the Hawaiian Islands was overthrown and some U.S. officials and businessmen were implicated as having been involved. Because of powerful business forces there, chiefly among planters involved in sugarcane and pineapple crop production, many Americans began to pay attention to political developments in that small Pacific nation. A secret society called the Annexation Club had been formed in 1892 in Hawaii. Its goal was to press for U.S. annexation of the islands and to plan ways of implementing formal opposition to Queen Liliuokalani's rule.

While the U.S. government exercised some measure of control over Hawaii, it remained passive in its official behavior in that no official declaration of war was ever made. The turn of events on the islands attracted attention within the U.S., however, and after Cleveland was inaugurated for his second term in March, he withdrew the pending Hawaiian annexation treaty. He did so to enable a full Senate investigation into the overthrow of the monarchy and to deflect any questions of U.S. involvement in that overthrow.

Questions of labor conditions were ever-present nationwide. In some cases, groups concerned with promoting certain labor issues often disagreed with workers seeking a different sort of consideration. In 1893, for example, Illinois enacted a law limiting women to an eight-hour workday. Reformers seeking better conditions applauded this law; women's rights activists decried protective legislation, saying it limited women's employment opportunities.

In 1892 Victor L. Berger, founded the *Wisconsin Vorwarts*, a socialist newspaper. He later became a close associate of Eugene V. Debs, who would lead the American Railway Union strike in 1894 and who founded the American Socialist party. Also in 1892, Terence V. Powderly, leader of the Noble Order of the Knights of Labor, resigned his office as Grand Master Workman, a post he had held for over 15 years. The International Longshoremen's Association was founded in 1892, and owners of the mining project at the Coeur d'Alene in Idaho shut down operations and refused to reopen until striking miners there accepted a wage cut. Such development indicate the various ways in which labor activists sought fair treatment for workers and how workers themselves sought control over issues most affecting their lives, on and off the job.

CHRONICLE OF EVENTS

1892:

January 1: A facility at Ellis Island, in New York Harbor, opens to receive immigrants to the United States.

January 29: In Kansas, members of the Republican party celebrate Kansas Day to commemorate the admission of their state to the Union in 1861.

May 5: Restrictive immigration legislation is passed that will affect Chinese immigrants who wish to come to the U.S.

June 7: The Republican National Convention opens in Minneapolis, Minnesota; Benjamin Harrison and Whitelaw Reid are nominated for president and vice president, respectively.

June 21: Chicago is once more the site of the Democratic National Convention. Grover Cleveland and Adlai Stevenson are named candidates for president and vice president, respectively.

June 29: The Prohibition party opens its national convention in Cincinnati, Ohio, nominating John Bidwell and James Cranfill for president and vice president, respectively.

July 1: In Pennsylvania, Henry Clay Frick closes the Carnegie-owned Homestead Steel Mill, provoking a labor strike. Secretly, Frick hires Pinkerton guards to protect strikebreakers, although organized workers discover Frick's plan and rioting soon breaks out.

July 4: The Northern and Southern Alliances join in Omaha, Nebraska, to form the People's (Populist) party. Their national convention immediately follows on the same day; James B. Weaver is named the party's presidential candidate, with James G. Field running as vice president.

July 6: Within several days of Pinkerton guards' arrival at the Homestead Steel Mill, at least nine striking workers and seven Pinkerton men are killed. Many others are shot during labor rioting there.

July 10: The governor of Pennsylvania sends in the state militia to the steelworks in Homestead, Pennsylvania, to break up the labor strike and restore order.

August 27: A fire nearly destroys New York City's Metropolitan Opera House.

August 28: In New York City, the Socialist Labor party convenes and nominates Simon Wing as its presidential candidate and Charles H. Matchett as his running mate.

September: Charles and Frank Duryea, of Chicopee, Massachusetts, build the first gasoline-powered automobile.

William Morrison, of Des Moines, Iowa, builds an electric automobile.

September 7: The first heavy weight boxing champ to win under Marquess of Queensbury rules and wearing gloves, James J. Corbett, knocks out John L. Sullivan in New Orleans, Louisiana.

September 8: The Youth's Companion magazine publishes the Pledge of Allegiance to the flag. Its author is Francis Bellamy, of the magazine's editorial staff.

October 3: The University of Idaho is opened.

October 5: While attempting a robbery, the infamous Dalton gang is all but eliminated in Coffeyville, Kansas.

October 15: Land owned by the Crow Indians is opened to white settlers by the federal government.

October 20: The Columbian Exposition in Chicago, Illinois, is dedicated by Vice President Levi Morton. John Philip Sousa conducts the band at the ceremonies.

October 28: A fire in Milwaukee, Wisconsin, destroys over $5 million in property.

November 8: Democrat Grover Cleveland is elected president by an electoral vote of 277–145, defeating Benjamin Harrison.

November 20: The Homestead Steel Mill strike ends when union workers decide to give up and return to their jobs. State militia had been at the site since July 9.

November 26: At their annual football game, Navy defeats Army, 12–4.

December 2: Railroad tycoon Jay Gould dies at

age 56. His estate is estimated to be $72 million.

December 19: The University of Oklahoma opens in Norman.

December 27: Construction begins on the Cathedral of St. John the Divine in New York City.

1893:

January 4: The federal government offers amnesty to all polygamists, hoping to appease the Mormon Church and lessen tensions in Utah.

January 14: The Annexation Club in Hawaii meets to draw up opposition strategy to Queen Liliuokalani's plans for a new constitution. As a response to these activities, U.S. marines once again arrive in the islands and land in Honolulu.

January 17: Members of the Annexation Club march to government headquarters in Honolulu and announce that the monarchy is overthrown and a provisional government is established.

Queen Liliuokalani steps down as the head of the Hawaiian government.

February 1: John Stevens, U.S. minister to Hawaii, declares that the islands are under the protection of the United States.

February 20: The Pennsylvania and Reading Railroads go into receivership as the first waves of economic disaster hit the nation, forerunners of the upcoming panic of 1893.

March: President Grover Cleveland is inaugurated.

At the direction of President Cleveland, James Blount is sent to Hawaii as a special commissioner to investigate recent actions there. Blount issues a report critical of John Stevens's call for military backup and states that the Hawaiian people are not in favor of the overthrow of the monarchy on the island.

The General Manager's Association, a society comprising several dozen railroads in the Chicago area, establishes a pay scale for its switchmen.

March 1: Under the terms of the Diplomatic Appropriation Act, the rank of ambassador is created for U.S. citizens serving overseas. Thomas Bayard is named ambassador to Great Britain at this time, the first of all U.S. envoys to bear this title.

March 9: President Cleveland withdraws the Hawaiian annexation treaty submitted by John Stevens.

April 13: Commissioner James Blount removes U.S. troops from the Hawaiian Islands.

April 15: Gold certificates are no longer issued by the U.S. Treasury because gold reserves have fallen below the $100 million mark.

May: Labor leader "Big Bill" Haywood meets with others in Butte, Montana, to organize the Western Federation of Miners.

May 1: The president opens the Columbian Exposition in Chicago, Illinois.

Labor leader and Socialist Eugene V. Debs. Courtesy of the Library of Congress.

May 5: A run on the New York Stock Exchange causes further economic panic.

June 20: Eugene V. Debs forms the American Railway Union.

June 26: Pardons are issued to the three remaining anarchists involved in the 1886 Haymarket riot.

June 27: The New York stock market crashes.

July 1: President Cleveland undergoes surgery for mouth cancer. The procedure is kept secret for fear of even more widespread national disruption on the economic scene.

August 7: Congress convenes in special session, called by President Cleveland, to discuss repeal of the Sherman Silver Purchase Act.

August 13: A Minneapolis, Minnesota, fire leaves 1,500 homeless.

August 24: A cyclone kills 1,000 in Savannah, Georgia, and Charleston, South Carolina.

September 16: Land purchased by the federal government from the Cherokee nation is settled by more than 50,000 homesteaders.

October 2: A cyclone rips through the Gulf Coast region of Louisiana, killing over 2,000.

November 1: President Cleveland signs a repeal of the Sherman Silver Purchase Act.

November 7: Women are granted the right to vote in Colorado.

December 18: President Cleveland announces that he will not support a Hawaiian annexation treaty.

EYEWITNESS TESTIMONY

We are nearing a serious crisis. If the present strained relations between wealth owners and wealth producers continue much longer they will ripen into frightful disaster. This universal discontent must be quickly interpreted and its causes removed.

There is no power on earth that can defeat us. It is a fight between labor and capital, and labor is in the vast majority.

General James B. Weaver, Populist candidate for U.S. president, 1892, in Davis and Woodman's Conflict or Consensus in American History *(1966).*

Don't confine the fight to any one thing money or land. Let's make the fight for *human liberty* and for the rights of man.

Novelist and Populist reformer Hamlin Garland, to Populist Party presidential candidate General James B. Weaver during the 1892 campaign, in Davis and Woodman's Conflict or Consensus *(1966).*

A vast conspiracy against mankind has been organized on two continents, and it is rapidly taking possession of the world. If not met and overthrown at once it forebodes terrible social convulsions, the destruction of civilization, or the establishment of an absolute despotism.

Ignatius Donnelly, in a preamble to the Populist platform, 1892, in Dubofsky's Industrialism and the American Worker, 1865–1920 *(1975).*

Consider the barrenness of the isolated farmer's life—the dull round of work and sleep in which so much of it passes. Even the discomforts and evils of the crowded tenement house are not worse than the discomforts and evils of such a life.

Henry George, reformer and single-tax proponent, 1892, in Degler's The Age of the Economic Revolution 1876–1900 *(1977).*

Government control of railroads has not succeeded and never will succeed. So long as it is in the power of a board of directors to increase stocks, issue bonds, and give rebates in secret, the people will have to pay for all the water and the interest on the bonds. Favors are shown to trusts and combines; the trusts

and combines are made up of the directors and stockholders of the railroads; they secretly allow rebates to their favorites, such as institutions as have railroad directors on the roll of stockholders having an undoubted advantage over their competitors. No systems of governmental control can reach the offenders. Public control is inconsistent with the idea of private ownership, and private ownership of public institutions is not consistent with well-founded principles of public policy and welfare. Public control without public ownership is an impossibility. What the government has a right to control it has a right to own and operate. Ownership must precede control, and the question must be solved in a very short time, or those who own the railroads will own the government.

Terence V. Powderly, leader of the Knights of Labor, 1892, in Hoogenboom and Hoogenboom's The Gilded Age *(1967).*

This won't do. This won't do at all. Find out who owns this paper and buy it.

Henry Clay Frick, manager of the Homestead Steel Mill, remarking on an offensive item in a Pittsburgh newspaper, 1892, in Tuchman's The Proud Tower *(1966).*

Life is worth living again. First happy morning since July . . . congratulate all around—improve works—go ahead—clear track.

Andrew Carnegie, owner of the Homestead Steel Mill, cabling home from Italy after learning of the cessation of the strike, 1892, in Dubofsky's Industrialism *(1975).*

Organized labor in America still occupies an aristocratic position and wherever possible leaves the ordinarily badly paid occupations to the immigrants, only a small portion of whom enter the aristocratic trade unions.

Friedrich Engels, German socialist, 1892, in Dubofsky's Industrialism *(1975).*

There is no place yet in America for a *third* party . . . The divergence of interests even in the *same* class group is so great . . . that wholly different groups and interests are represented in each of the two big parties . . . and almost each particular section of the possessing class has its representatives in each of the two parties . . . Only when there is a generation of native-born workers that cannot expect

anything from speculation *any more [sic]* will we have a solid foothold in America.
Friedrich Engels, writing in 1892, in Dubof-sky's Industrialism *(1975).*

Habit is thus the enormous fly-wheel of society, its most precious conservative agent. It alone is what keeps us all within the bounds of ordinance.
William James, philosopher and psychologist, in Psychology, *(1892).*

If conditions in Hawaii compel you people to act as you have indicated and you come to Washington with an annexation proposition, you will find an exceedingly sympathetic administration here.
President Benjamin Harrison, to Hawaiian sugar planters who wished to annex the island nation, 1892, in Lockwood and Harris's Reasoning with Democratic Values *(1985).*

Teacher of important and much-needed reforms, she has been obliged to practice differently from her teachings. Advocating arbitration and conciliation as first steps in labor disputes, she has been forced to take upon her shoulders the responsibilities of the aggressor first and, when hope of arbitrating and conciliation failed, to beg of the opposing side to do what we should have applied for in the first instance.

Advising against strikes we have been in the midst of them.
Terence V. Powderly, leader of the Knights of Labor, on his resignation as Grand Master Workman and his concern over a call for strikes, 1893, in Powderly's Thirty Years of Labor 1859–1889 *(1967).*

Now, to avoid any collision of armed forces and perhaps the loss of life, I do under this protest . . . yield my authority until such time as the Government of the United States shall . . . undo the action . . . and reinstate me in authority.
Queen Liliuokalani, to Hawaii, after learning that the U.S. minister had recognized a provisional government of the Hawaiian Islands, 1893, in Lockwood and Harris's Democratic Values *(1985).*

I transmit herewith, with a view to its ratification, a treaty of annexation concluded on the 14th day of February, 1893 . . . The provisional treaty, it will be observed, does not attempt to deal in detail with the questions that grow out of annexation of the Hawai-ian Islands to the United States. The commissioners representing the Hawaiian Government have consented to leave to the future and to the just and benevolent purposes of the United States the adjustment of all such questions.
President Harrison, to Congress, February 1893, in Gianakos and Karson's American Diplomacy and the Sense of Destiny *(1966).*

The mission of our nation is to build up and make a greater country out of what we have, instead of annexing islands.
President Grover Cleveland, withdrawing his support for the annexation of Hawaii, 1893, in Ginger's People on the Move *(1975).*

The chief underlying principle of all Populist financial schemes is fiat money. Free silver, a sub-treasury, etc., are purely incidental. It is the cardinal faith of Populism, without which no man can be saved, that money can be created by the Government, in any desired quantity, out of any substance, with no basis but itself; and that such money will be good and legal tender, the Government stamp, only, being required . . .

The Government, say the Populists, which by Protection rolls wealth into the manufacturer's lap, which constructs great harbors, buildings and defences, which gave us free land, pensions bounties, railways, and created greenbacks, can do anything to increase our money supply.
Frank B. Tracy, a newspaperman, 1893, in Hoogenboom and Hoogenboom's Gilded Age *(1967).*

The best periodical in the world.
James Russell Lowell, poet and editor commenting on The Nation, *1893, in Tuchman's* Proud Tower *(1966).*

. . . the best paper printed in the English language.
James Bryce, author of The American Commonwealth, *describing E.L. Godkin's* Evening Post, *1893, in Tuchman's* Proud Tower *(1966).*

The trouble with the damned sheet is that every editor in New York State reads it.
New York Republican Governor Hill, concerning the Evening Post, *1893, in Tuchman's* Proud Tower *(1966).*

What a fearful mental degeneracy results from reading [the *Evening Post*] or the *Nation* as a steady thing.

Theodore Roosevelt, U.S. Civil Service Commissioner, to Alfred Thayer Mahan, letter of 1893, in Tuchman's Proud Tower *(1966).*

All my friends are going to Europe . . . The Hays, Camerons, Lodges, Blaines, all start before mid-summer.

Henry Adams, historian, 1893, in Smith's The Rise of Industrial America *(1984).*

14. Labor Unrest and Union Activity: 1894–1895

THE HISTORICAL CONTEXT

While both critics and reformers in the late 19th century worked for policy changes at the federal level, many recognized that local government was just as likely to bring about desired changes. The Populist movement was an outgrowth of local efforts to make politics more responsive, a movement that would become most effective by 1896, but some people worked in smaller groups. There, they focused on a specific problem or set of issues and sought a simple solution.

An example of this more specialized approach was an organization concerned with honest, effective local government—the National Municipal League. Founded in 1894 by urban mayors, its chief goal was to promote honest and responsive governments in cities and towns. Although the organization provided a forum in which community leaders could discuss common issues, it did little to alleviate the more serious problems facing those who made their homes in rapidly growing urban areas. Reformers like Jane Addams, Florence Kelley and Lester Frank Ward tried to eliminate slum tenements and worked hard to seek solutions to unemployment, poor working conditions and low wages. But despite their good intentions, corrupt city governments, along with foul air, dirty streets, illiteracy and other ills, were impossible to eradicate.

Chicago's history during this period particularly illustrates the problems facing U.S. cities in the late 19th century. In 1894, business and industry in this midwestern center were the targets of growing dissatisfaction among workers. This unrest and discontent were especially evident among laborers who belonged to the American Railway Union (ARU). These workers at the Pullman Company, a manufacturer of railroad cars, demanded better conditions and higher pay. They threatened to strike if their demands were not met. They were not, and this labor stoppage in 1894 was one of the most disruptive—and effective—in U.S. history. It involved some 60,000 workers and resulted in Attorney General Richard Olney deputizing nearly 4,000 men to maintain order in and around Chicago, largely to prevent disruption of mail de-

Coxey's army of unemployed workers leaves Massillon, Ohio, on March 25, 1894, for Washington, D.C. Courtesy of the Library of Congress.

livery. Taking action even before the violent outbreaks that later occurred and obtaining a court injunction against the strikers, Olney indicated that the federal government had little tolerance for strikers.

Olney's action involved the federal government in Illinois's issues, despite the fact that the governor there had not requested help. This uninvited federal intervention caused more violence and resulted in President Cleveland's dispatch of federal troops to Illinois. Strikers caused a mail train derailment there, substantiating federal fears of problems with mail delivery. As troops arrived in the state on July 4, the leader of the ARU strike, Eugene V. Debs, was arrested and imprisoned.

The American Railway Union strike showed other labor groups that desperate measures were the best way to gain public sympathy. Even though the government moved swiftly to crush any strikes threatening the stability of the nation's industrial network, ARU strikers had been successful. Privately, many people recognized the degree of unhappiness among workers and became angry with the president for calling out federal troops to quell workers in Illinois.

The economic picture grew more discouraging as 1894 drew to a close. Greater numbers of people were unemployed and voters, worried about Cleveland's ineffectiveness, made their views clear. Signaling for change, during the November congressional elections voters defeated the Democrats virtually everywhere in the nation and gave Republicans control of Congress.

Union action in Chicago was merely one focal point in a much larger picture of disgruntled laborers nationwide. In 1894, there were a total of 1,400 industrial strikes, involving over 700,000 workers. But even more reflective of economic unease were demands made by groups of unemployed, homeless men. In the spring of 1894, they came from cities and towns everywhere and marched on the nation's capital, hoping to provoke action by Congress or the president on their behalf. The most famous of these groups was known as "Coxey's Army," named for Jacob S. Coxey, a businessman from Ohio who spearheaded one of these grassroots efforts. Coxey's Army comprised over 500 despairing and desperate men who, upon arrival in Washington, D.C., demanded that the federal government set up relief programs to provide them with work and wages. They were unsuccessful in achieving their goal of a federal work relief effort, but their protest further publicized the economic plight of many Americans.

Equally persuasive efforts to rally another oppressed group to advance its position were made by Booker T. Washington, head of the Tuskegee Institute. He emphasized the importance of self-help for the thousands of former slaves who eked out a living in rural and urban homes. At the 1895 Atlanta Exposition, Washington delivered a speech that made clear his dreams and desires for all African-American citizens.

As the desire for more timely information created better markets for daily newspapers, considerable competition developed among established—and aspiring—publishers. In 1895, William Randolph Hearst purchased the *New York Morning Journal*. By doing so, he became a competitor of Joseph Pulitzer's *World*. He also launched a rivalry that would only grow more intense as the months passed.

Hearst's correspondents grew infamous for their particularly lurid reporting and writing style, a style that was described by the term "yellow journalism." Their aggressive, inflammatory prose was popular, however. Some believed that these reporters were to blame for an increase in expansionism and war fever in Washington. It was certainly true that more and more stories appeared that encouraged a greater sense of nationalism. But these journalists generally reflected what was already being discussed in Congress: that the U.S. had a duty to act as the protector of the Western Hemisphere, and that it was obligatory that America fund military power sufficient to maintain that watch dog role.

This increasing interest in the rest of the world by Americans concerned about the future occurred at the same time that the domestic economy entered another period of depression. In 1893 the nation's gold reserve had dropped to below $100 million and the Sherman Silver Purchase Act was repealed as a result. But Cleveland's administration was doomed to failure, as evidenced by the fact that in the 1894 congressional elections the Republicans made a strong comeback. It would only be another two years before the executive branch of government, too, was controlled by the G.O.P.

CHRONICLE OF EVENTS

1894:

January 8: A fire causes $2 million in damage as it destroys nearly all the structures at the Columbian Exposition in Chicago.

January 17: The U.S. Treasury issues bonds as a means of building up gold reserves.

February 8: Congress repeals the Enforcement Act of 1871, leaving control of elections to the states.

February 13: Thirteen miners are killed in a Pennsylvania coal mine collapse.

April 5: Rioting breaks out in Pennsylvania as striking miners clash over working conditions.

April 20: Nearly 150,000 coal miners are on strike in Columbus, Ohio, in protest of low wages.

April 30: Coxey's Army marches on the nation's capital to protest unemployment. Their leader, Jacob Coxey, will press for legislation that will favor the working classes over business interests.

May 11: Workers at the Pullman Palace Car Company in Chicago go out on strike over low wages and reduced working hours.

June: Under the leadership of organizer and president Eugene V. Debs, over 20,000 American Railway Union (ARU) members go on strike in and around Chicago, Illinois. The ARU shows active support for other organized workers at the Pullman Palace Car Company, whose union has also gone out on strike to protest wage cuts and rent hikes.

June 21: William Jennings Bryan speaks out in favor of free silver at the Democratic National Convention in Omaha, Nebraska.

July 3: Rioting occurs on one of the striking railway lines going into Chicago. Strike leaders anticipate federal intervention to break up the work stoppage.

July 4: Two thousand federal troops arrive in Chicago to end the American Railway Union strike. Outbreaks of severe violence result in over 20 deaths and the destruction of several thousand railway cars.

The Republic of Hawaii is declared.

July 10: Under U.S. cavalry escort, the first stock train leaves the Chicago stockyards following the American Railway Union strike.

A forest fire in Minnesota destroys six towns and claims 480 lives; an area of over 480 square miles is destroyed.

1895:

January 12: The Government Printing Office is established.

January 14: A trolley strike begins in Brooklyn, New York. State militia are eventually called in to quell ensuing riots.

January 22: In Cincinnati, Ohio, the National Association of Manufacturers gathers for its first meeting.

February 4: The nation's first rolling lift bridge is operational in Chicago, Illinois.

February 8: The United States Treasury purchases $62 million in gold from private banking houses.

February 17: Gratz College, the first Hebrew teacher's training school, is established in Philadelphia, Pennsylvania.

February 24: Cuban rebel Jose Marti, based in New York City, leads a revolt in Cuba against Spain.

February 26: M.J. Owens patents a glassblowing machine in Toledo, Ohio.

March 5: Democrats in the U.S. House of Representatives request free coinage of silver. Two of the most vociferous supporters of this fiscal move are Representatives Bland (Missouri) and Bryan (Nebraska).

March 13: The U.S. Navy awards its first submarine construction contract to J.P. Holland.

March 18: Several hundred former slaves emigrate to Liberia, Africa.

March 28: In Boston, Massachusetts, construction begins on the nation's first city subway system.

April 10: The first round-the-world bicycle trip begins in Chicago, Illinois.

April 17: The Hennepin Canal at Rock Island, Illinois, is opened. The locks in this canal are the nation's first to be constructed of concrete.

April 21: In New York City, a motion picture is shown on a projection screen for the first time.

April 29: The U.S. Postal Service issues its first watermarked stamp, depicting Benjamin Franklin.

May 8: The first cat show in the nation opens at Madison Square Garden in New York City.

May 15: In Chicago, Illinois, the first electric elevated railroad in the country is operational.

May 20: The U.S. Supreme Court declares the income-tax clause of the 1894 tariff act invalid.

May 25: Golf in America, is published by J.P. Lee.

May 27: The U.S. Supreme Court upholds a federal injunction that prohibits strikers from interfering with interstate commerce.

June 11: Charles Duryea of Chicopee, Massachusetts, is issued a patent for the first gasoline-driven automobile.

August 31: The nation's first professional football game is played in Latrobe, Pennsylvania.

September 9: The American Bowling Congress is founded in Beethoven Hall, New York.

November 5: The Utah Territory adopts a constitution that permits women to vote.

December 21: President Cleveland is permitted by Congress to appoint a Venezuelan Boundary Commission.

EYEWITNESS TESTIMONY

I am just now not reading but devouring Captain Mahan's book and am trying to learn it by heart.

Kaiser Wilhelm II of Germany, after reading Mahan's The Influence of Sea Power on History, 1894, in Tuchman's The Proud Tower (1966).

The people's part is more than the organized discontent of the people. It is the organized aspiration of the people of a fuller, nobler, richer, kindlier life for every man, woman and child in the ranks of humanity.

Henry Demarest Lloyd, reformer and writer, at the Tattersall Rally in Chicago, during the Populist (People's) Party campaign, 1894, in Smith's The Rise of Industrial America (1984).

We of the People's party believe that the men who created our wonderful industrial system have the right to enjoy the institution which they have created.

Clarence Darrow, at the Tattersall Rally in Chicago, during the Populist (People's) Party campaign, 1894, in Smith's Industrial American (1984).

[Although] steam electricity, compressed air, are utilized to do the work of man, [they] have been made the monopoly of the few . . . In the face of the power exerted by the monopolists of these tremendous engines of industry and commerce the Republican and Democratic parties stand paralyzed—hypnotized, as it were, unable to control it or give direction and shape for common good . . . The failure to adapt the legislation of the country to the strange conditions which this new life has forced upon us is the cause in greater part of our industrial ills.

Frank Doster, Kansas leader of the Populist Party, in a Labor Day speech, 1894, in Davis and Woodman's Conflict or Consensus in American History.

We will send a petition to Washington with boots on.

Jacob S. Coxey, leader of "Coxey's Army," on the march to the nation's capital, 1894, in Morgan's The Gilded Age (1970).

I am beginning to feel that the movement [Coxey's Army] has some meaning, that it is a manifestation of the prevailing unrest and dissatisfaction among the labor class. When such an ugly and grotesque fungus can grow out so prominently on the body politic there must be something wrong.

Ray Stannard Baker, journalist, 1894, in Morgan's Gilded Age (1970).

I believe that every novel should have an intention. A man should mean something when he writes. Ah, this writing merely to amuse people—why, it seems to me altogether vulgar . . .

It is the business of the novel to picture the daily life in the most exact terms possible, with an absolute and clear sense of proportion. That is the important matter—the proportion. As a usual thing, I think, people have absolutely no sense of proportion . . .

[The novel] is a perspective made for the benefit of people who have no true use of their eyes. The novel, in its real meaning, adjusts the proportion. It preserves the balances. It is in this way that lessons are to be taught and reforms to be won. When people are introduced to each other they will see the resemblances, and won't want to fight so badly.

William Dean Howells, novelist and critic, in Ginger's People on the Move (1975).

Along about the latter part of March or 1st of April, 1894, we began to organize, and in order to do so we had to go to Grand Crossing, as the Pullman company would not tolerate any union in their shops. If a man belonged to a union, if the company knew it, he was discharged; we had to go down to Grand Crossing for the purpose of organizing the first local union . . .

The conditions became worse; in April there was another cut, which made it impossible for us to maintain our families and pay our rent; we had to do something; times were hard and men could not get money enough to move away from Pullman; we did not really know what to do. I used my utmost endeavors to keep the men from striking . . . but it was utterly impossible for me to control those who wanted to strike; we then held meetings until we had about 35 percent of the men organized; and on the 10th of May . . . after they had used every effort with the Pullman company to make some concessions . . . a strike was ordered.

Federal troops keeping order during the Pullman strike of 1894. Courtesy of the Library of Congress.

Thomas W. Heathcoate, of the American Railway Union, 1894, in Hoogenboom and Hoogenboom's The Gilded Age *(1967).*

As soon as the firing began, of course the crowd scattered, but it was hemmed in on each side by long rows of box cars which they could not get between very well and so they had to run in the direction of the firing, and a number of men, women, and children were injured, or rather men and women, there were no children, and none of those who were injured were members of the mob that was trying to overturn the Pullman cars. I saw the man who was killed; he stood in the crowd not a great distance from me. He did not have hold of the ropes and he was apparently merely a spectator. The men who did have hold of the ropes were not strikers. I know that, because this big fellow who led the mob I looked up afterwards and found him to be a tough from Chicago . . .

In all that mob that had hold of the ropes I do not think there were many American Railway Union

men. I think they were mostly roughs from Chicago who had been brought there by the excitement.

Ray Stannard Baker, journalist, on events following the ARU strike 1894, in Hoogenboom and Hoogenboom's Gilded Age *(1967).*

Let the Populist party triumph in the approaching election, and capital will shun Colorado as people avoid a city stricken with plague. Our reviving mining interests will be stunted in their growth, and Colorado men will appeal in vain to Eastern and European capitalists for money with which to develop any of our natural resources or to embark in new industries.

Denver Republican, *editorial of 1894, in* Smith's The Rise of Industrial America *(1984).*

New York seems to be the dirtiest wealthy city that I have seen. There are portions of the city that are so packed with empty vehicles of every size and shape that one is apt to think, from a view of the filthy state of all their surroundings, that after eight o'clock at night the commercial portion of the city is converted into a huge dirty public stable, unsightly and disgustingly hideous, viewed from whatever point it may be looked at.

J.S. Da Costa, to a friend in Brazil, letter of
1894, in Hoogenboom and Hoogenboom's
Gilded Age *(1967).*

The rules of life which orthodox Hebrews so unflinchingly obey as laid down in the Mosaic code . . . are designed to maintain health. These rules are applied to the daily life of the individuals as no other sanitary laws can be . . . Food must be cooked properly, and hence the avenues through which the germs of disease may enter are destroyed. Meat must be 'kosher,' and this means that it must be perfectly healthy. Personal cleanliness is at times strictly compelled, and at least one day in the week the habitation must be thoroughly cleaned.

Dr. Anne Daniel, outlining health conditions in
some urban tenements, 1894, in Callow's
American Urban History *(1973).*

There are two or three sides to the question of Americanism, and two or three senses in which the word "Americanism" can be used to express the antithesis of what is unwholesome and undesirable. In the first place we wish to be broadly American and national, as opposed to being local or sectional.

Theodore Roosevelt, Civil Service Commissioner
in "What Americanism Means," in The
Forum XVII *1894, in Callow's* Urban History
(1973).

The states of America, South as well as North, by geographical proximity, by natural sympathy, by similarity of governmental constitutions, are friends and allies, commercially and politically, of the United States. To allow the subjugation of any of them by an European power is, of course, to completely reverse that situation and signifies the loss of all the advantages incident to their natural relations to us . . .

Today the United States is practically sovereign on this continent, and its fiat is law upon the subjects to which it confines its interposition. Why? It is not because of the pure friendship or good will felt for it. It is not simply by reason of its high character as a civilized state, nor because wisdom, justice, and equity are the invariable characteristics of the dealings of the United States. It is because, in addition

Attorney General Richard Olney. Courtesy of the Library of Congress.

to all other grounds, its infinite resources combined with its isolated position render it master of the situation, and practically invulnerable as against any or all other powers.

Secretary of State Richard Olney, to the British
prime minister, regarding a boundary dispute
between Great Britain and Venezuela, 1895, in
Ginger's People *(1975).*

It is sea power which is essential to every splendid people.

. . . We are a great people; we control this continent; we are dominant in this hemisphere; we have too great an inheritance to be trifled with or parted with. It is ours to guard and extend.

Senator Henry Cabot Lodge (R-Massachusetts),
1895, in Ginger's People *(1975).*

In the interests of our commerce . . . we should build the Nicaragua Canal and for the sake of our commercial supremacy in the Pacific we should control the Hawaiian Islands and maintain our influence in Samoa. England has studded the West Indies with strong places which are a standing menace to our Atlantic seaboard. We should have among those is-

lands at least one strong naval station, and . . . the island of Cuba, still sparsely settled and of almost unbounded fertility, will become to us a necessity. Commerce follows the flag, and we should build up a navy strong enough to give protection to Americans in every quarter of the globe and sufficiently powerful to put our coasts beyond the possibility of successful attack.
Senator Henry Cabot Lodge (R-Massachusetts), in the Forum, March 1895, in Kelley's The Shaping of the American Past *(1978).*

Cuba should become an American colony.
Senator Morgan (D-Alabama), chair of the Senate Foreign Relations Committee, 1895, in Tuchman's Proud Tower *(1966).*

. . . we certainly ought to have the island [Cuba] in order to round out our possessions. If we cannot buy it, I for one, should like an opportunity to acquire it by conquest.
Senator Frye (R-Maine), 1895, in Tuchman's Proud Tower *(1966).*

The present assault upon capital is but the beginning. It will be but the stepping-stone to others, larger and more sweeping, 'til our political contests will become a war of the poor against the rich; a war constantly growing in intensity and bitterness.
Stephen J. Field, Supreme Court associate justice, on the recent income-tax law, 1895, in Degler's The Age of the Economic Revolution 1876–1900 *(1977).*

It is time that some one woke up and realized the necessity of annexing some property. We want all this northern hemisphere, and when we begin to reach out to secure these advantages we will begin to have a nation and our lawmakers will rise above the grade of politicians and become true statesmen.
Senator Shelby M. Cullom (R-Illinois), 1895, in Paterson's American Imperialism and Anti-Imperialism *(1973).*

The antics of the bankers, brokers and anglo-maniacs generally are humiliating to a degree . . . Personally I rather hope the fight will come soon. The clamor of the peace faction has convinced me that this country needs a war.
Theodore Roosevelt, U.S. Civil Service Commissioner, 1895, in Paterson's American Imperialism *(1973).*

[The United States] finds itself in possession of enormous power and is eager to use it in brutal fashion against anyone who comes along without knowing how to do so and is therefore constantly on the brink of some frightful catastrophe.
E.L. Godkin, editor of The Nation, *to a friend, letter of 1895, in Tuchman's* Proud Tower *(1966).*

The wisest among my race understand that the agitation of questions of social equality is the extremist folly, and that progress in the enjoyment of all the privileges that will come to us must be the result of severe and constant struggle, rather than artificial forcing. No race that has anything to contribute to the markets of the world is long in any degree ostracized. It is important and right that all privileges of the law be ours, but it is vastly more important that we be prepared for the exercises of these privileges. The opportunity to earn a dollar in a factory just now is worth infinitely more than the opportunity to spend a dollar in an opera house.
Booker T. Washington, African-American leader, to the Atlanta Exposition, 1895, in Ginger's People *(1975).*

Editor and outspoken critic of U.S. imperialism Edwin Lawrence Godkin. Courtesy of the Library of Congress.

Booker T. Washington. *Courtesy of the Library of Congress.*

In the inside shops the sanitary conditions are fairly good; and power is frequently, though by no means uniformly, furnished for running machines . . . The sweating-system has affected disastrously the condition of the employees in the inside shops, since any demand of the inside hands for increased wages or shorter hours is promptly met by transfer of work from the inside shop to a sweater; and the cutters alone remain secure from this competition.

It is preposterous, on the face of it, that a trade employing from 25,000 to 30,000 persons in a single city, with an annual output of many millions of dollars, should be carried on with the same primitive machines which were used thirty years ago. In every other branch of manufacture the watchword of the present generation has been concentration. Everywhere steam, electricity, and human ingenuity have been pressed into service for the purpose of organization and centralization; but in the garment trades this process has been reversed, and the division of labor has been made a means of demoralization, disorganization, and degradation, carried to a point beyond which it is impossible to go.

Florence Kelley, state inspector of factories and workshops for Illinois, 1895, in Hoogenboom and Hoogenboom's Gilded Age *(1967).*

. . . modern society is suffering from the very opposite of paternalism—from under-government, from the failure of government to keep pace with the change which civilization has wrought in substituting intellectual for physical qualities as the workers of injustice. Government to-day is powerless to perform its primary and original function of protecting society.

Plutocracy is the modern brigandage and can be dislodged only by . . . the power of the state . . . The true function of government is not to fetter but to liberate the forces of society, not to diminish but to increase their effectiveness. Unbridled competition destroys itself. The only competition that endures is that which goes on under judicious regulation.

Sociologist Lester F. Ward, 1895, in Hoogenboom and Hoogenboom's Gilded Age *(1967).*

So far from New York children being duller at their play than those of other cities and lands, I believe the reverse to be true. They lack neither spirit nor inventiveness. I watched a crowd of them having a donkey party in the street one night, when those parties were all the rage. The donkey hung in the window of a notion store, and a knot of tenement-house children with tails improvised from a newspaper and dragged in the gutter to make them stick, were staggering blindly across the sidewalk trying to fix them in place on the pane. They got a heap of fun out of the game, quite as much, it seemed to me, as any crowd of children could have got in a fine parlor, until the storekeeper came out with his club. Every cellar-door becomes a toboggan-slide when the children are around, unless it is hammered full of envious nails; every block a ball-ground when the policeman's back is turned, and every roof a kite-field; for that innocent amusement is also forbidden by city ordinance "below Fourteenth Street."

Jacob A. Riis, writer and photographer, 1895, in Hoogenboom and Hoogenboom's Gilded Age *(1967).*

Every few years our industrial system gets the jim-jams. Capital flies to cover, factories close and labor goes tramping across the country seeking honest employment and receiving a warm welcome—from militia companies with shotted guns. Cheerful idiots begin to prattle of "over-production," the economic M.D.'s to refurbish all the old remedies, from conjure-bags to communism. They all know exactly what caused the "crisis" and what to do for it; but despite the doctors the patient usually—survives. And the M.D. who succeeds in cramming his pet panacea down its throat claims all the credit for the recovery. We are slowly emerging from the crash of '93, and the cuckoos are cock-sure that a country fairly bursting with wealth was saved . . . by the blessed expedient of going into debt.

William Cowper Brann, controversial Texas newspaper publisher, in a speech titled "Slave or Sovereign," 1895, in Bartlett's Familiar Quotations *(1951).*

For more than thirty years we have been so much absorbed with grave domestic questions that we have lost sight of these vast interests which lie just outside our borders. They ought to be neglected no longer.

They are not only of material importance, but they are matters which concern our greatness as a nation and our future as a great people. They appeal to our national honor and dignity and to the pride of country and of race. If the humiliating foreign policy of the present Administration has served to call attention to these questions and to remind us that they are quite as important at least as tariffs and currency, it will perhaps prove to have been a blessing in disguise.

Senator Henry Cabot Lodge (R-Massachusetts), 1895, in Gianakos and Karson's American Diplomacy and the Sense of Destiny *(1966).*

Cleveland and Olney have relapsed into their normal hog-like attitudes of indifference, and Congress is disorganized, stupid and child-like as ever.

Historian Henry Adams, to his brother Brooks Adams, letter of 1895, in Smith's Industrial America *(1984).*

15. A Republican Victory and the Push for World Power: 1896–1897

THE HISTORICAL CONTEXT

The year 1896 was one of excitement and drama in the nation's political arena. When the former U.S. Representative from Nebraska, William Jennings Bryan, claimed his sweeping victory at the Democratic National Convention, he galvanized supporters into frenetic campaign activity. His appeal was so strong that the People's party named him their nominee as well. Even his detractors spoke of Bryan with grudging respect, although there were many who believed his ideas were unsound and felt his election would lead the country further into economic depression. Bryan's rousing "Cross of Gold" speech at the convention, and his relentless, unrestrained attack on eastern business and industrial interests, made him the topic of virtually every editorial or opinion column in the country. After their disappointment with Grover Cleveland, the Democrats felt they now had someone who, if elected president, would speak out on behalf of everything the party stood for.

The clash of ideologies between the nation's two principal parties had seldom been more clearly defined. The Republicans, who nominated William McKinley for president, supported a high tariff and the gold standard. Conversely, the issue of free silver coinage was a major plank in the Democratic platform, along with a lower tariff and a national income tax.

The Populist party had long called for an end to the gold standard, and it supported Bryan because of his position on money, although Populists suggested Bryan run with their nominee for vice president, Thomas E. Watson. And some Democrats who were unhappy with Bryan's demand for free silver coinage withdrew their backing of the

William Jennings Bryan, Democratic nominee for president in 1896. Courtesy of the Library of Congress.

ex-congressman, left the party, and formed their own, dubbing it the National Democratic party.

Republicans believed Bryan's election would ensure financial disaster. So to prevent a Democratic victory, they poured money into McKinley's campaign coffers. Hundreds of thousands of dollars meant victory for McKinley. His win over Bryan represented one of the most definitive electoral margins—271 to 176—in the nation's history, and the fact that McKinley claimed 7.1 million popular votes indicated a landslide of support in virtually every district in the country. Bryan's support, while enthusiastic, was limited to the South, some of the Plains states and the West.

Americans followed the campaigning, but foreign policy captured their attention as well. Congress became embroiled in debate over how—and if—the U.S. would take action with respect to Cuba. Expansionists believed the Spanish territory could be advantageous to U.S. interests. And since this island nation off the coast of Florida had rebelled against Spain and was now in the midst of civil war, those hoping to obtain control pushed for military intervention on the side of the freedom fighters in Cuba. Contributing to this internal conflict was the United States' passage of the Wilson–Gorman Tariff in 1894, which ended Cuban sugar merchants' virtual monopoly on U.S. markets. Since these merchants were no longer guaranteed favored prices, an

The gold or silver standard debate, from the Washington Post, 1896. *Courtesy of the Library of Congress.*

economic crisis was provoked in their homeland, a crisis that preceded the Cuban move for independence.

After much discussion, Congress decreed in 1896 that the U.S. would side with Cuba against Spain. Despite this, President Cleveland—nearing the end of his term—refused to send American troops to Cuba. Not until late 1897, after McKinley had been inaugurated, did the U.S. consider military action.

In March 1897 there also came an increase in the tariff, as McKinley had promised during his campaign. In passing the Dingley Tariff, Congress raised rates on foreign imports to their highest ever. And in addition to his support of this bill, McKinley upheld other campaign promises. He wanted to ensure that the U.S. would be strongly competitive in world markets, and therefore encouraged the nation to consider reciprocity agreements with other nations. The president also

President William McKinley.

*W.E.B. Du Bois. Courtesy of
the Library of Congress.*

worked to secure the gold standard, although this legislation would not pass for another three years.

Although the Republicans had established control via the election, and mainstream America felt optimistic about the future, there were some who looked ahead more warily. Among them was a young African-American, William E.B. Du Bois, newly appointed to the faculty at Atlanta University in 1897. Along with Booker T. Washington, Du Bois advocated activism by—and for—American blacks. His ideas soon diverged from those of Washington, who favored cooperation, not separatism, but until the 20th century the two were perhaps the most powerful in the nation's black community.

CHRONICLE OF EVENTS

1896:

January 4: Utah becomes the nation's 45th state.

The Actors' National Protective Union is formed.

January 16: The first intercollegiate five-man basketball game is held in Iowa City, Iowa.

January 18: The nation's first X-ray machine is exhibited in New York City.

January 29: X-ray technology is used in the treatment of breast cancer for the first time in the U.S.

February 28: Congress passes a resolution giving U.S. support to Cuban revolutionaries. Spain subsequently rejects the president's offer to help arrange a peace settlement for the island nation.

March 11: The national command of the Military Order of Foreign Wars is established.

March 31: The hookless fastener—known also as the zipper—is patented in Chicago, Illinois.

April 2: The College of Notre Dame of Maryland, in Baltimore, is incorporated.

April 6: At the first Olympic Games held in modern times, U.S. athletes win nine out of the 12 events held.

April 23: The first successful showing of a motion picture takes place in New York City at Koster and Bial's Music Hall.

May 12: In New York City, a health ordinance is enacted that prohibits spitting on public streets.

May 18: A Louisiana law, known as the Jim Crow Law, is declared constitutional by the U.S. Supreme Court. In its decision in *Plessy v. Ferguson*, the high court rules that segregated facilities are legal if they are offered equally to both races.

May 27: A tornado in St. Louis, Missouri, kills more than 100 people and leaves thousands homeless.

May 28: At the Prohibition party's national convention, Joshua Levering is nominated for president of the United States. Hale Johnson is selected as the vice-presidential candidate.

May 30: The nation's first automobile accident occurs in New York City.

June 4: In Detroit, Michigan, the first automobile rolls off the assembly line at Henry Ford's factory.

June 16: Republicans convene in St. Louis, Missouri, to nominate their candidates for president and vice president. William McKinley receives the nomination, along with running mate Garret A. Hobart.

June 22: Mary Stone becomes the first Chinese woman to receive an M.D. degree in the United States, in Ann Arbor, Michigan.

June 30: The first electric stove is patented by W.S. Hadaway in New York City.

July: Physical Education Magazine publishes the first rules for the game of volleyball.

July 4: The Socialist Labor party convention opens in New York City. Charles H. Matchett and Matthew Maguire are nominated for president and vice president, respectively.

July 11: The Democrats meet in Chicago, Illinois, for their national convention. William Jennings Bryan of Nebraska is nominated for president, and Arthur Sewall of Maine as vice president.

July 22: The National Silver party, known as "Silverites," holds its national convention in St. Louis, Missouri. It votes to uphold the Democratic candidates for president and vice president.

July 25: At the People's party convention, the Democratic nomination of William Jennings Bryan is supported, and Thomas E. Watson is put forth as the Populist candidate for vice president.

August 11: Harvey Hubbell patents the first electric light socket with a pull chain.

August 12: In Yukon Territory, gold is discovered on Klondike Creek, provoking the second major gold rush in U.S. history.

August 15: William Allen White, influential editor of the *Emporia Gazette*, publishes an editorial entitled "What's the Matter with Kansas?"

William Jennings Bryan (left) and his wife (right) greet supporters from the platform of his campaign train, 1896. Courtesy of the Library of Congress.

It wins him instant notoriety and provokes intense interest in his newspaper's comments on national politics.

September 2: The National Democratic party holds a convention in Indianapolis, Indiana, and nominates John M. Palmer for president. This group represents the so-called "sound money" Democrats who had no use for the free silver plank in Bryan's campaign platform.

September 7: In Cranston, Rhode Island, the first automobile race to be held on a track takes place.

September 15: A free hospital for the care of cancer patients opens in New York City.

October: *Argosy*, the nation's first all-fiction magazine, is published.

October 1: The U.S. Postal Service first offers free delivery for rural areas.

October 7: Beatrice Hoyt of Morristown, New Jersey, is the first winner of the U.S. Women's Amateur Golf Championship.

October 15: In Providence, Rhode Island, a cornerstone is laid for the State House, the first building with an all-marble dome.

November: McKinley defeats Bryan in the presidential election, becoming the nation's 25th chief executive.

November 15: A hydroelectric power plant at Niagara Falls provides electricity to Buffalo, New York.

November 24: Vermont enacts the nation's first absentee-voting law.

December 1: Frank Broaker becomes the nation's first certified public accountant.

December 10: The first intercollegiate basketball game is played in New Haven, Connecticut.

1897:

January 7: The first amateur handball championship match is held in Jersey City, New Jersey.

January 12: The National Monetary Conference meets in Indianapolis, Indiana. Following this conference, a commission is established to set up a plan for a permanent gold standard in the U.S.

January 25: The American Forestry Association is established.

February 2: In Harrisburg, Pennsylvania, fire destroys the state capitol building.

February 17: The National Congress of Mothers, a parent–teacher association, is formed in Washington, D.C.

February 25: Assistant Secretary of the Navy Theodore Roosevelt is left in charge of the Naval Department for several hours and nearly precipitates a series of confrontations in the Pacific by his take-charge attitude.

March 2: In one of the final acts of his presidency, Grover Cleveland vetoes an immigration law that, if passed, would require passage of a literacy test for those wishing to enter the U.S.

March 17: E.G. Briggs is the first woman to graduate from a theological seminary—the Union Theological Seminary in New York City.

  In a 14-round contest in Carson City, Nevada, "Gentleman Jim" Corbett defeats Bob Fitzsimmons in the first prizefight recorded on motion picture film.

March 30: The New York State Society of Certified Public Accountants is formed.

April 15: The nation's first indoor flycasting tournament opens in New York City.

April 19: The first annual marathon race in the nation is held with a course that goes from Hopkinton to Boston, Massachusetts.

April 20: The submarine *Argonaut* is fitted with an internal combustion engine, the first of its type, in Baltimore, Maryland.

May 1: C.G. Bothner is the first fencing champion to win three titles in one year in the U.S.

May 24: Congress approves $50,000 to be sent to Cuba for relief of victims of the civil war there.

July 2: Over 75,000 coal miners strike in Pennsylvania, Ohio, and West Virginia.

July 7: Congress passes the Dingley Tariff, which means that imports will be tagged with a higher tariff prior to their sale in the U.S.

September 10: Deputies fire on striking coal miners in Pennsylvlania, killing nearly two dozen men.

September 11: Striking coal miners settle their differences with owners, and are granted an eight-hour workday.

October 22: The United American Zionists is formed in New York City.

EYEWITNESS TESTIMONY

Our ancestors, when but three millions in number, had the courage to declare their political independence of every other nation; shall we, their descendants, when we have grown to seventy millions, declare that we are less independent than our forefathers? No my friends, that will never be the verdict of our people. Therefore, we care not upon what lines the battle is fought . . . If they dare to come out in the open field and defend the gold standard as a good thing, we will fight them to the uttermost. Having behind us the producing masses of this nation and the world, supported by the commercial interests, the laboring interests, and the toilers everywhere, we will answer their demand for a gold standard by saying to them: You shall not press down upon the brow of labor this crown of thorns, you shall not crucify mankind upon a cross of gold.

William Jennings Bryan, to the Democratic National Convention in Chicago, July 1896, in Kelley's The Shaping of the American Past *(1978).*

I have been thinking over Bryan's speech. What did he say, anyhow?

Illinois Governor John P. Altgeld, at the Democratic National Convention, 1896, in Tuchman's The Proud Tower *(1966).*

What's the matter with Kansas? We all know; yet here we are at it again. We have an old mossback Jacksonian who shouts and howls because there is a bathtub in the State house. We are running that old jay again for governor . . . We have raked the ashheap of failure in the State and found an old human hoop-skirt who has failed as a business man, who has failed as an editor, who has failed as a preacher, and we are going to run him for congressman-at-large . . . Then for fear some hint that the State had become respectable might percolate through the civilized portions of the nation, we have decided to send three or four harpies out lecturing, telling the people that Kansas is raising hell and letting the corn go to weeds.

Progressive newspaper editor William Allen White, in the Emporia Gazette, *August 1896, in an editorial used by the McKinley campaign, in Hoogenboom and Hoogenboom's* The Gilded Age *(1967).*

Illinois Governor John Peter Altgeld. Courtesy of the Library of Congress.

. . . a disorganized mob, at first out of which burst into sight, hearing, and force—one man [Bryan], but such a man! Alone, penniless, without backing, without money, with scarce a paper, without speakers, that man fought such a fight that even those in the East can call him a Crusader, an inspired fanatic—a prophet! It has been marvellous.

Mrs. Henry Cabot Lodge, the Republican senator's wife, 1896, in Kelley's American Past *(1978).*

The hatred of the East among many Westerners, and the crude ignorance of even elementary finance among such a multitude of well-meaning, but puzzleheaded, voters, give cause for serious alarm throughout this campaign.

Theodore Roosevelt, to Henry Cabot Lodge, letter of 1896, in Smith's The Rise of Industrial America *(1984).*

. . . the position and power of the Rocky Mountain states . . . are certainly as foreign to democracy as anything can possibly be.

Senator Marcus Alonzo Hanna. Courtesy of the Library of Congress.

William Graham Sumner, economist and sociologist, 1896, in Smith's Industrial America (1984).

Few rich men own their own property. The property owns them.
Robert Ingersoll, lawyer and orator, to the McKinley League at Carnegie Hall, New York City, 1896, in Bartlett's Familiar Quotations (1951).

The white race deems itself to be the dominant race in this country. And so it is, in prestige, in achievement, in education, in wealth and in power . . . But in view of the Constitution, in the eye of the law, there is in this country no superior, ruling class of citizens. There is no caste here. Our Constitution is color blind, and neither knows nor tolerates classes among citizens.
Marshall Harlan, Supreme Court associate justice, on his dissenting vote in Plessy v. Ferguson, 1896, in Degler's The Age of the Economic Revolution 1876–1900 (1977).

[The workers] have come to look upon the [Protestant] church and the ministry as the apologists and defenders of the wrongs committed against the interests of the people by employers and men of wealth.
Samuel Gompers, president of the American Federation of Labor, 1896, in Degler's Economic Revolution (1977).

We are bound to share in the commerce of the Far East, and it is better to strike for it while the iron is hot.
Senator Mark Hanna (R-Ohio), concerning a U.S. takeover of the Philippines, 1896, in Degler's Economic Revolution (1977).

There are far more human beings materially well off today than ever before in the history of the world. How interesting our times have been and still are!
Charles Eliot Norton, scholar and editor, 1896, in Tuchman's Proud Tower (1966).

In strict confidence . . . I should welcome almost any war, for I think this country needs one.
Theodore Roosevelt, Assistant Secretary of the Navy, to a friend, letter of 1897, in Degler's Economic Revolution (1977).

Do nothing unrighteous but take the [Hawaiian] islands first and solve afterward.
Alfred Thayer Mahan, naval historian, to Theodore Roosevelt, 1897, in Tuchman's Proud Tower (1966).

All religions are based upon a fundamental error.
Lester Frank Ward, Dynamic Sociology, 1883.

The men were assured that their future rested solely with themselves; that if they did their work faithfully and well, kept away from drink, treated citizens civilly, and tried to make themselves a credit to the department, there was no power in the city [New York City] that could get them out of their places, so long as I stayed in mine. On the other hand, if they were drunkards . . . no power could keep them in. When they found that I really meant what I said . . . they took on a new heart of hope and turned their eyes to the front. From that day their improvement has been constant and most satisfactory.
What has really been done has been to put a man instead of a voter at the other end of the broom-

Fashionable streets, like New York City's Fifth Avenue, were virtual parade grounds for the wealthy and well-dressed in the Gilded Age. Courtesy of the National Archives.

handle . . . A trusted sweeper, for example, will stand on a windy dock-log all night long, and night after night, protecting the city against the wiles and tricks of the snow-carters, He gets no extra pay for this, but his extra service and his hardship are compensated by the consciousness that he is doing good work, that his good work is appreciated by his officers, and that the force to which he belongs is winning public favor partly because of what he himself is doing. In other words, the whole department is actuated by a real esprit de corps, without which no organization of men can do its best, either in war or peace.

New York is now thoroughly clean in every part

Commissioner George E. Waring Jr., of New York City, 1897 in Hoogenboom and Hoogenboom's Gilded Age (1967).

No modern industry has gone with such leaps from primitive methods to the most highly developed mechanical perfection as that of oil; but these leaders of the trust did not invent nor introduce one of these improved processes—neither the pipe line nor the tank car nor the drill or still . . .

. . . the stock exchange value of the trust is in round numbers over $225,000,000.

The men who had "nothing" in the early sixties now have control of this fabulous sum in oil alone. The trust is a combination of corporations—a score or more. Hundreds of corporations all over the world have been condensed to make this score. Perhaps this lubrication of poverty into almost unaccountable millions is a triumph of co-operation.

. . . But the records show, on the sworn testimony of the organizers of the combination, that substantially the same men own the majority of this vast aggregation as began with nothing, and then formed the Standard Oil Company in 1870 with one million dollars capital.

Henry Demarest Lloyd, reformer and journalist, 1897, in Hoogenboom and Hoogenboom's Gilded Age (1967).

Everywhere [in America] the machine goes very rapidly, and it commands; the workman has to follow . . .

Even when the machine only plays a secondary role it is customary to go quickly and to lose no time, a necessary result of competition. The employer will not tolerate an idle or listless laborer, who causes him loss . . . The improvement of machinery and the growing power of industrial establishments, have diminished the price of a great number of goods, and this is one of the most laudable forward movements of industry whose object is to satisfy, as well as possible, the needs of man.

The laboring classes do not share this optimism. They reproach the machine with exhausting the physical powers of the laborer; but this can only apply to a very small number of cases to those where the workman is at the same time the motive power, as in certain sewing-machines. They reproach it with demanding such continued attention that it enervates, and of leaving no respite to the laborer, through the continuity of its movements.

. . . There is no social evolution which does not produce friction. That which urges industry toward machinery and large factories appears to me to-day irresistible, because it leads to cheapness, which the consumer seeks first of all, and which is one of the objects of economic civilization. It is Utopia to believe that the world could come back by some modification of the social order, or of mechanical motive powers to the system of the little family workshop. Such a workshop is far from being an ideal, as the sweating system proves.

E. Levasseur, French economist, 1897, in Hoogenboom and Hoogenboom's Gilded Age *(1967).*

If ever we come to nothing as a nation it will be because the teaching of Carl Schurz, President Eliot, the *Evening Post* and futile sentimentalists of the international arbitration type [will produce] a flabby timid type of character which eats away at the great fighting features of our race.

Theodore Roosevelt, Assistant Secretary of the Navy, to Henry Cabot Lodge, letter of 1897, in Tuchman's Proud Tower *(1966).*

There is a depth of human feeling in the Jew that no other race ever possessed. We do no more than imitate and follow it. David, for instance, and his conduct about Uriah's wife and the child that died— and Absalom—and Jonathan. Compare the Greek— the Chinese, the Roman. These Jews are more human than any other men. It is the cause of the spread of their religion—for we are all adopted in Judah. The heart of the world is Jewish. There is the same spirit in the Old Testament as in the New. That monstrous perversion—that we should worship their God and despise themselves.

John Jay Chapman, essayist, 1897, in Baltzell's The Protestant Establishment *(1966).*

The West End Jews, who are a well-to-do class, did not differ much from Englishmen of the same class. Those from the East End, employed for the most part in sweat-shops upon the manufacture of cheap clothing, averaged more than three inches less in stature, and were inferior also in size of skull and in every particular covered by the measurements. The intellectual deterioration that goes with this cannot be measured, but that it must exist will hardly be doubted.

Charles H. Cooley, sociologist, 1897, in Baltzell's Establishment *(1966).*

The family, rather than the individual, is the important social unit. If society as a whole is to gain by mobility and openness of structure, those who rise

must stay up in successive generations, that the higher levels of society may be constantly enlarged, and that the proportion of pure, gentle, magnanimous, and refined persons may steadily be increased. New-risen talent should reinforce the upper ranks . . . The assured permanence of superior families is quite as important as the free starting of such families.

Charles W. Eliot, Harvard president, 1897, in Garraty's Labor and Capital *(1968).*

In writing "progress and poverty," he dipped his pen into the tears of the human race, and with celestial clearness wrote down what he conceived to be eternal truths.

When he died, there was nowhere a soul that cried out: "There is one iron hand less to grind us, one wolf less to tear our flesh," but everywhere a feeling that a friend of the race had gone.

Judge John Peter Altgeld, former Governor of Illinois, memorial address on the death of Henry George, 1897, in Bartlett's Familiar Quotations *(1951).*

Order the squadron except Monocacy to Hong Kong. Keep full of coal. In the event of declaration war Spain, your duty will be to see that the Spanish squadron does not leave the Asiatic coast, and then offensive operations in Philippine Islands.

Theodore Roosevelt, as acting secretary of the Navy, to Admiral Dewey, cable of 1897, in Paterson's American Imperialism and Anti-Imperialism *(1973).*

He immediately began to launch peremptory orders: distributing ships; ordering ammunition, which there is no means to move, to places where there is no means to store it; sending for Captain Barker to come on about the guns of the *Vesuvius* . . . sending messages to Congress for immediate legislation, authorizing the enlistment of an unlimited number of seamen; and ordering guns from the Navy Yard at Washington to New York . . . He has gone at things like a bull in a china shop.

Secretary of the Navy Long, remarking on Roosevelt's one afternoon as acting secretary of the navy, 1897, in Paterson's American Imperialism *(1973).*

16. War, Peace and Economic Stability: 1898–1899

The Historical Context

America had barely finished celebrating the New Year of 1898 when it applauded yet another event: the sailing of the battleship *Maine* as it began a voyage to Havana harbor on a "friendly" visit, following a rebellion in Cuba. The voyage was meant as a show of force and indicated that the United States was serious about protecting its citizens living on the island nation. Pleased with this development, and with the recent election fresh on their minds, Republicans awaited the inauguration of William McKinley in March, feeling generally satisfied about the direction in which the nation was headed. Most hoped for a peaceful settlement in Cuba, although they realized the rebellion there had grown to proportions exceeding the ability of the United States to manage through diplomacy alone.

Two weeks into February, the nation's optimistic mood was shattered by the sinking of the *Maine*. By April, the U.S. was at war with Spain. It was a horrifying turn of events, although there was a strong feeling, especially among liberal intellectuals, that Cuban rebels were justified in seeking independence from Spain. These liberals, who actively and vocally encouraged such independence for its own sake, were joined by others who had somewhat different motives for urging the U.S. to intervene militarily in Cuba.

A large group of aggressive U.S. expansionists saw in the Cuban rebellion and subsequent Spanish–American conflict a perfect opportunity for the U.S. to increase its influence over rich but underdeveloped nations. Throughout the war, they sought expansion and made the case for a strong U.S. naval force and for a highly visible American profile worldwide. Among the more outspoken of those pushing for an American empire was Theodore Roosevelt. During the war he revelled in his role as a leader of the "Rough Riders," enjoying rising popularity and a strengthened political career due to his exploits—in November 1898 he was elected governor of New York.

Although it captured a lion's share of attention in the popular press, the war with Spain was not the sole concern of American citizens at the century's end. Innovative ideas in education, a rising tide of feminist protest and support for woman suffrage and growing affluence in America were transforming the national character. This transformation, although gradual, was discussed and analyzed in books, magazines and newspapers with greater frequency as the century drew to a close.

Labor issues continued to cause problems for owners of factories, mines and railroads, and these concerns generated a steady flow of federal legislation. In 1898, the Western Federation of Miners formed the Western Labor Union to increase its leverage in contract negotiations. In 1899, the Team Drivers International Union was founded. Later renamed the Teamsters' Union, it grew into the largest labor union in the nation.

In response to the growing strength of these groups, and because of lobbyists' demands, Congress enacted the Erdman Arbitration Act in 1898. This law arranged for government mediation in railroad labor disputes and prohibited the use of yellow-dog contracts by the railroads. As a condition of employment, a yellow-dog contract required a worker to agree not to join a union. Although it suggested an improvement in the government's attitude toward labor, the Erdman Act only softened the federal pro-business bias. Legislative and judicial actions remained slanted toward business interests until well into the 20th century.

While it would be several decades before women were granted federal voting rights, they had claimed a larger share of rights and responsibilities by the end of the century. They also had made an impression in many professions. In 1898, feminist theorist and writer Charlotte Perkins Gilman published her seminal work, *Women and Economics.* Thought by many to be an outrageous attack on traditional values and on conventional family structure, Gilman's work attracted much attention. While her ideas for releasing women from domestic drudgery never attained widespread acceptance, she nevertheless provoked much discussion about the role of women in society. The following year, novelist Kate Chopin published *The Awakening.* Another feminist work, it was assailed by critics because it dealt openly with sexual feelings and with the question of individual freedom within marriage.

Another work published in 1899 that received much attention and publicity was by the educator John Dewey. He wrote *The School and Society* to explain his theory that learning could be accomplished only "by doing." It was an idea that would completely transform education in America, making Dewey's name synonymous with educational reform.

In 1899, economist Thorstein Veblen published *The Theory of the Leisure Class.* This incisive, controversial analysis of the buying and spending habits of Americans provoked instant response. According to

Veblen, "conspicuous consumption" was a way for the dominant economic class to display its power. Veblen, a contemporary of Richard Ely and others in the college-trained crop of late 19th-century economists, was the most radical of those who applied economic theory to real-life situations.

CHRONICLE OF EVENTS

1898:

January: John Mitchell is elected vice president of the United Mine Workers. He is soon elected president of this powerful labor group.

January 25: The U.S. battleship *Maine* arrives in the harbor at Havana, Cuba.

February 9: Hearst's *New York Journal* publishes a private letter written by the Spanish minister to the U.S., Senor Dupuy de Lome. The letter angers U.S. readers, causes international embarrassment and provokes the minister's resignation, since in the letter the Spanish minister maligns the character and abilities of U.S. President McKinley.

February 15: The U.S. battleship *Maine* blows up in the harbor at Havana; 260 lives are lost. Spanish saboteurs are blamed and President McKinley is called upon to act in the nation's defense.

March 31: Spain refuses to arbitrate with the U.S. over the *Maine* affair. President McKinley drafts a declaration of war.

April 5: President McKinley recalls American consuls from Cuba.

April 11: McKinley requests that Congress issue permission for the U.S. to use force in expelling Spain from Cuba.

April 19: Congress adopts resolutions that call for Cuban independence and for the president to use military force against Spanish authority there.

April 22: The U.S. initiates a blockade of Cuban ports.

Congress passes the Volunteer Army Act, which permits the 1st Regiment of U.S. Cavalry Volunteers to form. Commanded by Colonel Leonard Wood and Lieutenant Colonel Theodore Roosevelt, it is best known by its nickname, the "Rough Riders."

The U.S. gunboat *Nashville* captures a Spanish ship, the *Buena Ventura*.

April 23: President McKinley calls for 125,000 volunteers to fight against Spain.

April 24: Spain recognizes a state of war against the U.S.

April 25: Congress passes a declaration of war against Spain. It dates the declaration to the

A group picture taken at the White House: (left to right) Andrew Carnegie, U.S. Steel Company; William Jennings Bryan, presidential nominee; J.J. Hill, railway president; and John Mitchell, president of the United Mine Workers of America. Courtesy of the Library of Congress.

Wreck of the U.S.S. Maine, *1898. Courtesy of the National Archives.*

21st of the month, however, to ensure that naval action by the U.S. on the 22nd would fall under the declaration's terms.

May 1: Commodore George Dewey sinks the Spanish Fleet at Manila Bay in the Philippines after a seven-hour battle. The U.S. sustains no casualties, while Spain loses nearly 400 men in the encounter.

May 25: The president calls for an additional 75,000 military volunteers.

May 28: The U.S. Supreme Court rules that citizenship is a right of any person born in this country, regardless of the parents' nationality.

June 1: Congress passes the Erdman Arbitration Act, which permits federal mediation between interstate carriers and employees in cases of discrimination against union workers.

June 10: Congress passes the War Revenue Bill, which authorizes issuance of government bonds up to $400 million as a means of supporting the war effort.

June 11: U.S. Marines land at Guantanamo Bay in Cuba.

June 12: American troops leave Key West, Florida, on a mission to Santiago, Cuba.

June 15: At Guantanamo Bay, Cuba, U.S. Marines engage Spanish forces and push them back.

Congress passes a law allowing for annexation of the Hawaiian Islands. President McKinley signs the law on July 7.

June 20: The island of Guam surrenders to the U.S.

June 24: In the first land battle of the Spanish–American war, the U.S. defeats opposing Spanish forces at Las Guasimas, Cuba. Troops leading the offensive include the Rough Riders, under the command of Theodore Roosevelt.

July 2: After two days of fighting at El Caney and San Juan, Cuba, U.S. troops defeat Spanish forces there.

July 3: U.S. ships destroy the Spanish fleet as they leave Santiago.

July 8: Commodore Dewey occupies Isla Granda in Subic Bay, near Manila in the Philippines.

July 17: Twenty-four thousand Spanish troops surrender to the U.S. at Santiago. There would be a total of 5,462 American deaths, most of them due to disease. Over 1,600 men were wounded.

July 21: In waters off the Cuban coast near Nipe, the last sea encounter of the war occurs. American ships seize the port there.

July 25: U.S. troops seize Guanica, Puerto Rico.

July 26: Spain requests terms of peace from the U.S.

July 31: At Malate, near Manila, U.S. troops suffer significant casualties in an encounter with Spanish troops.

August 1: The death toll mounts in a yellow-fever epidemic in Cuba. Over 4,200 U.S. troops are sick.

August 9: American troops defeat Spanish military forces at Coamo, Puerto Rico.

August 9: Spain accepts peace terms proffered by the U.S.

August 12: An armistice is signed with Spain as Cuba is freed and Puerto Rico and Guam are ceded to the United States.

September: John Hay, U.S. ambassador to Great Britain, is named by President McKinley to serve as secretary of state.

September 9: The U.S. Peace Commission, headed by Judge W.R. Day, prepares to sail for France to sign a peace treaty with Spain.

October 1: U.S. and Spanish peace commissioners meet to discuss the disposition of the Philippine Islands. The ensuing debate lasts for two years, during which time Philippine insurrectionists stage a revolt.

November 8: Theodore Roosevelt is elected governor of New York.

November 26: Off the shores of Cape Cod, Massachusetts, the vessel *City of Portland* is wrecked, with a resulting loss of 157 lives.

December 10: The United States and Spain sign a peace treaty in Paris. Under its terms, the U.S. gains control of Puerto Rico and Guam, and pays $20 million for control of the Philippines, which remains under U.S. jurisdiction until 1949.

1899:

January 20: The Commission on the Philippines is established by President McKinley. Its role is to map out strategies for how the islands will be ruled prior to instituting self-government there.

January 24: In Lowell, Massachusetts, a process for manufacturing the first rubber heel for shoes is patented.

January 28: The American Social Science Association is established.

February 6: The U.S. Senate ratifies the Treaty of Paris. During the debate, imperialists—led by Senator Henry Cabot Lodge—argue for the economic and political advantages the treaty represents. Opponents say the treaty embraces ideas in opposition to the Monroe Doctrine.

February 12: An international bicycle race is held in New York City.

February 14: Voting machines are authorized for use in federal elections in states where such machines are available.

March 1: The Union Reform party adopts its platform at a convention in Cincinnati, Ohio.

March 2: Congress calls for additional volunteers for army duty in order to help suppress a rebellion in the Philippines led by Emilio Aguinaldo.

March 2: Commodore George Dewey, the hero of Manila Bay, is named Admiral of the Navy, only the third naval officer on whom this rank is conferred. Admirals Farragut and Porter held this rank before him.

March 3: The Isthmian Canal Commission is established by Congress, the third commission to propose such a waterway in the history of the U.S.

March 20: At Sing Sing prison in Ossining, New York, the first woman is executed by electrocution.

April 21: An intercollegiate chess tournament is held via telephone cable between New York City and London.

April 24: In Wardner, Idaho, a miners' strike turns violent as demands are rejected by mine owners there.

April 27: The federal government opens a hospital for tuberculosis patients in Fort Stanton, New Mexico.

Missouri is struck by a tornado that kills several dozen people and leaves scores injured.

April 28: The Filipinos request peace terms, a request that is rejected by General Otis since the U.S. demands an unconditional surrender of insurrectionists.

May 18: The first Hague Peace Conference opens in Paris. At this conference, the United States requests—and obtains—the formation of a permanent court of international arbitration.

May 20: The first arrest for automobile speeding occurs in New York City.

The American Physics Society is established in New York City.

May 24: A public automobile garage is established in Boston, Massachusetts.

June 23: G.H. Wanton becomes the first black American to receive the Medal of Honor, for service in the Spanish–American War.

July 1: A juvenile court is opened in Chicago, Illinois.

The Christian Commercial Men's Association of America organizes the Gideons, which becomes famous for publishing Bibles that are placed in hotel rooms across the nation.

July 6: The nation's first automobile licensing board is established in Chicago, Illinois.

July 8: H.M. Harriman becomes the first American-born professional golf champion, in Lake Forest, Illinois.

July 18: Secretary of War Russell A. Alger resigns under heavy criticism after it is discovered that military commands were insufficiently prepared for service during the Spanish–American War.

July 29: A motorcycle-paced bicycle race is held in New York City at the Manhattan Beach Track. This marks the first time that gasoline-powered pacers are used in such an event.

August 8: A.T. Marshall of Brockton, Massachusetts, patents the first home refrigerator.

September 6: Secretary of State John Hay requests establishment of an "open door" policy in China, so as to ensure free access to all economic opportunities there. This request will be consented to in early 1900 by Britain, France, Germany, Italy, Japan and Russia.

September 9: An automobile parade is held in Newport, Rhode Island.

September 13: In New York City, the first automobile-related death occurs.

October 4: Admiral Dewey sends additional troops to the Philippines.

October 14: President William McKinley rides in a Stanley Steamer, becoming the first U.S. president to ride in an automobile.

October 16: The first radio broadcast from a yacht takes place off Sandy Hook, New Jersey.

November 10: In a New Orleans, Louisiana, hospital, a spinal operation is performed using anesthesia, the first such procedure of its kind.

November 12: Vice President Garret A. Hobart dies in Paterson, New Jersey.

November 24: Reports from Central Luzon in the Philippines indicate that General Otis has taken three important prisoners: the Philippine president, secretary of state and treasurer.

December 4: The U.S. Supreme Court rules, in *Addyston Pipe & Steel Co. v. United States,* that companies cannot make noncompetition agreements without violating the Sherman Anti-Trust Law.

December 5: In his third address to Congress, President McKinley warns of the growing power of trusts in the U.S., a statement that is seen as a bold move for the relatively conservative Republican president.

December 10: In Denver, Colorado, the National Jewish Hospital opens and offers free, nonsectarian service to tuberculosis patients.

December 12: The golf tee is patented in Boston, Massachusetts.

December 16: The nation's first children's museum is opened in Brooklyn, New York.

EYEWITNESS TESTIMONY

Every boy and man, many of the girls, and some of the women, regard an afternoon or an evening at the Dime now and then as an indispensable part of their lives. The Dime is to them that the theatre, the opera, and the symphony are to the more fortunate classes in the community. It is the only means by which they can obtain the enjoyment that is derived from the imagination. That the craving is strong is shown by the crowded houses always to be seen at this resort.

Long-time Boston resident Frederick Haynes, describing the most popular theater in South Boston, 1898, in Hoogenboom and Hoogenboom's The Gilded Age *(1967).*

An elaborate form of this game [rounders] has become the national game of the United States.

Alice Bertha Gomme, observing the popularity of baseball in the United States, 1898, in Bowman and Zoss's Diamonds in the Rough *(1989).*

If the Philippines are annexed, what is to prevent the Chinese, the negritos, and the Malays coming to our own country?

Samuel Gompers, President of the American Federation of Labor, speech of 1898, in Paterson's American Imperialism and Anti-Imperialism *(1973).*

How much has happened since I last heard from you! To say nothing of the Zola trial, we now have the Cuban war! A curious episode of history, showing how a nation's ideals can be changed in the twinkling of an eye, by a succession of outward events partly accidental. It is possible that, without the explosion of the Maine, we should still be at peace, though, since the basis of the whole American attitude is the persuasion on the part of the people that the cruelty and misrule of Spain in Cuba call for her expulsion . . . it is hardly possible that peace could have been maintained indefinitely longer, unless Spain had gone out—a consummation hardly to be expected by peaceful means.

. . . The self-conscious feeling of our people has been entirely based in a sense of philanthropic duty, without which not a step would have been taken . . . once the excitement of action gets loose, the taxes

Philosopher William James. Courtesy of the Library of Congress.

levied, the victories achieved, etc., the old human instincts will get into play with all their old strength, and the ambition and sense of mastery which our nation has will set up new demands.

William James, philosopher and psychologist, to Francois Pilon, letter of 1898, in Hoogenboom and Hoogenboom's Gilded Age *(1967).*

We shall have Hawaii, of course, if not in one way, in another, and there is nothing in the special pleas of lawyers or the public quirks of other public men, that will prevent our people from having their own way.

Murat Halstead, imperialist associate of Theodore Roosevelt, 1898, in Campbell's Expansionism and Imperialism *(1970).*

We need Hawaii just as much and a good deal more than we did California. It is Manifest Destiny.

President William A. McKinley, 1898, in Ginger's People on the Move *(1975).*

I think . . . possibly the President could have worked the business without a war, but the current was too strong, the demagogues too numerous, and the fall elections too near.

Senator John Spooner (R-Wisconsin), on the annexation of Hawaii, 1898, in Degler's The Age of Economic Revolution 1876–1900 *(1977).*

We are the conquering race. We must obey our blood and occupy new markets and if necessary new lands. . . . In the Almighty's infinite plan . . . debased civilizations and decaying races [disappear] before the higher civilization of the nobler and more virile types of man.

Albert J. Beveridge, expansionist, 1898, in Tuchman's The Proud Tower *(1966).*

I would give anything if President McKinley would order the fleet to Havana tomorrow . . . the *Maine* was sunk by an act of dirty treachery on the part of the Spaniards.

Theodore Roosevelt, writing Assistant Secretary of the Navy, of the Maine affair, 1898, in Kelley's The Shaping of the American Past *(1978).*

About three months.

Alfred Thayer Mahan, naval historian, responding to a question about how long the war with Spain might last, 1898, in Tuchman's Proud Tower *(1966).*

There is no question that you stand head and shoulders above the rest of us. You have given us just the suggestions we want.

Theodore Roosevelt, a member of the U.S. Naval War Board, responding to suggestions for a campaign in the Philippines, 1898, in Tuchman's Proud Tower *(1966).*

You may fire when ready, Gridley.

Commodore George Dewey, giving the command to begin attacking the Spanish fleet, in Manila Bay, April 30, 1898, in Tuchman's Proud Tower *(1966).*

We must on no account let the islands go . . . The American flag is up and it must stay.

Senator Henry Cabot Lodge (R-Massachusetts), 1898, in Tuchman's Proud Tower *(1966).*

It has been a splendid little war, carried on with magnificent intelligence and spirit, favored by that Fortune which loves the Brave.

Admiral George Dewey, and his faithful companion Bob, who defeated the Spanish Fleet at Manila Bay in the Philippines. Courtesy of the Library of Congress.

Secretary of State John Hay, then Assistant Secretary of the Navy, to Theodore Roosevelt during the assault on Spanish troops in Cuba, letter of 1898, in Ginger's People *(1975).*

It was a most happy-go-lucky expedition, run with real American optimism and readiness to take big chances, and with the spirit of a people who recklessly trust that it will come out all right in the end, and that the barely possible may not happen . . . As one of the generals on board said, 'This is God Almighty's war, and we are only His agents.' "

Richard Harding Davis, journalist and war correspondent, 1898, in Degler's Economic Revolution *(1977).*

Tell the President for Heaven's sake to send us every regiment and above all every battery possible. We have won so far at a heavy cost, but the Spaniards fight very hard and charging these intrenchments

Roosevelt and his troops. Courtesy of the Library of Congress.

against modern rifles is terrible . . . We *must* have help—thousands of men, batteries, and *food* and ammunition.

Theodore Roosevelt, leader of the volunteer Rough Riders, 1898, in Ginger's People *(1975).*

American character will be still better understood when the whole world clearly perceives that the purpose of the war is only to remove from our very doors this cruel and inefficient piece of medievalism which is one of the . . . scandals of the closing years of the century; for it is not a want of conquest . . . Once free, let [Cuba] govern itself . . .

Walter Hines Page, editor of Atlantic Monthly, *June 1898.*

. . . it will be my aim to subserve our large interests in that quarter [China] by all means appropriate to the constant policy of our Government.

President McKinley, to Congress, annual message of 1898, in Campbell's Expansionism *(1970).*

. . . act vigorously for the protection of Americans.

John Hay, secretary of state, to the U.S. foreign minister in China, 1898, in Campbell's Expansionism *(1970).*

. . . unless a vigorous policy is pursued on the part of the United State Government, these markets will be eventually closed to our trade, as has recently been the case in Madagascar . . . We earnestly call attention to the above facts, and ask that our repre-

Secretary of State John Hay, who was instrumental in encouraging China's "Open Door" policy, spoke strongly in support of U.S. commercial interests in Asia. Courtesy of the Library of Congress.

sentatives at St. Petersburgh [*sic*] be instructed to give special attention to the subject.

Fifty-three U.S. manufacturers and exporters of cotton textiles, to Congress, expressing joint concern over Russia's apparent interest in restricting or monopolizing trade with China, letter of 1899, in Campbell's Expansionism *(1970).*

We are, of course, opposed to the dismemberment of that Empire [China], and we do not think that the public opinion of the United States would justify this Government in taking part on the great game of spoliation now going on. At the same time we are keenly alive to the importance of safeguarding our great commercial interests in that Empire and representatives there have orders to watch closely everything that may seem calculated to injure us, and to prevent it by energetic and timely representations.

Secretary of State John Hay, to the editor of the New York Sun, *1899, in Campbell's* Expansionism *(1970).*

If they become states on an equal footing with the other states they will not only be permitted to govern themselves as to their home concerns, but will take part in governing the whole republic, in governing us, by sending senators and representatives into our Congress to help make our laws, and by voting for president and vice-president to give our national government its executive. The prospect of the consequences which would follow the admission of the

Spanish creoles and the negroes of the West India islands and of the Malays and Tagals of the Philippines to participation in the conduct of our government is so alarming that you instinctively pause before taking the step.

Carl Schurz, liberal Republican and former Secretary of the Interior, 1899, in Paterson's American Imperialism *(1973).*

Neither the people nor the institutions of the United States can ever occupy the Philippines. The American home cannot endure there, the town-meeting cannot exist.

David Starr Jordan, president of Stanford University, 1899, in Paterson's American Imperialism *(1973).*

Civilization is, as it were, suffocated in the tropics.

David Starr Jordan, president of Stanford University, 1899, in Degler's Economic Revolution *(1977).*

We want to send the products of our farms, our factories, and our mines into every market of the world; make the foreign peoples familiar with our products; and the way to do that is to make them familiar with our flag.

President McKinley, discussing the nation's economy following the Spanish–American conflict, 1899, in Ginger's People *(1975).*

. . . our yellow journals have abundant time in which to raise new monuments of capitols to the victories of Old Glory, and in which to extol the unrestrained eagerness of our brave soldiers . . .

. . . It is horrible, simply horrible. Surely there cannot be many born and bred Americans who, when they look at the bare fact of what we are doing, the fact taken all by itself, do not feel this . . .

. . . But these are passions that interfere with the reasonable settlement of any affair; and in this affair we have to deal with a factor altogether peculiar with our belief, namely, in a national destiny which must be "big" at any cost . . . We are to be missionaries of civilization, and to bear the white man's burden, painful as it often is.

William James, philosopher and psychologist, to the Boston Evening Transcript, *letter of March 1, 1899.*

Before you go I would like to say just a word about the Philippine business. I have been criticized a good deal about the Philippines, but don't deserve it. The truth is I didn't want the Philippines, and when they came to us, as a gift from the gods, I did not know what to do with them. When the Spanish war broke out Dewey was at Hongkong [sic], and I ordered him to go to Manila and to capture or destroy the Spanish fleet, and he had to; because, if defeated, he had no place to refit on that side of the globe, and if the Dons were victorious they would likely cross the Pacific and ravage our Oregon and California coasts. And so he had to destroy the Spanish fleet, and did it! But that was as far as I thought then.

When next I realized that the Philippines had dropped into our laps I confess I did not know what to do with them. I sought counsel from all sides—Democrats as well as Republicans—but, got little help.

President William McKinley, to a delegation
from the General Missionary Committee of the
Methodist Episcopal Church, November 21,
1899, in Ginger's People *(1975).*

From a nation of shopkeepers we become a nation of warriors. We escape the menace and peril of socialism and agrarianism, as England has escaped them, by a policy of colonization and conquest. From a provincial huddle of petty sovereignties held together by a rope of sand we rise to the dignity and prowess of an imperial republic incomparably greater than Rome. It is true that we exchange domestic dangers for foreign dangers; but in every direction we multiply the opportunities of the people. We risk Caesarism, certainly; but even Caesarism is preferable to anarchism. We risk wars; but a man has but one time to die, and either in peace or war, he is not likely to die until his time comes . . . In short, anything is better than the pace we were going before these present forces were started into life. Already the young manhood of the country is as a goodly brand snatched from the burning, and given a perspective replete with noble deeds and elevating ideas.

Henry Watterson, editor of the Louisville
Courier-Journal, *promoting U.S. expansion,*
1899, in Kelley's American Past *(1978).*

It is an evil thing for any man of education to forget that education should intensify patriotism, and that patriotism must not only be shown by striving to do good to the country from within, but by readiness to uphold its interests and honor, at any cost, when menaced from without. Educated men owe to the community the serious performance of this duty.

Theodore Roosevelt, Governor of New York,
1899, in Hoogenboom and Hoogenboom's
Gilded Age *(1967).*

The great foe of democracy now and in the near future is plutocracy. Every year that passes brings out this antagonism more distinctly. It is to be the social war of the twentieth century. In that war militarism, expansion and imperialism will all favor plutocracy. In the first place, war and expansion will favor jobbery, both in the dependencies and at home. In the second place, they will take away the attention of the people from what the plutocrats are doing. In the third place, they will cause large expenditures of the people's money, the return for which will not go into the treasury but into the hands of a few schemers. In the fourth place, they will call for a large public debt and taxes, and these things especially tend to make men unequal, because any social burdens bear more heavily on the weak than on the strong, and so make the weak weaker and the strong stronger. Therefore expansion and imperialism are a grand onslaught on democracy.

William Graham Sumner, sociologist and econ-
omist, lecturing at Yale University, January
1899, in Gianakos and Karson's American Diplomacy and the Sense of Destiny *(1966).*

. . . I felt certain that you must be opposed to the mad folly, not to say crime, of Imperialism. A man possessing such clear discernment as your public career has given rare evidence of could not fail to see that Imperialism is the new treason which now confronts our republic; treason to those high ideals that have given us all the greatness and glory which we can rightly claim to among the nations of history.

. . . We in Massachusetts who love the old ideals of our republic hang our heads with shame when we see only one of our senators at Washington contending for these ideals . . . Hoar, [Senator George F. Hoar, R-Mass.] whom I have never had any use for until now, is standing up nobly against the treaty which treats for war rather than peace, and I only hope that he will "stick," as Sumner advised Stanton to. We Anti-Imperialists in Massachusetts have done what we could to stem the tide of McKinley's cussedness. . .

A.W. Stevens, writer, to Representative George
W. Julian, letter of 1899, in Hoogenboom and
Hoogenboom's Gilded Age *(1967).*

. . . [a] class poet, blazoning an empty race prejudice.
John Jay Chapman, reformer and friend of Henry Adams, on Rudyard Kipling, 1899, in Baltzell's The Protestant Establishment *(1966).*

Miss Arlington might do as a pitcher among amateurs, but the sluggers of the Atlantic league would soon put her out of the business. She, of course, hasn't the strength to get much speed on and has poor control. But, for a woman, she is a success.
The Reading, Pennsylvania, newspaper, describing female baseball pitcher, Lizzie Arlington, 1899, in Bowman and Zoss's Diamonds *(1989).*

The ordinary "horseless carriage" is at present a luxury for the wealthy; and although its price will probably fall in the future, it will never, of course, come into as common use as the bicycle.
Literary Digest, report of October 1899.

The walking-stick serves the purpose of an advertisement that the bearer's hands are employed otherwise than in useful effort, and it therefore has utility as an evidence of leisure . . . The adoption of the cap and gown is one of the striking atavistic features of modern college life . . . The classics have scarcely lost in absolute value as a voucher of scholastic respectability, since for this purpose it is only necessary that the scholar should be able to put in evidence some learning which is conventionally recognized as evidence of wasted time.
Thorstein Veblen, in The Theory of the Leisure Class, *1899.*

Whether the Spanish war shall be known in history as a war for liberty or a war of conquest; whether the principles of self-government shall be strengthened or abandoned; whether this nation shall remain a homogeneous republic or become a heterogeneous empire—these questions must be answered by the American people—when they speak, and not until then, will destiny be revealed.

Destiny is not a matter of chance, it is a matter of choice; it is not a thing to be waited for, it is a thing to be achieved.

. . . If we embark upon a career of conquest no one can tell how many islands we may be able to seize or how many races we may be able to subjugate; neither can anyone estimate the cost, immediate and remote, to the nation's purse and to the nation's character, but whether we shall enter upon such a career is a question which the people have a right to decide for themselves.
William Jennings Bryan, Populist Party leader, a speech in Washington, D.C., 1899, in Gianakos and Karson's American Diplomacy *(1966).*

17. Election, Assassination and the New Century: 1900–1901

THE HISTORICAL CONTEXT

Since the end of Reconstruction in the 1870s, the United States had forged a stronger federal system, built great cities, established a successful transportation network and founded an empire of industry and commerce unrivaled elsewhere in the world.

These changes provided for a handy set of campaign issues during the months preceding the presidential election of 1900. Domestic policy combined with foreign policy to fuel substantial debate between Republicans and Democrats, labor party supporters and big business interests, expansionists and anti-imperialists. Those eager to lead the country knew that the challenges of the 20th century meant even greater change for the United States. Yet they believed also that the nation still cherished dreams of equal opportunity, financial success and tolerance and freedom for all loyal citizens, and that change brought opportunity as well as problems.

Many of these same powerful politicians prided themselves on U.S. involvement in Cuba's independence from Spain, since this activism had been based on a desire to win democracy for Cuban citizens. But few were prepared for an American military hero of that war to become vice president of the United States in 1900. Even fewer anticipated that they would watch this hero reverently assume the presidency as a grieving nation mourned McKinley's assassination in 1901.

The president's death, coming so violently and without warning, shocked Americans. Always aware of his goodness and integrity, the country belatedly praised his skills as an executive. It then turned to its new president, wondering—some hopefully, many with more than a little trepidation—how this jaunty, outspoken patriot and war hero would govern.

And as the U.S. paid its final respects to its martyred leader and feted its new president, debate continued over the proper role of the federal government in regulating private business and industry. The

179

glittering decades of financial excess could not be instantly erased by legions of reformers, although 1900 marked a delineation between the power of laissez-faire government policies and that of policymakers who favored an aggressive federal role. Over the first two decades of the 1900s, social, political and economic reforms would limit the previously untrammeled growth of private corporations.

A clearly defined sense of moral and civic duty was articulated in books and newspapers and from pulpits and speakers' platforms as Americans tried to make social and political structures more responsive. An example of this revived interest in responsibility toward one's tasks was perhaps most cogently stated in Elbert Hubbard's essay "A Message to Garcia." While Hubbard merely voiced his personal philosophy in this short treatise on personal duty, he nonetheless struck a chord in the hearts and minds of his readers. Published in 1900, "A Message to Garcia" sold over 80 million copies. A scant year later, when President Roosevelt told Congress of his desire to restrain government tendencies to lavish legislative and judicial approval on business interests, he appealed to his audience's sense of responsibility.

Roosevelt termed this new approach to federal action and decision making the principle of "public interest." And far from being an isolated, Rooseveltian quirk, it was a principle that guided a whole new era of leaders, reformers and civil servants. Their "progressive" approach to problem solving resulted in informed public policy and helped in setting federal, state and local agendas right up until the outbreak of the First World War.

CHRONICLE OF EVENTS

1900:

January 2: An electric bus seating eight people begins service along Fifth Avenue in New York City.

January 25: Congress votes 268–50 to unseat Brigham H. Young, a Congressman-elect from Utah, because he has three wives.

January 27: The Social Democratic party of America holds its first convention in Rochester, New York.

January 29: The American Baseball League is formed in Chicago, Illinois.

February 6: Theodore Roosevelt, governor of New York, states flatly that he will not accept the nomination for vice president of the United States. Roosevelt's opponents are eager to see him in this essentially powerless position.

February 16: The nation's first Chinese daily newspaper, *Ching Sai Yat Po*, is published in San Francisco, California.

March 5: At New York University, the first Hall of Fame is established by Mrs. Finley J. Shepard's gift of $250,000. Members are elected to the Hall of Fame every five years by a committee of 100 people.

March 14: McKinley signs the Gold Standard Act, returning the nation to a single monetary standard, and establishing a gold dollar of 25.8 grains in weight.

March 24: In New Jersey, the new Carnegie Steel Company is incorporated. Formation of the company directly challenges the Sherman Anti-Trust Law.

March 25: The United States' Socialist party is founded in Indianapolis, Indiana.

March 31: The nation's first automobile advertisement appears in a magazine.

April 12: Puerto Rico is confirmed as a U.S. territory with passage of the Foraker Act, although Puerto Ricans will not become U.S. citizens until passage of the 1916 Jones Act.

The first couple to be married in a ceremony conducted by telegraph is held in Kansas City, Missouri.

April 14: A 50-mile automobile cross-country race is held between Springfield and Babylon, on Long Island, New York.

April 16: The U.S. Postal Service issues the first book of stamps.

April 30: Hawaii becomes a U.S. territory by an act of Congress.

May 1: In a coal mine in Scofield, Utah, a blasting powder explosion kills 200 people.

May 10: The Populist (Fusion) National Convention is held in Sioux Falls, South Dakota. William Jennings Bryan is nominated for president, with Charles A. Town his vice-presidential running mate.

In Cincinnati, Ohio, the Populist (middle-of-the-road) party breaks away from the main party group and holds a convention. It nominates Wharton Barker for president and names Ignatius Donnelly, the labor leader, as its nominee for vice president.

May 14: Sanford Dole becomes governor of the territory of Hawaii.

The U.S. Supreme Court rules, in *Knowlton v. Moore*, that an inheritance tax imposed under the War Revenue Act of 1898 is constitutional.

Women's Christian Temperance Union (WCTU) leader Carrie Nation begins her anti-saloon campaign in Kansas.

May 22: A pneumatic player piano is patented in Detroit, Michigan.

May 23: The Army Medal of Honor goes for the first time to a black American, W.H. Carney.

May 26: Congress approves an appropriation to establish the Army War College.

June: The International Ladies' Garment Workers Union is established in New York City by delegates from seven unions, representing 2,000 members. The group does not wield any significant power until a strike in 1909.

The nation's first society of orthodontists is founded in St. Louis, Missouri.

June 2: The Socialist Labor party holds a convention in New York City. The party nominees for president and vice president are Joseph P. Maloney and Valentine Remmel.

June 12: The nation's first trapshooting tournament is held in Interstate Park, New York.

June 16: The first international revolver-shooting competition is held in Greenville, New Jersey.

June 19: The Republican National Convention opens in Philadelphia, Pennsylvania. Despite his previous protestations to the contrary, Theodore Roosevelt is nominated for vice president by acclamation and accepts the nomination to run alongside incumbent President William McKinley.

June 20: A wholesale uprising against foreign influence occurs in China, with a violent episode known as the "Boxer Rebellion."

June 21: Filipino insurgents are granted amnesty.

June 27: The Prohibition party convenes in Chicago, Illinois, and nominates John G. Woodley for president and Henry B. Metcalf for vice president.

June 30: At the piers of the North German Lloyd Steamship concern in Hoboken, New Jersey, a fire breaks out and kills 326 people.

July 1: In Camden, Maine, the nation's first six-masted schooner is launched.

July 3: Following events of the Boxer Rebellion in China, Secretary of State John Hay sends out a circular note to foreign nations, indicating that it is the United States' intention to "preserve Chinese territorial and administrative integrity." This communication with America's allies is a way of further establishing the nation's Open Door policy.

July 4: Kansas City, Missouri, is the site of the Democratic National Convention, which opens today. William Jennings Bryan is nominated for the presidency and Adlai E. Stevenson, of Illinois, receives the vice-presidential nomination.

July 5: Elizabeth Cohn makes a second speech at the Democratic National Convention, be-coming the first woman delegate in the nation to do so at a major political party convention.

July 18: The nation's first duckpin bowling match is held in Union Hill, New Jersey.

July 20: The first woman astronomer is employed at the U.S. Naval Observatory in Washington, D.C.

August 8: The Davis Cup lawn tennis match opens in Brookline, Massachusetts.

September: The nation's first industrial research laboratory is opened in Schenectady, New York.

September 3: The Union Reform party holds its first national convention in Baltimore, Maryland.

September 8: A hurricane in Galveston, Texas, kills at least 6,000 people. The winds are clocked at 120 miles per hour and Gulf waters flood inland, causing at least $20 million in damage.

September 17: A coal strike increases the cost of anthracite coal from $1 to $6.50 per ton.

September 18: In Minneapolis, Minnesota, the nation's first primary presidential election is held.

November 6: President McKinley is reelected, defeating William Jennings Bryan with an electoral college vote of 292–155.

November 15: The Carnegie Institute of Technology, known as Carnegie Tech, is established by millionaire steel magnate Andrew Carnegie.

1901:

January 1: In Providence, Rhode Island, the nation's first building with an all-marble dome, the Rhode Island State House, is occupied.

January 8: The American Bowling Congress opens its first tournament in Chicago, Illinois.

January 10: In Beaumont, Texas, the Spindletop oil claim produces the first of what will be millions of gallons of "black gold."

February 2: Congress creates the U.S. Army Dental Corps, and the Army Nurse Corps. The latter is formed as a branch of the U.S. Army.

February 5: Edwin Prescott patents the centrifugal railway.

February 25: U.S. Steel Corporation is incorporated in New Jersey by J. P. Morgan, in defiance of the Sherman Anti-Trust Law.

March 2: Congress adopts the Platt Amendment as part of the Army Appropriations Act. The amendment establishes provisions under which the U.S. will withdraw military troops from the island of Cuba.

March 3: The U.S. Bureau of Standards is established.

March 4: President McKinley is inaugurated for his second term of office.

March 13: Former President Benjamin Harrison dies.

Filipino insurgent leader Emilio Aguinaldo is captured by an American patrol in the province of Luzon in the Philippines.

April 19: The Philippine Rebellion is ended by special proclamation.

May 3: A fire in Jacksonville, Florida, destroys over $11 million in property and leaves 10,000 people without shelter.

May 9: A struggle for control of the Great Northern and Northern Pacific railroads results in stock values increasing from $100 to $1,000 per share. Panic ensues as other stocks fall rapidly. Hill-Morgan and Kuhn, Loeb and Company, the two rival companies fighting for possession of the railroad lines, are obliged to come to an agreement in order to preserve national economic stability.

May 27: As a means of determining future tariff policy toward Puerto Rico and the Philippines, the Supreme Court determines that territories falling into U.S. hands during the Spanish–American War were not foreign nations at the time, nor were they part of the U.S. The ruling, *De Lima v. Bidwell,* will be followed later this year by other high court decisions affecting trade with former foreign territories.

September 6: An avowed anarchist, Leon F. Czolgosz, shoots President McKinley at close range as the chief executive attends a reception for the Pan-American Exhibition in Buffalo, New York.

September 14: At 2:15 A.M., President McKinley dies as a result of gunshot wounds received a week earlier. Vice President Theodore Roosevelt is sworn in that afternoon at 3:00 P.M. and becomes the nation's 26th—and youngest—president. Roosevelt is 42 years old.

October 16: Booker T. Washington is invited to be a guest at the White House by President Roosevelt.

November 18: The U.S. signs the Hay–Pauncefote Treaty. This agreement will authorize construction of a U.S.-built and -operated canal across the isthmus of Panama.

December 3: President Roosevelt announces his intention to launch efforts to regulate trusts in the U.S. Soon to be known as an aggressive champion of reform, Roosevelt determines such regulation of big business to be in "the public interest."

December 16: Congress ratifies the recently signed Hay–Paunceforte Treaty.

EYEWITNESS TESTIMONY

Briefly, if I were czar, I would make no dividends upon the common stock; save all surplus and spend it for a hoop and cotton-tie mill, for wire and nail mills, for tube mills, for lines of boats upon the Lakes.

Andrew Carnegie, steel magnate, to mill managers, letter of June 11, 1900, in DeNovo's The Gilded Age and After *(1972).*

The question we are called to consider dwarfs in importance all other issues now before the country or the world. When Dreyfus shall have been forgotten, when the war in the Philippines shall be regarded only as one of the episodes of history, when men shall speak no longer of the tariff or the currency, the present era may well be remembered by coming generations as the epoch of that great organic change when the system of competition began to give way to the system of co-operation—a change leading inevitably (whether for good or ill we cannot clearly see) to the radical reconstruction of the world's industrial and social life.

William Dudley Foulke, reformer, to the Chicago Conference on Trusts, speech of 1900, in Hoogenboom and Hoogenboom's The Gilded Age *(1967).*

I want to start with the declaration that a monopoly in private hands is indefensible from any standpoint, and intolerable. I make no exceptions to the rule. I do not divide monopolies in private hands into good monopolies and bad monopolies. There is no good monopoly in private hands. There can be no good monopoly in private hands until the Almighty sends us angels to preside over the monopoly. There may be a despot who is better than another despot, but there is no good despotism. One trust may be less harmful than another. One trust magnate may be more benevolent than another, but there is no good monopoly in private hands . . .

. . . the government that created must retain control, and . . . the man-made man must be admonished: "Remember now thy Creator in the days of thy youth"—and throughout thy entire life.

What government gives, the government can take away. What the government creates, it can control; and I insist that both the state government and the federal government must protect the God-made man from the man-made man.

William Jennings Bryan, Populist party leader, to the Chicago Conference on Trusts, 1900, in Hoogenboom and Hoogenboom's Gilded Age *(1967).*

I am convinced that the office of the President is not such a very difficult one to fill, his duties being mainly to execute the laws of Congress.

Admiral George Dewey, in the New York World, *April 4, 1900.*

It is not book learning young men need, nor instruction about this and that, but a stiffening of the vertebrae which will cause them to be loyal to a trust, to act promptly, concentrate their energies, do a thing—"carry a message to Garcia."

Elbert Hubbard, in the introduction to his popular essay, "A Message to Garcia," 1900.

The Philippines are ours forever, "territory belonging to the United States," as the Constitution calls them. And just beyond the Philippines are China's illimitable markets. We will not retreat from either. We will not repudiate our duty in the archipelago. We will not abandon our opportunity in the Orient. We will not renounce our part in the mission of our race, trustee, under God, of the civilization of the world. And we will move forward to our work, not howling out regrets like slaves whipped to their burdens, but with gratitude for a task worthy of our strength, and thanksgiving to Almighty God that He has marked us as His chosen people, henceforth to lead in the regeneration of the world.

This island empire is the last land left in all the oceans. If it should prove a mistake to abandon it, the blunder once made would be irretrievable. If it proves a mistake to hold it, the error can be corrected when we will. Every other progressive nation stands ready to relieve us.

But to hold it will be no mistake. Our largest trade henceforth must be with Asia. The Pacific is our ocean. More and more Europe will manufacture the most it needs, secure from its colonies the most it consumes. Where shall we turn for consumers of our surplus? Geography answers the question. China is our natural consumer. She is nearer to us than England, Germany, or Russia, the commercial powers of the present and the future. They have moved nearer to China by securing permanent bases on her borders. The Philippines give us a base at the door of all the East.

Senator Albert J. Beveridge (R-Indiana), to Congress, speech of January 9, 1900, in Kelley's The Shaping of the American Past *(1978).*

[Religion] is the most fundamental thing in our civilization.

John R. Mott, leader of the Student Volunteers and founder of the YMCA, 1900, in Smith's The Rise of Industrial America *(1984).*

I have always been fond of the West African proverb. 'Speak softly and carry a big stick, you will go far.'

Theodore Roosevelt, vice president-elect of the United States, 1900, in Kelley's American Past *(1978).*

It receives and expends more money every year than any but the very greatest of the world's national governments; its debt is larger than that of many of the lesser nations of Europe; it absolutely controls the destinies of a population nearly as large as that of Maryland and Nebraska, and indirectly influences twice that number.

Ray Stannard Baker, journalist, in "What the United States Steel Corporation Really Is and How It Works," McClure's, *1901, in Denovo's* Gilded Age *(1972).*

Shall we? That is, shall we go on conferring our Civilizations upon the peoples that sit in darkness, or shall we give those poor things a rest? Shall we bang right ahead in our old-time, loud, pious way, and commit the new century to the game; or shall we sober up and sit down and think it over first? Would it not be prudent to get our Civilization tools together, and see how much stock is left on hand in the way of Glass Beads and Theology, and Maxim Guns and Hymn Books, and Trade Gin and Torches of Progress and Enlightenment (patent adjustable ones, good to fire villages with, upon occasion), and balance the books, and arrive at the profit and loss, so that we may intelligently decide whether to continue the business or sell out the property and start a new Civilization Scheme on the proceedings?

Mark Twain, in the North American Review, *1901, in Current and Garraty's* Words that Made American History, since the Civil War *(1965).*

Good-bye, all. Good-bye. It is God's way. His will be done.

President William A. McKinley, dying words, September 14, 1901, in Kelley's American Past *(1978).*

Appendix A
Documents

1. The Constitution of the United States

2. Lincoln's Proclamation of Amnesty and Reconstruction, December 8, 1863

3. Second Inaugural Address, March 4, 1865

4. Johnson's Proclamation of Amnesty and Reconstruction, May 29, 1865

5. The Civil Rights Act, 1866

6. The Fourteenth Amendment, 1866

7. The First Reconstruction Act, March 2, 1867

8. The Second Reconstruction Act, March 23, 1867

9. The Third Reconstruction Act, July 19, 1867

10. The Fourth Reconstruction Act, March 8, 1868

11. The Platform of the Populist Party, Omaha, Nebraska, 1892

1. The Constitution of the United States

We the People of the United States, in Order to form a more perfect Union, establish Justice, insure domestic Tranquility, provide for the common defense, promote the general Welfare, and secure the Blessings of Liberty to ourselves and our Posterity, do ordain and establish this Constitution for the United States of America.

ARTICLE I.

SECTION 1. All legislative Powers herein granted shall be vested in a Congress of the United States, which shall consist of a Senate and House of Representatives.

SECTION 2. The House of Representatives shall be composed of Members chosen every second Year by the People of the several States, and the Electors in each State shall have the Qualifications requisite for Electors of the most numerous Branch of the State Legislature.

No Person shall be a Representative who shall not have attained to the Age of twenty five Years, and been seven Years a Citizen of the United States, and who shall not, when elected, be an Inhabitant of that State in which he shall be chosen.

Representatives and direct Taxes shall be apportioned among the several States which may be included within this Union, according to their respective Numbers, which shall be determined by adding to the whole Number of free Persons, including those bound to Service for a Term of Years, and excluding Indians not taxed, three fifths of all other Persons. the actual Enumeration shall be made within three Years after the first Meeting of the Congress of the United States, and within every subsequent Term of ten Years, in such Manner as they shall by Law direct. The Number of Representatives shall not exceed one for every thirty Thousand, but each State shall have at Least one Representative; and until such enumeration shall be made, the State of New Hampshire shall be entitled to chuse three, Massachusetts eight, Rhode-Island and Providence Plantations one, Connecticut five, New-York six, New Jersey four, Pennsylvania eight, Delaware one, Maryland six, Virginia ten, North Carolina five, South Carolina five, and Georgia three.

When vacancies happen in the Representation from any State, the Executive Authority thereof shall issue Writs of Election to fill such Vacancies.

The House of Representatives shall chuse their Speaker and other Officers; and shall have the sole Power of Impeachment.

SECTION 3. The Senate of the United States shall be composed of two Senators form each State, chosen by the Legislature thereof, for six Years; and each Senator shall have one Vote.

Immediately after they shall be assembled in Consequence of the first Election, they shall be divided as equally as may be into three Classes. The Seats of the Senators of the first Class shall be vacated at the Expiration of the second Year, of the second Class at the Expiration of the fourth Year, and of the third Class at the Expiration of the sixth Year, so that one third may be chosen every second Year; and if Vacancies happen by Resignation, or otherwise, during the Recess of the Legislature of any State, the Executive thereof may make temporary Appointments until the next Meeting of the Legislature, which shall then fill such Vacancies.

No Person shall be a Senator who shall not have attained to the Age of thirty Years, and been nine Years a Citizen of the United States, and who shall not, when elected, be an Inhabitant of that State for which he shall be chosen.

The Vice President of the United States shall be President of the Senate, but shall have no Vote, unless they be equally divided.

The Senate shall chuse their other Officers, and also a President pro tempore, in the Absence of the Vice President, or when he shall exercise the Office of President of the United States.

The Senate shall have the sole Power to try all Impeachments. When sitting for that Purpose, they shall be on Oath or Affirmation. When the President of the United States is tried, the Chief Justice shall preside: And no Person shall be convicted without the Concurrence of two thirds of the Members present.

Judgment in Cases of Impeachment shall not extend further than to removal from Office, and disqualification to hold and enjoy any Office of honor, Trust or Profit under the United States: but the Party convicted shall nevertheless be liable and subject to Indictment, Trial, Judgment and Punishment, according to Law.

SECTION 4. The Times, Places and Manner of holding Elections for Senators and Representatives, shall be prescribed in each State by the Legislature thereof; but the Congress may at any time by Law make or alter such Regulations, except as to the Places of chusing Senators.

The Congress shall assemble at least once in every Year, and such Meeting shall be on the first Monday in December, unless they shall by Law appoint a different Day.

SECTION 5. Each House shall be the Judge of the Elections, Returns and Qualifications of its own Members, and a Majority of each shall constitute a Quorum to do Business; but a smaller Number may adjourn from day to day, and may be authorized to compel the Attendance of absent Members, in such Manner, and under such Penalties as each House may provide.

Each House may determine the Rules of its Proceedings, punish its Members for disorderly Behaviour, and, with the Concurrence of two thirds, expel a Member.

Each House shall keep a Journal of its Proceedings, and from time to time publish the same, excepting such Parts as may in their Judgment require Secrecy; and the Yeas and Nays of the Members of either House on any question shall, at the Desire of one fifth of those Present, be entered on the Journal.

Neither House, during the Session of Congress, shall, without the Consent of the other, adjourn for more than three days, nor to any other Place than that in which the two Houses shall be sitting.

SECTION 6. The Senators and Representatives shall receive a Compensation for their Services, to be ascertained by Law, and paid out of the Treasury of the United States. They shall in all Cases, except Treason, Felony and Breach of Peace, be privileged from Arrest during their Attendance at the Session of their respective Houses, and in going to and returning from the same; and for any Speech or Debate in either House, they shall not be questioned in any other Place.

No Senator or Representative shall, during the Time for which he was elected, be appointed to any civil Office under the Authority of the United States, which shall have been created, or the Emoluments whereof shall have been encreased during such time; and no Person holding any Office under the United States, shall be a Member of either House during his Continuance in Office.

SECTION 7. All Bills for raising Revenue shall originate in the House of Representatives; but the Senate may propose or concur with amendments as on other Bills.

Every Bill which shall have passed the House of Representatives and the Senate, shall, before it become a Law, be presented to the President of the United States; If he approve he shall sign it, but if not he shall return it, with his Objections to that House in which it shall have originated, who shall enter the Objections at large on their Journal, and proceed to reconsider it. If after such Reconsideration two thirds of that House shall agree to pass the Bill, it shall be sent, together with the Objections, to the other House, by which it shall likewise be reconsidered, and if approved by two thirds of that House, it shall become a Law. But in all such Cases the Votes of both Houses shall be determined by Yeas and Nays, and the Names of the Persons voting for and against the Bill shall be entered on the Journal of each House respectively. If any Bill shall not be returned by the President within ten Days (Sundays excepted) after it shall have been presented to him, the Same shall be a Law, in like Manner as if he had signed it, unless the Congress by their Adjournment prevent its Return, in which Case it shall not be a Law.

Every Order, Resolution, or Vote to which the Concurrence of the Senate and House of Representatives may be necessary (except on a question of Adjournment) shall be presented to the President of the United States; and before the Same shall take Effect, shall be approved by him, or being disapproved by him, shall be repassed by two thirds of the Senate and House of Representatives, according to the Rules and Limitations prescribed in the Case of a Bill.

SECTION 8. The Congress shall have Power To lay and collect Taxes, Duties, Imposts and Excises, to pay the Debts and provide for the common Defence and general Welfare of the United States; but all Duties, Imposts and Excises shall be uniform throughout the United States;

To Borrow Money on the credit of the United States;

To regulate Commerce with foreign Nations, and among the several States, and with the Indian Tribes;

To establish an uniform Rule of Naturalization, and uniform Laws on the subject of Bankruptcies throughout the United States;

To coin Money, regulate the Value thereof, and of foreign Coin, and fix the Standard of Weights and Measures;

To provide for the Punishment of counterfeiting the Securities and current Coin of the United States;

To establish Post Offices and post Roads;

To promote the Progress of Science and useful Arts, by securing for limited Times to Authors and

Inventors the exclusive Right to their respective Writings and Discoveries;

To constitute Tribunals inferior to the supreme Court;

To define and punish Piracies and Felonies committed on the high Seas, and Offences against the Law of Nations;

To declare War, grant Letters of Marque and Reprisal, and make Rules concerning Captures on Land and Water;

To raise and support Armies, but no Appropriation of Money to that Use shall be for a longer Term than two Years;

To provide and maintain a Navy;

To make Rules for the Government and Regulations of the land and naval Forces;

To provide for calling forth the Militia to execute the Laws of the Union, suppress Insurrections and repel Invasions;

To provide for organizing, arming, and disciplining the Militia, and for governing such Part of them as may be employed in the Service of the United States, reserving to the States respectively, the Appointment of the Officers, and the Authority of training the Militia according to the discipline prescribed by Congress;

To exercise exclusive Legislation in all Cases whatsoever, over such District (not exceeding ten Miles square) as may, by Cession of Particular States, and the Acceptance of Congress, become the Seat of the Government of the United States, and to exercise like Authority over all Places purchased by the Consent of the Legislature of the State in which the Same shall be for the Erection of Forts, Magazines, Arsenals, dock-Yards, and other needful Buildings;—And

To make all Laws which shall be necessary and proper for carrying into Execution the foregoing Powers, and all other Powers vested by this Constitution in the Government of the United States, or in any Department or Officer thereof.

SECTION 9. The Migration or Importation of such Persons as any of the States now existing shall think proper to admit, shall not be prohibited by the Congress prior to the Year one thousand eight hundred and eight, but a Tax or duty may be imposed on such Importation, not exceeding ten dollars for each Person.

The Privilege of the Writ of Habeas Curpus shall not be suspended, unless when in Cases of Rebellion or Invasion the public Safety may require it.

No Bill of Attainder or ex post facto Law shall be passed.

No Capitation, or other direct, Tax shall be laid, unless in Proportion to the Census or Enumeration herein before directed to be taken.

No Tax or Duty shall be laid on Articles exported from any State.

No Preference shall be given by any Regulation of Commerce or Revenue to the Ports of one State over those of another; nor shall Vessels bound to, or from, one State, be obliged to enter, clear, or pay Duties in another.

No Money shall be drawn form the Treasury, but in Consequence of Appropriations made by Law; and a regular Statement and Account of the Receipts and Expenditures of all public Money shall be published from time to time.

No title of Nobility shall be granted by the United States: And no Person holding any Office of Profit or Trust under them, shall, without the Consent of Congress, accept any present, Emolument, Office, or Title, of any kind whatever, from any King, Prince, or foreign State.

SECTION 10. No State shall enter into any Treaty, Alliance, or Confederation; grant Letters of Marque and Reprisal; coin Money; emit Bills of Credit; make any Thing but gold and silver Coin a Tender in Payment of Debts; pass any Bill of Attainder, ex post facto Law, or Law impairing the Obligation of Contracts, or grant any Title of Nobility.

No State shall, without the Consent of the Congress, lay any Imposts or Duties on Imports or Exports, except what may be absolutely necessary for executing its inspection Laws: and the net Produce of all Duties and Imposts, laid by any State on Imports or Exports, shall be for the Use of the Treasury of the United States; and all such Laws shall be subjected to the Revision and Controul of the Congress.

No State shall, without the Consent of Congress, lay any Duty of Tonnage, keep Troops, or Ships of War in time of Peace, enter into any Agreement or Compact with another State, or with a foreign Power, or engage in War, unless actually invaded, or in such imminent Danger as will not admit of delay.

ARTICLE II.

SECTION 1. The executive Power shall be vested in a President of the United States of America. He shall hold his Office during the Term of four Years, and, together with the Vice President, chosen for the same term, be elected, as follows

Each State shall appoint, in such Manner as the Legislature thereof may direct, a Number of Electors, equal to the whole Number of Senators and Representatives to which the State may be entitled in the Congress: but no Senator or Representative, or Person holding an Office of Trust or Profit under the United States, shall be appointed an Elector.

The Electors shall meet in their respective States, and vote by Ballot for two Persons, of whom one at least shall not be an Inhabitant of the same State with themselves. And they shall make a List of all the Persons voted for, and of the Number of Votes for each; which List they shall sign and certify, and transmit sealed to the Seat of the Government of the United States, directed to the President of the Senate. The President of the Senate shall, in the Presence of the Senate and House of Representatives, open all the Certificates, and the Votes shall then be counted. The Person having the greatest Number of Votes shall be the President, if such Number be a Majority of the whole Number of Electors appointed, and if there be more than one who have such Majority, and have an equal Number of Votes, then the House of Representatives shall immediately chuse by Ballot one of them for President: and if no Person have a Majority, then from the five highest on the List the said House shall in like Manner chuse the President. But in chusing the President, the Votes shall be taken by States, the Representation from each State having one Vote; a quorum for this Purpose shall consist of a Member or Members from two thirds of the States, and a Majority of all the States shall be necessary to a Choice. In every Case, after the Choice of the President, the Person having the greatest Number of Votes of the Electors shall be the Vice President. But if there should remain two or more who have equal Votes, the Senate shall chuse from them by Ballot the Vice President.

The Congress may determine the Time of chusing the Electors, and the Day on which they shall give their Votes; which Day shall be the same throughout the United States.

No Person except a natural born Citizen, or a Citizen of the United States, at the time of Adoption of this Constitution, shall be eligible to the Office of President; neither shall any Person be eligible to that Office who shall not have attained to the Age of thirty five Years, and been fourteen Years a Resident within the United States.

In Case of the Removal of the President from Office, or of his Death, Resignation, or Inability to discharge the Powers and Duties of the said Office, the Same shall devolve on the Vice President, and the Congress may by Law provide for the Case of Removal, Death, Resignation or Inability, both of the

President and Vice President, declaring what Officer shall then act as President, and such Officer shall act accordingly, until the Disability be removed, or a President shall be elected.

The President shall, at stated Times, receive for his Services, a Compensation, which shall neither be encreased nor diminished during the Period for which he shall have been elected, and he shall not receive within that Period any other Emolument from the United States, or any of them.

Before he enter on the Execution of his Office, he shall take the following Oath or Affirmation:—"I do solemnly swear (or affirm) that I will faithfully execute the Office of President of the United States, and will to the best of my Ability, preserve, protect and defend the Constitution of the United States."

SECTION 2. The President shall be Commander in Chief of the Army and Navy of the United States, and of the Militia of the several States, when called into the actual Service of the United States; he may require the Opinion in writing, of the principal Officer in each of the executive Departments, upon any Subject relating to the Duties of their respective Offices, and he shall have Power to grant Reprieves and Pardons for Offences against the United States, except in Cases of Impeachment.

He shall have Power, by and with the Advice and Consent of the Senate, to make Treaties, provided two thirds of the Senators present concur; and he shall nominate, and by and with the Advice and Consent of the Senate; shall appoint Ambassadors, other public Ministers and Consuls, Judges of the supreme Court, and all other Offices of the United States, whose Appointments are not herein otherwise provided for, and which shall be established by Law: but the Congress may by Law vest the Appointment of such inferior Officers, as they think proper, in the President alone, in the Courts of Law, or in the Heads of Departments.

The President shall have Power to fill up all Vacancies that may happen during the Recess of the Senate, by granting Commissions which shall expire at the End of their next Session.

SECTION 3. He shall from time to time give to the Congress Information of the State of the Union, and recommend to their Consideration such Measures as he shall judge necessary and expedient; he may, on extraordinary Occasions, convene both Houses, or either of them, and in Case of Disagreement between them, with Respect to the Time of Adjournment, he may adjourn them to such Time as he shall think proper; he shall receive Ambassadors and other public Ministers; he shall take care that the Laws be faithfully executed, and shall Commission all the Officers of the United States.

SECTION 4. The President, Vice President and all civil Officers of the United States, shall be removed from Office on Impeachment for, and Conviction of, Treason, Bribery, or other High Crimes and Misdemeanors.

ARTICLE III.

SECTION 1. The judicial Power of the United States, shall be vested in one supreme Court, and in such inferior Courts as the Congress may from time to time ordain and establish. The Judges, both of the supreme and inferior Courts, shall hold their Offices during good Behaviour, and shall, at stated Times, receive for their Services a Compensation, which shall not be diminished during their Continuance in Office.

SECTION 2. The judicial Power shall extend to all Cases, in Law and Equity, arising under this Constitution, the Laws of the United States, and Treaties made, or which shall be made, under their Authority;—to all Cases affecting Ambassadors, other public Ministers and Consuls;—to all Cases of admiralty and maritime Jurisdiction;—to Controversies to which the United States shall be a Party;—to Controversies between two or more States;—between a State and Citizens of another State;—between Citizens of different States;—between Citizens of the same State claiming Lands under Grants of different States, and between a State, or the Citizens thereof, and foreign States, Citizens or Subjects.

In all Cases affecting Ambassadors, other public Ministers and Consuls, and those in which a State shall be Party, the supreme Court shall have original Jurisdiction. In all the other Cases before mentioned, the supreme Court shall have appellate Jurisdiction, both as to Law and Fact, with such Exceptions, and under such Regulations as the Congress shall make.

The Trial of all Crimes, except in Cases of Impeachment, shall be by Jury; and such Trial shall be held in the State where the said Crimes shall have been committed; but when not committed within any State, the Trial shall be at such a Place or Places as the Congress may by Law have directed.

SECTION 3. Treason against the United States, shall consist only in levying War against them, or in adhering to their Enemies, giving them Aid and Comfort. No Person shall be convicted of Treason unless on the Testimony of two Witnesses to the same overt Act, or on Confession in open Court.

The Congress shall have Power to declare the Punishment of Treason, but no Attainder of Treason shall work Corruption of Blood, or Forfeiture except during the Life of the Person attained.

ARTICLE IV.

SECTION 1. Full Faith and Credit shall be given in each State to the public Acts, Records, and judicial Proceedings of every other State. And the Congress may by general Laws prescribe the Manner in which such Acts, Records and Proceedings shall be proved, and the Effect thereof.

SECTION 2. The Citizens of each State shall be entitled to all Privileges and Immunities of Citizens in the several States.

A Person charged in any State with Treason, Felony, or other Crime, who shall flee from Justice, and be found in another State, shall on Demand of the executive Authority of the State from which he fled, be delivered up, to be removed to the State having Jurisdiction of the Crime.

No Person held to Service or Labour in one State, under the Laws thereof, escaping into another, shall, in Consequence of any Law or Regulation therein, be discharged from such Service or Labour, but shall be delivered up on Claim of the Party to whom such Service or Labour may be due.

SECTION 3. New States may be admitted by the Congress into this Union; but no new State shall be formed or erected within the Jurisdiction of any other State; nor any State be formed by the Junction of two or more States, or Parts of States, without the Consent of the Legislatures of the States concerned as well as of the Congress.

The Congress shall have Power to dispose of and make all needful Rules and Regulations respecting the Territory or other Property belonging to the United States; and nothing in this Constitution shall be so construed as to Prejudice any Claims of the United States, or of any particular State.

SECTION 4. The United States shall guarantee to every State in this Union a Republican Form of Government, and shall protect each of them against Invasion; and on Application of the Legislature, or of the Executive (when the Legislature cannot be convened) against domestic Violence.

ARTICLE V.

The Congress, whenever two thirds of both Houses shall deem it necessary, shall propose Amendments to this Constitution, or, on the Application of the Legislatures of two thirds of the several States, shall call a Convention for proposing Amendments, which, in either Case, shall be valid to all Intents and Purposes, as Part of this Constitution, when ratified by the Legislatures of three fourths of the several States, or by Conventions in three fourths thereof, as the one or the other Mode of Ratification may be proposed by the Congress; Provided that no Amendment which may be made prior to the Year One thousand eight hundred and eight shall in any Manner affect the first and fourth Clauses in the Ninth Section of the first Article; and that no State, without its Consent, shall be deprived of its equal Suffrage in the Senate.

ARTICLE VI.

All Debts contracted and Engagements entered into, before the Adoption of this Constitution shall be as valid against the United States under this Constitution, as under the Confederation.

This Constitution, and the Laws of the United States which shall be made in Pursuance thereof; and all Treaties made, or which shall be made, under the Authority of the United States, shall be the supreme Law of the Land; and the Judges in every State shall be bound thereby, any Thing in the Constitution or Laws of any State to the Contrary notwithstanding.

The Senators and Represenatives before mentioned, and the Members of the several State Legislatures, and all executive and judicial Officers, both of the United States and of the several States, shall be bound by Oath or Affirmation, to support this Constitution; but no religious Test shall ever be required as a Qualification to any Office or public Trust under the United States.

ARTICLE VII.

The Ratification of the Conventions of nine States, shall be sufficient for the Establishment of this Constitution between the States so ratifying the Same. Done in Convention by the Unanimous Consent of the States present the Seventeenth Day of September in the Year of our Lord one thousand seven hundred and Eighty seven and the Independence of the United States of America the Twelfth IN WITNESS WHEREOF We have hereunto subscribed our Names,

New Hampshire	John Langdon
	Nicholas Gilman
Massachusetts	Nathaniel Gorham
	Rufus King
Connecticut	Wm. Saml. Johnson
	Roger Sherman
New York	Alexander Hamilton
New Jersey	Wil.: Livingston
	David Brearley.
	Wm. Paterson.
	Jona. Dayton
Pennsylvania	B Franklin
	Thomas Mifflin
	Robt Morris
	Geo. Clymer
	Thos. FitzSimons
	Jared Ingersoll
	James Wilson
	Gouv Morris
Delaware	Geo: Read
	Gunning Bedford jun
	John Dickinson
	Richard Bassett
	Jaco: Broom
Maryland	James McHenry
	Dan of St Thos. Jenifer
	Danl Carroll
Virginia	John Blair—
	James Madison Jr.
North Carolina	Wm. Blount
	Richd. Dobbs Spaight.
	Hu Williamson
South Carolina	J. Rutledge
	Charles Cotesworth Pinckney
	Charles Pinckney
	Pierce Butler.
Georgia	William Few
	Abr Baldwin

In Convention Monday, September 17th 1787.
Present
The States of
New Hampshire, Massachusetts, Connecticut, Mr. Hamilton from New York, New Jersey, Pennsylvania, Delaware, Maryland, Virginia, North Carolina, South Carolina and Georgia.
Resolved,

That the preceeding Constitution be laid before the United States in Congress assembled, and that it is the Opinion of this Convention, that it should afterwards be submitted to a Convention of Delegates, chosen in each State by the People thereof, under the recommendation of its Legislature, for their Assent and Ratification; and that each Convention assenting to, and ratifying the Same, should give Notice thereof to the United States in Congress assembled. Resolved, That it is the Opinion of this Convention, that as soon as the Conventions of nine States shall have ratified this Constitution, the United States in Congress assembled should fix a Day on which the Electors should assemble to vote for the President, and the Time and Place for commencing Proceedings under this Constitution. That after such Publication the Electors should be appointed, and the Senators and Representatives elected: That the Electors should meet on the Day fixed for the Election of the President, and should transmit their Votes certified, signed, sealed and directed, as the Constitution requires, to the Secretary of the United States in Congress assembled, that the Senators and representatives should convene at the Time and Place assigned; that the Senators should appoint a President of the Senate, for the sole Purpose of receiving, opening and counting the Votes for President; and that after he shall be chosen, the Congress, together with the President, should, without Delay, proceed to execute this Constitution.

By the Unanimous Order of the Convention

Go. Washington—Presidt.

W. Jackson Secretary.

AMENDMENT I.
Congress shall make no law respecting an establishment of religion, or prohibiting the free exercise thereof; or abridging the freedom of speech, or of the press; or the right of the people peaceably to assemble, and to petition the Government for a redress of grievances.

AMENDMENT II.
A well regulated Militia, being necessary to the security of a free State, the right of the people to keep and bear Arms, shall not be infringed.

AMENDMENT III.
No Soldier shall, in time of peace, be quartered in any house, without the consent of the Owner, nor in time of war, but in a manner to be prescribed by law.

AMENDMENT IV.
The right of the people to be secure in their persons, houses, papers, and effects, against unreasonable searches and seizures, shall not be violated, and no Warrants shall issue, but upon probable cause, supported by Oath or affirmation, and particularly describing the place to be searched, and the persons or things to be seized.

AMENDMENT V.
No person shall be held to answer for a capital, or otherwise infamous crime, unless on a presentment or indictment of a Grand Jury, except in cases arising in the land or naval forces, or in the Militia, when in actual service in time of War or public danger; nor shall any person be subject for the same offence to be twice put in jeopardy of life or limb; nor shall be compelled in any criminal case to be a witness against himself, nor be deprived of life, liberty, or property, without due process of law; nor shall private property be taken for public use, without just compensation.

AMENDMENT VI.
In all criminal prosecutions, the accused shall enjoy the right to a speedy and public trial, by an impartial jury of the State and district wherein the crime shall have been committed, which district shall have been previously ascertained by law, and to be informed of the nature and cause of the accusation; to be confronted with the witnesses against him; to have compulsory process for obtaining witnesses in his favor, and to have the Assistance of Counsel for his defence.

AMENDMENT VII.
In Suits at common law, where the value in controversy shall exceed twenty dollars, the right of trial by jury shall be preserved, and no fact tried by a jury, shall be otherwise reexamined in any Court of the United States, than according to the rules of the common law.

AMENDMENT VIII.
Excessive bail shall not be required, nor excessive fines imposed, nor cruel and unusual punishment inflicted.

AMENDMENT IX.
The enumeration in the Constitution, of certain rights, shall not be construed to deny or disparage others retained by the people.

Amendment X.
The powers not delegated to the United States by the Constitution, nor prohibited by it to the States, are reserved to the States respectively, or to the people.

AMENDMENT XI.
(Adopted January 8, 1798)

The Judicial power of the United States shall not be construed to extend to any suit in law or equity, commenced or prosecuted against one of the United States by Citizens of another State, or by Citizens or Subjects of any Foreign State.

AMENDMENT XII.
(Adopted September 25, 1804)

The Electors shall meet in their respective states and vote by ballot for President and Vice-President, one of whom, at least, shall not be an inhabitant of the same state with themselves; they shall name in their ballots the person voted for as President, and in distinct ballots the person voted for as Vice-President, and they shall make distinct lists of all persons voted for as President, and of all persons voted for as Vice-President, and of the number of votes for each, which lists they shall sign and certify, and transmit sealed to the seat of the government of the United States, directed to the President of the Senate;—The President of the Senate shall, in presence of the Senate and House of Representatives, open all the certificates and the votes shall then be counted;—The person having the greatest number of votes for President, shall be the President, if such number be a majority of the whole number of Electors appointed; and if no person have such majority, then from the persons having the highest numbers not exceeding three on the list of those voted for as President, the House of Representatives shall choose immediately, by ballot, the President. But in choosing the President, the votes shall be taken by states, the representation from each state having one vote; a quorum for this purpose shall consist of a member or members from two-thirds of the states, and a majority of all the states shall be necessary to a choice. And if the House of Representatives shall not choose a President whenever the right of choice shall devolve upon them, before the fourth day of March next following, then the Vice-President shall act as President, as in the case of the death or other constitutional disability of the President.—The person having the greatest number of votes as Vice-President, shall be the Vice-President, if such number be a majority of the whole number of Electors appointed, and if no person have a majority, then from the two highest numbers on the list, the Senate shall choose the Vice-President; a quorum for the purpose shall consist of two-thirds of the whole number of Senators, and a majority of the whole number shall be necessary to a choice. But no person constitution-

ally ineligible to the office of President shall be eligible to that of Vice-President of the United States.

AMENDMENT XIII.
(Adopted December 18, 1865)

SECTION 1. Neither slavery nor involuntary servitude, except as a punishment for crime whereof the party shall have been duly convicted, shall exist within the United States, or any place subject to their jurisdiction.

SECTION 2. Congress shall have power to enforce this article by appropriate legislation.

Amendment XIV.
(Adopted July 28, 1868)

SECTION 1. All persons born or naturalized in the United States and subject to the jurisdiction thereof, are citizens of the United States and of the State wherein they reside. No State shall make or enforce any law which shall abridge the privileges or immunities of citizens of the United States; nor shall any State deprive any person of life, liberty, or property, without due process of law; nor deny to any person within its jurisdiction the equal protection of the laws.

SECTION 2. Representatives shall be apportioned among the several States according to their respective numbers, counting the whole number of persons in each State, excluding Indians not taxed. But when the right to vote at any election for the choice of electors for President and Vice-President of the United States, Representatives in Congress, the Executive and Judicial officers of a State, or the members of the Legislature thereof, is denied to any of the male inhabitants of such State, being twenty-one years of age, and citizens of the United States, or in any way abridged, except for participation in rebellion, or other crime, the basis of representation therein shall be reduced in the proportion which the number of such male citizens shall bear to the whole number of male citizens twenty-one years of age in such State.

SECTION 3. No person shall be a Senator or Representative in Congress, or elector of President and Vice-President, or hold any office, civil or military, under the United States, or under any State, who, having previously taken an oath, as a member of Congress, or as an officer of the United States, or as a member of any State legislature, or as an executive or judicial officer of any State, to support the Constitution of the United States, shall have engaged in insurrection or rebellion against the same, or given aid or comfort to the enemies thereof. But Congress may by a vote of two-thirds of each House, remove such disability.

SECTION 4. The validity of the public debt of the United States, authorized by law, including debts incurred for payment of pensions and bounties for services in suppressing insurrection or rebellion, shall not be questioned. But neither the United States nor any State shall assume or pay any debt or obligation incurred in aid of insurrection or rebellion against the United States, or any claim for the loss or emancipation of any slave; but all such debts, obligations and claims shall be held illegal and void.

SECTION 5. The Congress shall have power to enforce, by appropriate legislation, the provisions of this article.

AMENDMENT XV.
(Adopted March 30, 1870)

SECTION 1. The right of citizens of the United States to vote shall not be denied or abridged by the United States or by any State on account of race, color, or previous condition of servitude.

SECTION 2. The Congress shall have power to enforce this article by appropriate legislation.

AMENDMENT XVI.
(Adopted February 25, 1913)
The Congress shall have power to lay and collect taxes on incomes, from whatever source derived, without apportionment among the several States, and without regard to any census or enumeration.

AMENDMENT XVII.
(Adopted May 13, 1913)

SECTION 1. The Senate of the United States shall be composed of two Senators from each State, elected by the people thereof, for six years; and each Senator shall have one vote. The electors in each State shall have the qualifications requisite for electors of the most numerous branch of the State legislatures.

SECTION 2. When vacancies happen in the representation of any State in the Senate, the executive authority of such State shall issue writs of election to fill such vacancies: Provided, That the legislature of any State may empower the executive thereof to make temporary appointments until the people fill the vacancies by election as the legislature may direct.

SECTION 3. This amendment shall not be so construed as to affect the election or term of any Senator chosen before it becomes valid as part of the Constitution.

AMENDMENT XVIII.
(Adopted January 29, 1919)

SECTION 1. After one year from ratification of this article the manufacture, sale, or transportation of intoxicating liquors within, the importation thereof into, or the exportation thereof from the United States and all territory subject to the jurisdiction thereof for beverage purposes is hereby prohibited.

SECTION 2. The Congress and the several States shall have concurrent power to enforce this article by appropriate legislation.

SECTION 3. This article shall be inoperative unless it shall have been ratified as an amendment to the Constitution by the legislatures of the several States, as provided in the Constitution, within seven years from the date of the submission hereof to the States by the Congress.

AMENDMENT XIX.
(Adopted August 26, 1920)
The right of citizens of the United States to vote shall not be denied or abridged by the United States or by any State on account of sex.
Congress shall have power to enforce this article by appropriate legislation.

AMENDMENT XX.
(ADOPTED FEBRUARY 6, 1933)

SECTION 1. The terms of the President and Vice President shall end at noon on the 20th day of January, and the terms of Senators and Representatives at noon at the 3d day of January, of the years in which such terms would have ended if this article had not been ratified; and the terms of their successors shall then begin.

SECTION 2. The Congress shall assemble at least once in every year, and such meeting shall begin at noon on the 3d day of January, unless they shall by law appoint a different day.

SECTION 3. If, at the time fixed for the beginning of the term of the President, the President elect shall have died, the Vice President elect shall become President. If a President shall not have been chosen before the time fixed for the beginning of his term, or if the President elect shall have failed to qualify, then the Vice President elect shall act as President until a President shall have qualified; and the Congress may by law provide for the case wherein neither a President elect nor a Vice President elect shall have qualified, declaring who shall then act as President, or the manner in which one who is to act shall be selected, and such person shall act accordingly until a President or Vice President shall have qualified.

SECTION 4. The Congress may by law provide for the case of the death of any of the persons from whom the House of Representatives may choose a President whenever the right of choice shall have devolved upon them, and for the case of the death of any of the persons from whom the Senate may choose a Vice President whenever the right of choice shall have devolved upon them.

SECTION 5. Sections 1 and 2 shall take effect on the 15th day of October following the ratification of this article.

SECTION 6. This article shall be inoperative unless it shall have been ratified as an amendment to the Constitution by the legislatures of three-fourths of the several States within seven years from the date of its submission.

AMENDMENT XXI.
(Adopted December 5, 1933)

SECTION 1. The eighteenth article of amendment to the Constitution of the United States is hereby repealed.

SECTION 2. The transportation or importation into any State, Territory, or possession of the United States for delivery or use therein of intoxicating liquors, in violation of the laws thereof, is hereby prohibited.

SECTION 3. This article shall be inoperative unless it shall have been ratified as an amendment to the Constitution by conventions in the several States, as provided in the Constitution, within seven years from the date of the submission hereof to the States by the Congress.

AMENDMENT XXII.
(Adopted February 27, 1951)

SECTION 1.
No person shall be elected to the office of the President more than twice, and no person who has held the office of President, or acted as President, for more than two years of a term to which some other person was elected President shall be elected to the office of the President more than once. But this Article shall not apply to any person holding the office of President when this Article was proposed by the Congress, and shall not prevent any person who may be holding the office of President, or acting as President, during the term within which this Article becomes operative from holding the office of President or acting as President during the remainder of such term.

SECTION 2. This Article shall be inoperative unless it shall have been ratified as an amendment to the Constitution by the legislatures of three-fourths of the several States within seven years from the date of its submission to the States by the Congress.

AMENDMENT XXIII.
(Adopted March 29, 1961)

SECTION 1. The District constituting the seat of Government of the United States shall appoint in such manner as the Congress may direct:
A number of electors of President and Vice President equal to the whole number of Senators and Representatives in Congress to which the District would be entitled if it were a State, but in no event more than the least populous State; they shall be in addition to those appointed by the States, but they shall be considered, for the purposes of the election of President and Vice President, to be electors appointed by a State; and they shall meet in the District and perform such duties as provided by the twelfth article of amendment.

SECTION 2. The Congress shall have power to enforce this article by appropriate legislation.

AMENDMENT XXIV.
(Adopted January 23, 1964)

SECTION 1. The right of citizens of the United States to vote in any primary or other election for President or Vice President, for electors for President or Vice President, or for Senator or Representative in Congress, shall not be denied or abridged by the United States or any State by reason of failure to pay any poll tax or other tax.

SECTION 2. The Congress shall have the power to enforce this article by appropriate legislation.

AMENDMENT XXV.
(Adopted February 10, 1967)

SECTION 1. In case of the removal of the President from office or of his death or resignation, the Vice President shall become President.

SECTION 2. Whenever there is a vacancy in the office of the Vice President, the President shall nominate a Vice President who shall take the office upon confirmation by a majority vote of both houses of Congress.

SECTION 3. Whenever the President transmits to the President pro tempore of the Senate and the Speaker of the House of Representatives his written declaration that he is unable to discharge the powers and duties of his office, and until he transmits to them a written declaration to the contrary, such powers and duties shall be discharged by the Vice President as Acting President.

SECTION 4. Whenever the Vice President and a majority of either the principal officers of the executive departments or of such other body as Congress may by law provide, transmit to the President pro tempore of the Senate and the Speaker of the House of Representatives their written declaration that the President is unable to discharge the powers and duties of his office, the Vice President shall immediately assume the powers and duties of the office as Acting President.

Thereafter, when the President transmits to the President pro tempore of the Senate and the Speaker of the House of Representatives his written declaration that no inability exists, he shall resume the powers and duties of his office unless the Vice President and a majority of either the principal officers of the executive departments or of such other body as Congress may by law provide, transmit within four days to the President pro tempore of the Senate and the Speaker of the House of Representatives their written declaration that the President is unable to discharge the powers and duties of his office. Thereupon Congress shall decide the issue, assembling within forty-eight hours for that purpose if not in session. If the Congress, within twenty-one days after receipt of the latter written declaration, or, if Congress is not in session, within twenty-one days after Congress is required to assemble, determines by two-thirds vote of both houses that the President is unable to discharge the powers and duties of his office, the Vice President shall continue to discharge the same as Acting President; otherwise, the President shall resume the powers and duties of his office.

AMENDMENT XXVI.
(Adopted June 30, 1971)

SECTION 1. The right of citizens of the United States, who are 18 years of age or older, to vote shall not be denied or abridged by the United States or by any state on account of age.

SECTION 2. The Congress shall have power to enforce this article by appropriate legislation.

2. Lincoln's Proclamation of Amnesty and Reconstruction December 8, 1863

WHEREAS, in and by the Constitution of the United States, it is provided that the President "shall have power to grant reprieves and pardons for offences against the United States, except in cases of impeachment;" and

Whereas a rebellion now exists whereby the loyal State governments of several States have for a long time been subverted, and many persons have committed and are now guilty of treason against the United States; and

Whereas, with reference to said rebellion and treason, laws have been enacted by Congress declaring forfeitures and confiscation of property and liberation of slaves, all upon terms and conditions therein stated, and also declaring that the President was thereby authorized at any time thereafter, by proclamation, to extend to persons who may have participated in the existing rebellion, in any State or part thereof, pardon and amnesty, with such exceptions and at such times and on such conditions as he may deem expedient for the public welfare; and

Whereas the congressional declaration for limited and conditional pardon accords with well-established judicial exposition of the pardoning power; and

Whereas, with reference to said rebellion, the President of the United States has issued several proclamations, with provisions in regard to the liberation of slaves; and

Whereas it is now desired by some persons heretofore engaged in said rebellion to resume their allegiance to the United States, and to reinaugurate loyal State governments within and for their respective States; therefore,

I, Abraham Lincoln, President of the United States, do proclaim, declare, and make known to all persons who have, directly or by implication, participated in the existing rebellion, except as hereinafter excepted, that a full pardon is hereby granted to them and each of them, with restoration of all rights of property, except as to slaves, and in property cases where rights of third parties shall have intervened, and upon the condition that every such person shall take and subscribe an oath, and thenceforward keep and maintain said oath inviolate; and which oath shall be registered for permanent preservation, and shall be of the tenor and effect following, to wit:

"I,———, do solemnly swear, in presence of Almighty God, that I will henceforth faithfully support, protect and defend the Constitution of the United States, and the union of the States thereunder; and that I will, in like manner, abide by and faithfully support all acts of Congress passed during the existing rebellion with reference to slaves, so long and so far as not repealed, modified or held void by Congress, or by decision of the Supreme Court; and that I will, in like manner, abide by and faithfully support all proclamations of the President made during the existing rebellion having reference to slaves, so long and so far as not modified or declared void by decision of the Supreme Court. So help me God."

The persons excepted from the benefits of the foregoing provisions are all who are, or shall have been, civil or diplomatic officers or agents of the so-called confederate government; all who have left judicial stations under the United States to aid the rebellion; all who are, or shall have been, military or naval officers of said so-called confederate government above the rank of colonel in the army, or of lieutenant in the navy; all who left seats in the United States Congress to aid the rebellion; all who resigned commissions in the army or navy of the United States, and afterwards aided the rebellion; and all who have engaged in any way in treating colored persons or white persons, in charge of such, otherwise than lawfully as prisoners of war, and which persons may have been found in the United States

service, as soldiers, seamen, or in any other capacity.

And I do further proclaim, declare, and make known, that whenever, in any of the States of

Arkansas, Texas, Louisiana, Mississippi, Tennessee, Alabama, Georgia, Florida, South Carolina, and North Carolina, a number of persons, not less than one-tenth in number of the votes cast in such State at the Presidential election of the year of our Lord One thousand eight hundred and sixty, each having taken the oath aforesaid and not having since violated it, and being a qualified voter by the election law of the State existing immediately before the so-called act of secession, and excluding all others, shall re-establish a State government which shall be republican, and in no wise contravening said oath, such shall be recognized as the true government of the State, and the State shall receive thereunder the benefits of the constitutional provision which declares that "The United States shall guaranty to every State in this union a republican form of government, and shall protect each of them against invasion; and, on application of the legislature, or the executive, (when the legislature cannot be convened,) against domestic violence."

And I do further proclaim, declare, and make known that any provision which may be adopted by such State government in relation to the freed people of such State, which shall recognize and declare their permanent freedom, provide for their education, and which may yet be consistent, as a temporary arrangement, with their present condition as a laboring, landless, and homeless class, will not be objected to by the national Executive. And it is suggested as not improper, that, in constructing a loyal State government in any State, the name of the State, the boundary, the subdivisions, the constitution, and the general code of laws, as before the rebellion, be maintained, subject only to the modifications made necessary by the conditions hereinbefore stated, and such others, if any, not contravening said conditions, and which may be deemed expedient by those framing the new State government.

To avoid misunderstanding, it may be proper to say that this proclamation, so far as it relates to State governments, has no reference to States wherein loyal State governments have all the while been maintained. And for the same reason, it may be proper to further say that whether members sent to Congress from any State shall be admitted to seats, constitutionally rests exclusively with the respective Houses, and not to any extent with the Executive. And still further, that this proclamation is intended to present the people of the States wherein the national authority has been suspended, and loyal State governments have been subverted, a mode in and by which the national authority and loyal State governments may be re-established within said States, or in any of them; and, while the mode presented is the best the Executive can suggest, with his present impressions, it must not be understood that no other possible mode would be acceptable.

Given under my hand at the city, of Washington, the 8th. day of December, A.D. one thousand eight hundred and sixty-three, and of the independence of the United States of America the eighty-eighth.

ABRAHAM LINCOLN

By the President:

WILLIAM H. SEWARD,
Secretary of State.

3. Lincoln's Second Inaugural Address March 4, 1865

At this second appearing to take the oath of the presidential office, there is less occasion for an extended address than there was at the first. Then a statement, somewhat in detail, of a course to be pursued, seemed fitting and proper. Now, at the expiration of four years, during which public declarations have been constantly called forth on every point and phase of the great contest which still absorbs the attention, and engrosses the energies [sic] of the nation, little that is new could be presented. The progress of our arms, upon which all else chiefly depends, is as well known to the public as to myself; and it is, I trust, reasonably satisfactory and encouraging to all. With high hope for the future, no prediction in regard to it is ventured.

On the occasion corresponding to this four years ago, all thoughts were anxiously directed to an impending civil-war. All dreaded it—all sought to avert it. While the inaugural address was being delivered from this place, devoted altogether to *saving* the Union without war, insurgent agents were in the city seeking to *destroy* it without war—seeking to dissol[v]e the Union, and divide effects, by negotiation. Both parties deprecated war; but one of them would *make* war rather than let the nation survive; and the other would *accept* war rather than let it perish. And the war came.

One eighth of the whole population were colored slaves, not distributed generally over the Union, but localized in the Southern part of it. These slaves constituted a peculiar and powerful interest. All knew that this interest was, somehow, the cause of the war. To strengthen, perpetuate, and extend this interest was the object for which the insurgents would rend the Union, even by war; while the government claimed no right to do more than to restrict the territorial enlargement of it. Neither party expected for the war, the magnitude, or the duration, which it has already attained. Neither anticipated that the *cause* of the conflict might cease with, or even before, the conflict itself should cease. Each looked for an easier triumph, and a result less fundamental and astounding. Both read the same Bible, and pray to the same God; and each invokes His aid against the other. It may seem strange that any men should dare to ask a just God's assistance in wringing their bread from the sweat of other men's faces; but let us judge not that we be not judged. The prayers of both could not be answered; that of neither has been answered fully. The Almighty has His own purposes. "Woe unto the world because of offences! for it must needs be that offences come; but woe to that man by whom the offence cometh!" If we shall suppose that American Slavery is one of those offences which, in the providence of God, must needs come, but which, having continued through His appointed time, He now wills to remove, and that He gives to both North and South, this terrible war, as the woe due to those by whom the offence came, shall we discern therein any departure from those divine attributes which the believers in a Living God always ascribe to Him? Fondly do we hope—fervently do we pray—that this mighty scourge of war may speedily pass away. Yet, if God wills that it continue, until all the wealth piled by the bond-man's two hundred and fifty years of unrequited toil shall be sunk, and until every drop of blood drawn with the lash, shall be paid by another drawn with the sword, as was said three thousand years ago, so still it must be said "the judgments of the Lord, are true and righteous altogether."

With malice toward none; with charity for all; with firmness in the right, as God gives us to see the right, let us strive on to finish the work we are in; to bind up the nation's wounds; to care for him who shall have borne the battle, and for his widow, and his orphan—to do all which may achieve and cherish a just, and a lasting peace, among ourselves, and with all nations.

4. Johnson's Proclamation of Amnesty and Reconstruction, May 29, 1865

WHEREAS the President of the United States, on the 8th day of December, A.D. 1863, and on the 26th day of March, A.D. 1864, did, with the object to suppress the existing rebellion, to induce all persons to return to their loyalty, and to restore the authority of the United States, issue proclamations offering amnesty and pardon to certain persons who had, directly or by implication, participated in the said rebellion; and

Whereas many persons who had so engaged in said rebellion have, since the issuance of said proclamations, failed or neglected to take the benefits offered thereby; and

Whereas many persons who have been justly deprived of all claim to amnesty and pardon thereunder by reason of their participation, directly or by implication, in said rebellion and continued hostility to the Government of the United States since the date of said proclamations now desire to apply for and obtain amnesty and pardon.

To the end, therefore, that the authority of the Government of the United States may be restored and that peace, order, and freedom may be established, I, Andrew Johnson, President of the United States, do proclaim and declare that I hereby grant to all persons who have, directly or indirectly, participated in the existing rebellion, except as hereinafter excepted, amnesty and pardon, with restoration of all rights of property, except as to slaves and except in cases where legal proceedings under the laws of the United States providing for the confiscation of property of persons engaged in rebellion have been instituted; but upon the condition, nevertheless, that every such person shall take and subscribe the following oath (or affirmation) and thenceforward keep and maintain said oath inviolate, and which oath shall be registered for permanent preservation and shall be of the tenor and effect following, to wit:

I, —— ——, do solemnly swear (of affirm), in presence of Almighty God, that I will henceforth faithfully support, protect, and defend the Constitution of the United States and the Union of the States thereunder, and that I will in like manner abide by and faithfully support all laws and proclamations which have been made during the existing rebellion with reference to the emancipation of slaves. So help me God.

The following classes of persons are excepted from the benefits of this proclamation:

FIRST. All who are or shall have been pretended civil or diplomatic officers or otherwise domestic or foreign agents of the pretended Confederate government.

SECOND. All who left judicial stations under the United States to aid the rebellion.

THIRD. All who shall have been military or naval officers of said pretended Confederate government above the rank of colonel in the army or lieutenant in the navy.

FOURTH. All who left seats in the Congress of the United States to aid the rebellion.

FIFTH. All who resigned or tendered resignations of their commissions in the Army or Navy of the United States to evade duty in resisting the rebellion.

SIXTH. All who have engaged in any way in treating otherwise than lawfully as prisoners of war persons found in the United States service as officers, soldiers, seamen, or in other capacities.

SEVENTH. All persons who have been or are absentees from the United States for the purpose of aiding the rebellion.

EIGHTH. All military and naval officers in the rebel service who were educated by the Government in the Military Academy at West Point or the United States Naval Academy.

NINTH. All persons who held the pretended offices of governors of States in insurrection against the United States.

TENTH. All persons who left their homes within the jurisdiction and protection of the United States and passed beyond the Federal military lines into the pretended Confederate States for the purpose of aiding the rebellion.

ELEVENTH. All persons who have been engaged in the destruction of the commerce of the United States upon the high seas and all persons who have made raids into the United States from Canada or been engaged in destroying the commerce of the United States upon the lakes and rivers that separate the British Provinces from the United States.

TWELFTH. All persons who, at the time when they seek to obtain the benefits hereof by taking the oath herein prescribed, are in military, naval, or civil confinement or custody, or under bonds of the civil, military, or naval authorities or agents of the United States as prisoners of war, or persons detained for offenses of any kind, either before or after conviction.

THIRTEENTH. All persons who have voluntarily participated in said rebellion and the estimated value of whose taxable property is over $20,000.

FOURTEENTH. All persons who have taken the oath of amnesty as prescribed in the President's proclamation of December 8, A.D. 1863, or an oath of allegiance to the Government of the United States since the date of said proclamation and who have not thenceforward kept and maintained the same inviolate.

Provided, That special application may be made to the President for pardon by any person belonging to the excepted classes, and such clemency will be liberally extended as may be consistent with the facts of the case and the peace and dignity of the United States.

The Secretary of State will establish rules and regulations for administering and recording the said amnesty oath, so as to insure its benefit to the people and guard the Government against fraud.

In testimony whereof I have hereunto set my hand and caused the seal of the United States to be affixed.

Done at the city of Washington, the 29th day of May, A.D. *1865, and of the Independence of the United States the eighty-ninth.*

ANDREW JOHNSON

By the President:

WILLIAM H. SEWARD,
Secretary of State.

WHEREAS the fourth section of the fourth article of the Constitution of the United States declares that the United States shall guarantee to every State in the Union a republican form of government and shall protect each of them against invasion and domestic violence; and

Whereas the President of the United States is by the Constitution made Commander in Chief of the Army and Navy, as well as chief civil executive officer of the United States, and is bound by solemn oath faithfully to execute the office of President of the United States and to take care that the laws be faithfully executed; and

Whereas the rebellion which has been waged by a portion of the people of the United States against the properly constituted revolting form, but whose organized and armed forces have now been almost entirely overcome, has in its revolutionary progress deprived the people of the State of North Carolina of all civil government; and

Whereas it becomes necessary and proper to carry out and enforce the obligations of the United States to the people of North Carolina in securing them in the enjoyment of a republican form of government:

Now, therefore, in obedience to the high and solemn duties imposed upon me by the Constitution of the United States and for the purpose of enabling the loyal people of said State to organize a State government whereby justice may be established, domestic tranquillity insured, and loyal citizens protected in all their rights of life, liberty, and property, I, Andrew Johnson, President of the United States and Commander in Chief of the Army and Navy of the United States, do hereby appoint William W. Holden provisional governor of the State of North Carolina, whose duty it shall be, at the earliest practicable period, to prescribe such rules and regulations as may be necessary and proper for convening a convention composed of delegates to be chosen by that portion of the people of said State who are loyal to the United States, and no others, for the purpose of altering or amending the constitution thereof, and with authority to exercise within the limits of said State all the powers necessary and proper to enable such loyal people of the State of North Carolina to restore said State to its constitutional relations to the Federal Government and to present such a republican form of State government as will entitle the State to the guaranty of the United States therefor and its people to protection by the United States against invasion, insurrection, and domestic violence: *Provided,* That in any election that may be hereafter held for choosing delegates to any State convention as aforesaid no person shall be qualified as an elector or shall be eligible as a member of such convention unless he shall have previously taken and subscribed the oath of amnesty as set forth in the President's proclamation of May 29, A.D. 1865, and is a voter qualified as prescribed by the constitution and laws of the State of North Carolina in force immediately before the 20th day of May, A.D. 1861, the date of the so-called ordinance of secession; and the said convention, when convened, or the legislature that may be thereafter assembled, will prescribe the qualification of electors and the eligibility of persons to hold office under the constitution and laws of the State—a power the people of the several States composing the Federal Union have rightfully exercised from the origin of the Government to the present time.

And I do hereby direct—

FIRST. That the military commander of the department and all officers and persons in the military and naval service aid and assist the said provisional governor in carrying into effect this proclamation; and they are enjoined to abstain from in any way hindering, impeding, or discouraging the loyal people from the organization of a State government as herein authorized.

SECOND. That the Secretary of State proceed to put in force all laws of the United States the administration whereof belongs to the State Department applicable to the State Department applicable to the geographical limits aforesaid.

THIRD. That the Secretary of the Treasury proceed to nominate for appointment assessors of taxes and collectors of customs and internal revenue and such other officers of the Treasury Department as are authorized by law and put in execution the revenue laws of the United States within the geographical limits aforesaid. In making appointments the preference shall be given to qualified loyal persons residing within the districts where their respective duties are to be performed; but if suitable residents of the districts shall not be found, then persons residing in other States or districts shall be appointed.

FOURTH. That the Postmaster-General proceed to establish post-offices and post routes and put into execution the postal laws of the United States within the said State, giving to loyal residents the preference of appointment; but if suitable residents are not found, then to appoint agents, etc., from other States.

FIFTH. That the district judge for the judicial district in which North Carolina is included proceed to hold courts within said State in accordance with the provisions of the act of Congress. The Attorney-General will instruct the proper officers to libel and bring to judgment, confiscation, and sale property subject to confiscation and enforce the administration of justice within said State in all matters within the cognizance and jurisdiction of the Federal courts.

SIXTH. That the Secretary of the Navy take possession of all public property belonging to the Navy Department within said geographical limits and put in operation all acts of Congress in relation to naval affairs having application to the said State.

SEVENTH. That the Secretary of the Interior put in force the laws relating to the Interior Department applicable to the geographical limits aforesaid.

In testimony whereof I have hereunto set my hand and caused the seal of the United States to be affixed.

Done at the City of Washington, this 29th day of May, A.D. 1865, and of the Independence of the United States the eighty-ninth.

ANDREW JOHNSON

By the President:

WILLIAM H. SEWARD,
Secretary of State.

5. The Civil Rights Act 1866

Be it enacted by the Senate and House of Representatives of the United States of America in Congress assembled, That all persons born in the United States and not subject to any foreign power, excluding Indians not taxed, are hereby declared to be citizens of the United States; and such citizens, of every race and color, without regard to any previous condition of slavery or involuntary servitude, except as a punishment for crime whereof the party shall have been duly convicted, shall have the same right, in every State and Territory in the United States, to make and enforce contracts, to sue, be parties, and give evidence, to inherit, purchase, lease, sell, hold, and convey real and personal property, and to full and equal benefit of all laws and proceedings for the security of person and property, as is enjoyed by white citizens, and shall be subject to like punishment, pains, and penalties, and to none other, any law, statute, ordinance, regulation, or custom, to the contrary notwithstanding.

SECTION 2. *And be it further enacted,* That any person who, under color of any law, statute, ordinance, regulation, or custom, shall subject, or cause to be subjected, any inhabitant of any State or Territory to the deprivation of any right secured or protected by this act, or to different punishment, pains, or penalties on account of such person having at any time been held in a condition of slavery or involuntary servitude, except as a punishment for crime whereof the party shall have been duly convicted, or by reason of his color or race, than is prescribed for the punishment of white persons, shall be deemed guilty of a misdemeanor, and, on conviction, shall be punished by fine not exceeding one thousand dollars, or imprisonment not exceeding one year, or both, in the discretion of the court.

SECTION 3. *And be it further enacted,* That the district courts of the United States, within their respective districts, shall have, exclusively of the courts of the several States, cognizance of all crimes and offences committed against the provisions of this act, and also, concurrently with the circuit courts of the United States, of all causes, civil and criminal, affecting persons who are denied or cannot enforce in the courts or judicial tribunals of the State or locality where they may be any of the rights secured to them by the first section of this act; and if any suit or prosecution, civil or criminal, has been or shall be commenced in any State court, against any such person, for any cause whatsoever, or against any officer civil or military, or other person, for any arrest or imprisonment, trespasses, or wrongs done or committed by virtue or under color of authority derived from this act or the act establishing a Bureau for the relief of Freedmen and Refugees, and all acts amendatory thereof, or for refusing to do any act upon the ground that it would be inconsistent with this act, such defendant shall have the right to remove such cause for trial to the proper district or circuit court in the manner prescribed by the "Act relating to habeas corpus and regulating judicial proceedings in certain cases," approved March three, eighteen hundred and sixty-three, and all acts amendatory thereof. The jurisdiction in civil and criminal matters hereby conferred on the district and circuit courts of the United States shall be exercised and enforced in conformity with the laws of the United States, so far as such laws are suitable to carry the same into effect; but in all cases where such laws are not adapted to the object, or are deficient in the provisions necessary to furnish suitable remedies and punish offences against law, the common law, as modified and changed by the constitution and statutes of the State wherein the court having jurisdiction of the cause, civil or criminal, is held, so far as the same is not inconsistent with the Constitution and laws of the United States, shall be extended to and govern said courts in the trial and disposition of such cause, and, if of a criminal nature, in the infliction of punishment on the party found guilty.

SECTION 4. *And be it further enacted,* That the district attorneys, marshals, and deputy marshals of the United States, the commissioners appointed by the circuit and territorial courts of the United States, with powers of arresting, imprisoning, or bailing offenders against the laws of the United States, the officers and agents of the Freedmen's Bureau, and every other officer who may be specially empowered by the President of the United States, shall be, and they are hereby, specially authorized and required, at the expense of the United States, to institute proceedings against all and every person who shall violate the provisions of this act, and cause him or them to be arrested and imprisoned, or bailed, as the case may be, for trial before such court of the United States or territorial court as by this act has cognizance of the offence. And with a view to affording reasonable protection to all persons in their constitutional rights of equality before the law, without distinction of race or color, or previous condition of slavery or involuntary servitude, except as a punishment for crime, whereof the party shall have been duly convicted, and to the prompt discharge of the duties of this act,

it shall be the duty of the circuit courts of the United States and the superior courts of the Territories of the United States, from time to time, to increase the number of commissioners, so as to afford a speedy and convenient means for the arrest and examination of persons charged with a violation of this act; and such commissioners are hereby authorized and required to exercise and discharge all the powers and duties conferred on them by this act, and the same duties with regard to offences created by this act, as they are authorized by law to exercise with regard to other offences against the laws of the United States.

SECTION 5. *And be it further enacted,* That it shall be the duty of all marshals and deputy marshals to obey and execute all warrants and precepts issued under the provisions of this act, when to them directed; and should any marshal or deputy marshal refuse to receive such warrant or other process when tendered, or to use all proper means diligently to execute the same, he shall, on conviction thereof, be fined in the sum of one thousand dollars, to the use of the person upon whom the accused is alleged to have committed the offence. And the better to enable the said commissioners to execute their duties faithfully and efficiently, in conformity with the Constitution of the United States and the requirements of this act, they are hereby authorized and empowered, within their counties respectively, to appoint, in writing, under their hands, any one or more suitable persons, from time to time, to execute all such warrants and other processes as may be issued by them in the lawful performance of their respective duties; and the persons so appointed to execute any warrant or process as aforesaid shall have authority to summon and call to their aid the bystanders or posse comitatus of the proper county, or such portion of the land or naval forces of the United States, or of the militia, as may be necessary to the performance of the duty with which they are charged, and to insure a faithful observance of the clause of the Constitution which prohibits slavery, in conformity with the provisions of this act; and said warrants shall run and be executed by said officers anywhere in the State or Territory within which they are issued.

SECTION 6. *And be it further enacted,* That any person who shall knowingly and wilfully obstruct, hinder, or prevent any officer, or other person charged with the execution of any warrant or process issued under the provisions of this act, or any person or persons lawfully assisting him or them, from arresting any person for whose apprehension such warrant or process may have been issued, or shall rescue or attempt to rescue such person from the custody of the officer, other person or persons, or those lawfully assisting as aforesaid, when so arrested pursuant to the authority herein given and declared, or shall aid, abet, or assist any person so arrested as aforesaid, directly or indirectly, to escape from the custody of the officer or other person legally authorized as aforesaid, or shall harbor or conceal any person for whose arrest a warrant or process shall have been issued as aforesaid, so as to prevent his discovery and arrest after notice or knowledge of the fact that a warrant has been issued for the apprehension of such person, shall, for either of said offences, be subject to a fine not exceeding one thousand dollars, and imprisonment not exceeding six months, by indictment and conviction before the district court of the United States for the district in which said offence may have been committed, or before the proper court of criminal jurisdiction, if committed within any one of the organized Territories of the United States.

SECTION 7. *And be it further enacted*, That the district attorneys, the marshals, their deputies, and the clerks of the said district and territorial courts shall be paid for their services the like fees as may be allowed to them for similar services in other cases; and in all cases where the proceedings are before a commissioner, he shall be entitled to a fee of ten dollars in full for his services in each case, inclusive of all services incident to such arrest and examination. The person or persons authorized to execute the process to be issued by such commissioners for the arrest of offenders against the provisions of this act shall be entitled to a fee of five dollars for each person he or they may arrest and take before any such commissioner as aforesaid, with such other fees as may be deemed reasonable by such commissioner for such other additional services as may be necessarily performed by him or them, such as attending at the examination, keeping the prisoner in custody, and providing him with food and lodging during his detention, and until the final determination of such commissioner, and in general for performing such other duties as may be required in the premises; such fees to be made up in conformity with the fees usually charged by the officers of the courts of justice within the proper district or county, as near as may be practicable, and paid out of the Treasury of the United States on the certificate of the judge of the district within which the arrest is made, and to be recoverable from the defendant as part of the judgment in case of conviction.

SECTION 8. *And be it further enacted*, That whenever the President of the United States shall have reason to believe that offences have been or are likely to be committed against the provisions of this act within any judicial district, it shall be lawful for him, in his discretion, to direct the judge, marshal, and district attorney of such district to attend at such place within the district, and for such time as he may designate, for the purpose of the more speedy arrest and trial of persons charged with a violation of this act; and it shall be the duty of every judge or other officer, when any such requisition shall be received by him, to attend at the place and for the time therein designated.

SECTION 9. *And be it further enacted*, That it shall be lawful for the President of the United States, or such person as he may empower for that purpose, to employ such part of the land or naval forces of the United States, or of the militia, as shall be necessary to prevent the violation and enforce the due execution of this act.

SECTION 10. *And be it further enacted*, That upon all questions of law arising in any cause under the provisions of this act a final appeal may be taken to the Supreme Court of the United States.

6. The Fourteenth Amendment 1866

Be it resolved by the Senate and House of Representatives of the United States of America in Congress assembled, (two thirds of both Houses concurring.) That the following article be proposed to the legislatures of the several States as an amendment to the Constitution of the United States, which, when ratified by three fourths of said legislatures, shall be valid as part of the Constitution, namely:—

ARTICLE XIV.

SECTION 1. All persons born or naturalized in the United States, and subject to the jurisdiction thereof, are citizens of the United States and of the State wherein they reside. No State shall make or enforce any law which shall abridge the privileges or immunities of citizens of the United States; nor shall any State deprive any person of life, liberty, or property, without due process of law, nor deny to any person within its jurisdiction the equal protection of the laws.

SECTION 2. Representatives shall be apportioned among the several States according to their respective numbers, counting the whole number of persons in each State, excluding Indians not taxed. But when the right to vote at any election for the choice of electors for President and Vice-President of the United States, representatives in Congress, the executive and judicial officers of a State, or the members of the legislature thereof, is denied to any of the male inhabitants of such State, being twenty-one years of age, and citizens of the United States, or in any way abridged, except for participation in rebellion or other crime, the basis of representation therein shall be reduced in the proportion which the number of such male citizens shall bear to the whole number of male citizens twenty-one years of age in such State.

SECTION 3. No person shall be a senator, or representative in Congress, or elector of President and Vice-President, or hold any office, civil or military under the United States, or under any State, who having previously taken an oath, as a member of Congress, or as an officer of the United States, or as a member of any State legislature, or as an executive or judicial officer of any State, to support the Constitution of the United States, shall have engaged in insurrection or rebellion against the same, or given aid or comfort to the enemies thereof. But Congress may by a vote of two thirds of each house remove such disability.

SECTION 4. The validity of the public debt of the United States, authorized by law, including debts incurred for payment of pensions and bounties for services in suppressing insurrection or rebellion, shall not be questioned. But neither the United States nor any State shall assume or pay any debt or obligation incurred in aid of insurrection or rebellion against the United States, or any claim for the loss or emancipation of any slave; but all such debts, obligations, and claims shall be held illegal and void.

SECTION 5. The Congress shall have power to enforce, by appropriate legislation, the provisions of this article.

7. The First Reconstruction Act March 2, 1867

WHEREAS no legal State governments or adequate protection for life or property now exists in the rebel States of Virginia, North Carolina, South Carolina, Georgia, Mississippi, Alabama, Louisiana, Florida, Texas, and Arkansas; and whereas it is necessary that peace and good order should be enforced in said States until loyal and republican State governments can be legally established: Therefore,

Be it enacted . . . , That said rebel States shall be divided into military districts and made subject to the military authority of the United States as hereinafter prescribed, and for that purpose Virginia shall constitute the first district; North Carolina and South Carolina the second district; Georgia, Alabama, and Florida the third district; Mississippi and Arkansas the fourth district; and Louisiana and Texas the fifth district.

SECTION 2. *And be it further enacted,* That it shall be the duty of the President to assign to the command of each of said districts an officer of the army, not below the rank of brigadier-general, and to detail a sufficient military force to enable such officer to perform his duties and enforce his authority within the district to which he is assigned.

SECTION 3. *And be it further enacted.* That it shall be the duty of each officer assigned as aforesaid, to protect all persons in their rights of person and property, to suppress insurrection, disorder, and violence, and to punish, or cause to be punished, all disturbers of the public peace and criminals; and to this end he may allow local civil tribunals to take jurisdiction of and to try offenders, or, when in his judgment it may be necessary for the trial of offenders, he shall have power to organize military commissions or tribunals for that purpose, and all interference under color of State authority with the exercise of military authority under this act, shall be null and void.

SECTION 4. *And be it further enacted,* That all persons put under military arrest by virtue of this act shall be tried without unnecessary delay, and no cruel or unusual punishment shall be inflicted, and no sentence of any military commission or tribunal hereby authorized, affecting the life or liberty of any person, shall be executed until it is approved by the officer in command of the district, and the laws and regulations for the government of the army shall not be affected by this act, except in so far as they conflict with its provisions: *Provided,* That no sentence of death under the provisions of this act shall be carried into effect without the approval of the President.

SECTION 5. *And be it further enacted,* That when the people of any one of said rebel States shall have formed a constitution of government in conformity with the Constitution of the United States in all respects, framed by a convention of delegates elected by the male citizens of said State, twenty-one years old and upward, of whatever race, color, or previous condition, who have been resident in said State for one year previous to the day of such election, except such as may be disfranchised for participation in the rebellion or for felony at common law, and when such constitution shall provide that the elective franchise shall be enjoyed by all such persons as have the qualifications herein stated for electors of delegates, and when such constitution shall be ratified by a majority of the persons voting on the question of ratification who are qualified as electors for delegates, and when such constitution shall have been submitted to Congress for examination and approval, and Congress shall have approved the same, and when said State, by a vote of its legislature elected under said constitution, shall have adopted the amendment to the Constitution of the United States, proposed by the Thirty-ninth Congress, and known as article fourteen and when said article shall have become a part of the Constitution of the United States said State shall be declared entitled to representation in Congress, and senators and representatives shall be admitted therefrom on their taking the oath prescribed by law, and then and thereafter the preceding sections of this act shall be inoperative in said State: *Provided,* That no person excluded from the privilege of holding office by said proposed amendment to the Constitution of the United States, shall be eligible to election as a member of the convention to frame a constitution for any of said rebel States, nor shall any such person vote for members of such convention.

SECTION 6. *And be it further enacted,* That, until the people of said rebel States shall be by law admitted to representation in the Congress of the United States, any civil governments which may exist there in shall be deemed provisional only, and in all respects subject to the paramount authority of the United States at any time to abolish, modify, control, or supersede the same; and in all elections to any office under such provisional governments all persons shall be entitled to vote, and none others, who are entitled to vote, under the provisions of the fifth section of this act; and no persons shall be eligible to any office under any such provisional governments who would be disqualified from holding office under the provisions of the third article of said constitutional amendment.

8. The Second Reconstruction Act **March 23, 1867**

Be it enacted . . . , That the first day of September, eighteen hundred and sixty-seven, the commanding general in each district defined by an act entitled "An act to provide for the more efficient government of the rebel States," passed March second, eighteen hundred and sixty-seven, shall cause a registration to be made of the male citizens of the United States, twenty-one years of age and upwards, resident in each county or parish in the State or States included in his district, which registration shall include only those persons who are qualified to vote for delegates by the act aforesaid, and who shall have taken and subscribed the following oath or affirmation: "I, —— —— ——, do solemnly swear (or affirm), in the presence of Almighty God, that I am a citizen of the State of ——; that I have resided in said State for —— months next preceding this day, and now reside in the county of——, or the parish of——, In said State (as the case may be); that I am twenty-one years old; that I have not been disfranchised for participation in any rebellion or civil war against the United States, or for felony committed against the laws of any State or of the United States; that I have never been a member of any State legislature, nor held any executive or judicial office in any State, and afterwards engaged in insurrection or rebellion against the United States, or given aid or comfort to the enemies thereof; that I have never taken an oath as a member of Congress of the United States, or as an officer of the United States, or as a member of any State legislature, or as an executive or judicial officer of any State, to support the Constitution of the United States, and afterwards engaged in insurrection or rebellion against the United States, or given aid or comfort to the enemies thereof; that I will faithfully support the Constitution and obey the laws of the United States, and will, to the best of my ability, encourage others so to do, so help me God"; which oath or affirmation may be administered by any registering officer.

SECTION 2. *And be it further enacted,* That after the completion of the registration hereby provided for in any State, at such time and places therein as the commanding general shall appoint and direct, of which at least thirty days' public notice shall be given, an election shall be held of delegates to a convention for the purpose of establishing a constitution and civil government for such State loyal to the Union, said convention in each State, except Virginia, to consist of the State legislature of such State in the year eighteen hundred and sixty, to be appointed among the several districts, counties, or parishes of such State by the commanding general, giving to each representation in the ratio of voters registered as aforesaid as nearly as may be. The convention in Virginia shall consist of the same number of members as represented the territory now constituting Virginia in the most numerous branch of the legislature of said State in the year eighteen hundred and sixty, to be apportioned as aforesaid.

Section 3. *And be it further enacted,* That at said election the registered voters of each State shall vote for or against a convention to form a constitution therfor under this act. . . . Those voting in favor of such a convention shall have written or printed on the ballots by which they vote for delegates, as aforesaid, the words "For a convention," and those voting against such a convention shall have written or printed on such ballots the words "Against a convention." The persons appointed to superintend said election, and to make return of the votes given thereat, as herein provided, shall count and make return of the votes given for and against a convention; and the commanding general to whom the same shall have been returned shall ascertain and declare the total vote in each State for and against a convention. If a majority of the votes given on that question shall be for a convention, then such a convention shall be held as hereinafter provided; but if a majority of said votes shall be against a convention, then no such convention shall be held under this act: *Provided,* That such convention shall not be held unless a majority of all such registered voters shall have voted on the question of holding such convention.

Section 4. *And be it further enacted,* That the commanding general of each district shall appoint as many boards of registration as may be necessary, consisting of three loyal officers or persons, to make and complete the registration, superintend the election, and make return to him of the votes, lists of voters, and of the persons elected as delegates by a plurality of the votes cast at said election; and upon receiving said returns he shall open the same, ascertain the persons elected as delegates, according to the returns of the officers who conducted said election, and make proclamation thereof; and if a majority of the votes given on that question shall be for a convention, the commanding general, within sixty days from the date of election, shall notify the dele-

gates to assemble in convention, at a time and place to be mentioned in the notification, and said convention, when organized, shall proceed to frame a constitution and civil government according to the provisions of this act, and the act to which it is supplementary; and when the same shall have been framed, said constitution shall be submitted by the convention for ratification to the persons registered under the provisions of this act at an election to be conducted by the officers or persons appointed or to be appointed by the commanding general, as hereinbefore provided, and to be held after the expiration of thirty days from the date of notice thereof, to be given by said convention; and the returns thereof shall be made to the commanding general of the district.

Section 5. *And be it further enacted,* That if, according to said returns, the constitution shall be ratified by a majority of the votes of the registered electors qualified as herein specified, cast at said election, at least one half of all the registered voters voting upon the question of such ratification, the president of the convention shall transmit a copy of the same, duly certified, to the President of the United States, who shall forthwith transmit the same to Congress, if then in session, and if not in session, then immediately upon its next assembling; and if it shall moreover appear to Congress that the election was one at which all the registered and qualified electors in the State had an opportunity to vote freely and without restraint, fear, or the influence of fraud, and if the Congress shall be satisfied that such constitution meets the approval of a majority of all the qualified electors in the State, and if the said constitution shall be declared by Congress to be in conformity with the provisions of the act to which this is supplementary, and the other provisions of said act shall have been complied with, and the said constitution shall be approved by Congress, the State shall be declared entitled to representation, and senators and representatives shall be admitted therefrom as therein provided.

Section 6. *And be it further enacted,* That all elections in the States mentioned in the said "Act to provided for the more efficient government of the rebel States," shall, during the operation of said act, be by ballot; and all officers making the said registration of voters and conducting said elections shall, before entering upon the discharge of their duties, take and subscribe the oath prescribed by the act approved July second, eighteen hundred and sixty two, entitled "An act to prescribe an oath of office": *Provided*, That if any person shall knowingly and falsely take and subscribe any oath in this act prescribed, such person so offending and being thereof duly convicted shall be subject to the pains, penalties, and disabilities which by law are provided for the punishment of the crime of wilful and corrupt perjury.

SECTION 7. *And be it further enacted*, That all expenses incurred by the several commanding generals, or by virtue of any orders issued, or appointments made, by then, under or by virtue of this act, shall be paid out of any moneys in the treasury not otherwise appropriated.

SECTION 8. *And be it further enacted*. That the convention for each State shall prescribe the fees, salary, and compensation to be paid to all delegates and other officers and agents herein authorized or necessary to carry into effect the purposes of this act not herein otherwise provided for, and shall provide for the levy and collection of such taxes on the property in such State as may be necessary to pay the same.

SECTION 9. *And be it further enacted*, That the word "article," in the sixth section of the act to which this is supplementary, shall be construed to mean "section."

9. The Third Reconstruction Act July 19, 1867

Be it enacted . . . , That it is hereby declared to have been the true intent and meaning . . . [of the acts of March 2 and March 23, 1867] . . . , that the governments then existing in the rebel States of Virginia, North Carolina, South Carolina, Georgia, Mississippi, Alabama, Louisiana, Florida, Texas, and Arkansas were not legal State governments; and that thereafter said governments, if continued, were to be continued subject in all respects to the military commanders of the respective districts, and to the paramount authority of Congress.

SECTION 2. *And be it further enacted*, That the commander of any district named in said act shall have power, subject to the disapproval of the General of the army of the United States, and to have effect till disapproved, whenever in the opinion of such com-

mander the proper administration of said act shall require it, to suspend or remove from office, or from the performance of official duties and the exercise of official powers, any officer or person holding or exercising, or professing to hold or exercise, any military office or duty in such district under any power, election, appointment or authority derived from, or granted by, or claimed under, any so-called State or the government thereof, or any municipal or other division thereof, and upon such suspension or removal such commander, subject to the disapproval of the General as aforesaid, shall have power to provide from time to time for the performance of the said duties of such officer or person so suspended or removed, by the detail of some competent officer or soldier of the army, or by the appointment of some other person, to perform the same, and to fill vacancies occasioned by death, resignation, or otherwise.

SECTION 3. *And be it further enacted*, That the General of the army of the United States shall be invested with all the powers of suspension, removal, appointment, and detail granted in the preceding section to district commanders.

SECTION 4. *And be it further enacted*, That the acts of the officers of the army already done in removing in said districts persons exercising the functions of civil officers, and appointing others in their stead, are hereby confirmed: *Provided*, That any person heretofore or hereafter appointed by any district commander to exercise the functions of any civil office, may be removed either by the military officer in command of the district, or by the General of the army. And it shall be the duty of such commander to remove from office as aforesaid all persons who are disloyal to the government of the United States, or who use their official influence in any manner to hinder, delay, prevent, or obstruct the due and proper administration of this act and the acts to which it is supplementary.

SECTION 5. *And be it further enacted*, That the boards of registration provided for in the act . . . [of March 23, 1867] . . . , shall have power, and it shall be their duty before allowing the registration of any person, to ascertain, upon such facts or information as they can obtain, whether such person is entitled to be registered under said act, and the oath required by said act shall not be conclusive on such question, and no person shall be registered unless such board shall decide that he is entitled thereto; and such board shall also have power to examine, under oath, (to be administered by any member of such board,) any one touching the qualification of any person claiming registration; but in every case of refusal by the board to register an applicant, and in every case of striking his name from the list as hereinafter provided, the board shall make a note or memorandum, which shall be returned with the registration list to the commanding general of the district, setting forth the grounds of such refusal or such striking from the list: *Provided*, That no person shall be disqualified as member of any board of registration by reason of race or color.

SECTION 6. *And be it further enacted*, That the true intent and meaning of the oath prescribed in said supplementary act is, (among other things,) that no person who has been a member of the legislature of any State, or who has held any executive or judicial office in any State, whether he has taken an oath to support the Constitution of the United States or not, and whether he was holding such office at the commencement of the rebellion, or had held it before, and who has afterwards engaged in insurrection or rebellion against the United States, or given aid or comfort to the enemies thereof, is entitled to be registered or to vote; and the words "executive or judicial office in any State" in said oath mentioned shall be construed to include all civil offices created by law for the administration of any general law of a State, or for the administration of justice.

SECTION 7. *And be it further enacted*, That the time for completing the original registration provided for in said act may, in the discretion of the commander of any district, be extended to the first day of October, eighteen hundred and sixty-seven; and the boards of registration shall have power, and it shall be their duty, commencing fourteen days prior to any election under said act, and upon reasonable public notice of the time and place thereof, to revise, for a period of five days, the registration lists, and upon being satisfied that any person not entitled thereto has been registered, to strike the name of such person from the list, and such person shall not be allowed to vote. And such board shall also, during the same period, add to such registry the names of all persons who at that time possess the qualifications required by said act who have not been already registered; and no person shall, at any time, be entitled to be registered or to vote by reason of any executive pardon or amnesty for any act or thing which, without such pardon or amnesty, would disqualify him from registration or voting.

SECTION 8. *And be it further enacted*, That section four of said last-named act shall be construed to authorize the commanding general named herein, whenever he shall deem it needful, to remove any member of a board of registration and to appoint another in his stead, and to fill any vacancy in such board.

SECTION 9. *And be it further enacted*, That all members of said boards of registration and all persons hereafter elected or appointed to office in said military districts, under any so-called State or municipal authority, or by detail or appointment of the district commanders, shall be required to take and to subscribe the oath of office prescribed by law for officers of the United States.

SECTION 10. *And be it further enacted*, That no district commander or member of the board of registration, or any of the officers or appointees acting under them, shall be bound in his action by any opinion of any civil officer of the United States.

SECTION 11. *And be it further enacted*, That all the provisions of this act and of the acts to which this is supplementary shall be construed liberally, to the end that all the intents thereof may be fully and perfectly carried out.

10. The Fourth Reconstruction Act March 8, 1868

Be it enacted . . . , That hereafter any election authorized by the act [of March 23, 1867] . . . , shall be decided by a majority of the votes actually cast; and at the election in which the question of the adoption or rejection of any constitution is submitted, any person duly registered in the State may vote in the election district where he offers to vote when he has resided therein for ten days next preceding such election, upon presentation of his certificate of registration, his affidavit, or other satisfactory evidence, under such regulations as the district commanders may prescribe.

SECTION 2. *And be it further enacted*, That the constitutional convention of any of the States mentioned in the acts to which this is amendatory may provide that at the time of voting upon the ratification of the constitution the registered voters may vote also for members of the House of Representatives of the United States, and for all elective officers provided for by the said constitution; and the same election officers who shall make the return of the votes cast on the ratification or rejection of the constitution, shall enumerate and certify the votes cast for members of Congress.

11. The Platform of the Populist Party, Omaha, Nebraska, 1892

Assembled upon the 116th anniversary of the Declaration of Independence, the People's Party of America, in their first national convention, invoking upon their action the blessing of Almighty God, put forth in the name and on behalf of the people of this country, the following preamble and declaration of principles:

PREAMBLE

The conditions which surround us best justify our co-operation; we meet in the midst of a nation brought to the verge of moral, political, and material ruin. Corruption dominates the ballot-box, the Legislatures, the Congress, and touches even the ermine of the bench. The people are demoralized; most of the States have been compelled to isolate the voters at the polling places to prevent universal intimidation and bribery. The newspapers are largely subsidized or muzzled, public opinion silenced, business prostrated, homes covered with mortgages, labor impoverished, and the land concentrating in the hands of capitalists. The urban workmen are denied the right to organize for self-protection, imported pauperized labor beats down their wages, a hireling standing army, unrecognized by our laws, is established to shoot them down, and they are rapidly degenerating into European conditions. The fruits of the toil of millions are boldly stolen to build up colossal fortunes for a few, unprecedented in the history of mankind; and the possessors of these, in turn, despise the Republic and endanger liberty. From the same prolific womb of governmental injustice we breed the two great classes—tramps and millionaires.

The national power to create money is appropriated to enrich bondholders; a vast public debt payable in legal-tender currency has been funded into gold-bearing bonds, thereby adding millions to the burdens of the people.

Silver, which has been accepted as coin since the dawn of history, has been demonetized to add to the purchasing power of gold by decreasing the value of all forms of property as well as human labor, and the supply of currency is purposely abridged to fatten usurers, bankrupt enterprise, and enslave industry. A vast conspiracy against mankind has been organized on two continents, and it is rapidly taking possession of the world. If not met and overthrown at once it forbodes terrible social convulsions, the destruction of civilization, or the establishment of an absolute despotism.

We have witnessed for more than a quarter of a century the struggles of the two great political parties for power and plunder, while grevious wrongs have been inflicted upon the suffering people. We charge that the controlling influences dominating both these parties have permitted the existing dreadful conditions to develop without serious effort to prevent or restrain them. Neither do they now promise us any substantial reform. They have agreed together to ignore, in the coming campaign, every issue but one. They propose to drown the outcries of a plundered people with the uproar of a sham battle over the tariff, so that capitalists, corporations, national banks, rings, trusts, watered stock, the demonetization of silver and the oppressions of the usurers may all be lost sight of. They propose to sacrifice our homes, lives, and children on the altar of mammon; to destroy the multitude in order to secure corruption funds from the millionaires.

Assembled on the anniversary of the birthday of the nation, and filled with the spirit of the grand general and chief who established our independence, we seek to restore the government of the Republic to the hands of the "plain people," with which class it originated. We assert our purposes to be identical with the purposes of the National Constitution; to form a more perfect union and establish justice, insure domestic tranquillity, provide for the common defence, promote the general welfare, and secure the blessings of liberty for ourselves and our posterity.

We declare that this Republic can only endure as a free government while built upon the love of the people for each other and for the nation; that it cannot be pinned together by bayonets; that the Civil War is over, and that every passion and resentment which grew out of it must die with it, and that we must be in fact, as we are in name, one united brotherhood of free men.

Our country finds itself confronted by conditions for which there is no precedent in the history of the world; our annual agricultural productions amount to billions of dollars in value, which must, within a few weeks or months, be exchanged for billions of dollars' worth of commodities consumed in their production; the existing currency supply is wholly inadequate to make this exchange; the results are falling prices, the formation of combines and rings, the impoverishment of the producing class. We pledge ourselves that if given power we will labor to correct these evils by wise and reasonable legislation, in accordance with the terms of our platform.

We believe that the power of government—in other words, of the people—should be expanded (as in the case of the postal service) as rapidly and as far as the good sense of an intelligent people and the teachings of experience shall justify, to the end that oppression, injustice, and poverty shall eventually cease in the land.

While our sympathies as a party of reform are naturally upon the side of every proposition which will tend to make men intelligent, virtuous, and temperate, we nevertheless regard these questions, important as they are, as secondary to the great issues now pressing for solution, and upon which not only our individual prosperity but the very existence of free institutions depend; and we ask all men to first help us to determine whether we are to have a republic to administer before we differ as to the conditions upon which it is to be administered, believing that the forces of reform this day organized will never cease to move forward until every wrong is righted and equal rights and equal privileges securely established for all the men and women of this country.

PLATFORM

We declare, therefore—

First.—That the union of the labor forces of the United States this day consummated shall be permanent and perpetual; may its spirit enter into all hearts for the salvation of the Republic and the uplifting of mankind.

Second.—Wealth belongs to him who creates it, and every dollar taken from industry without an equivalent is robbery. "If any will not work, neither shall he eat." The interests of rural and civil labor are the same; their enemies are identical.

Third.—We believe that the time has come when the railroad corporations will either own the people or the people must own the railroads; and should the government enter upon the work of owning and managing all railroads, we should favor an amendment to the constitution by which all persons engaged in the government service shall be placed under a civil-service regulation of the most rigid character, so as to prevent the increase of the power of the national administration by the use of such additional government employes.

FINANCE.—We demand a national currency, safe, sound, and flexible issued by the general government only, a full legal tender for all debts, public and private, and that without the use of banking corporations; a just, equitable, and efficient means of distribution direct to the people, at a tax not to exceed 2 percent, per annum, to be provided as set forth in the sub-treasury plan of the Farmers' Alliance, or a better system; also by payments in discharge of its obligations for public improvements.

1. We demand free and unlimited coinage of silver and gold at the present legal ratio of 16 to 1.
2. We demand that the amount of circulating medium be speedily increased to not less than $50 per capita.
3. We demand a graduated income tax.
4. We believe that the money of the country should be kept as much as possible in the hands of the people, and hence we demand that all State and national revenues shall be limited to the necessary expenses of the government, economically and honestly administered.
5. We demand that postal savings banks be established by the government for the safe deposit of the earnings of the people and to facilitate exchange.

TRANSPORTATION.—Transportation being a means of exchange and a public necessity, the government should own and operate the railroads in the interest of the people. The telegraph and telephone, like the post-office system, being a necessity for the transmission of news, should be owned and operated by the government in the interest of the people.

LAND.—The land, including all the natural sources of wealth, is the heritage of the people, and should not be monopolized for speculative purposes, and alien ownership of land should be prohibited. All land now held by railroads and other corporations in excess of their actual needs, and all lands now owned by aliens should be reclaimed by the government and held for actual settlers only.

EXPRESSION OF SENTIMENTS

Your Committee on Platform and Resolutions beg leave unanimously to report the following:

Whereas, Other questions have been presented for our consideration, we hereby submit the following, not as a part of the Platform of the People's Party, but as resolutions expressive of the sentiment of this Convention.

1. RESOLVED, That we demand a free ballot and a fair count in all elections, and pledge ourselves to secure it to every legal voter without Federal intervention, through the adoption by the States of the unperverted Australian or secret ballot system.
2. RESOLVED, That the revenue derived from a graduated income tax should be applied to the reduction of the burden of taxation now levied upon the domestic industries of this country.
3. RESOLVED, That we pledge our support to fair and liberal pensions to ex-Union soldiers and sailors.
4. RESOLVED, That we condemn the fallacy of protecting American labor under the present system, which opens our ports to the pauper and criminal classes of the world and crowds out our wage-earners; and we denounce the present ineffective laws against contract labor, and demand the further restriction of undesirable emigration.
5. RESOLVED, That we cordially sympathize with the efforts of organized workingmen to shorten the hours of labor, and demand a rigid enforcement of the existing eight-hour law on Government work, and ask that a penalty clause be added to the said law.
6. RESOLVED, That we regard the maintenance of a large standing army of mercenaries, known as the Pinkerton system, as a menace to our liberties, and we demand its abolition; and we condemn the recent invasion of the Territory of Wyoming by the hired assassins of plutocracy, assisted by Federal officers.
7. RESOLVED, That we commend to the favorable consideration of the people and the reform press the legislative system known as the initiative and referendum.
8. RESOLVED, That we favor a constitutional provision limiting the office of President and Vice-President to one term, and providing for the election of Senators of the United States by a direct vote of the people.
9. RESOLVED, That we oppose any subsidy or national aid to any private corporation for any purpose.
10. RESOLVED, That this convention sympathizes with the Knights of Labor and their righteous contest with the tyrannical combine of clothing manufacturers of Rochester, and declare it to be a duty of all who hate tyranny and oppression to refuse to purchase the goods made by the said manufacturers, or to patronize any merchants who sell such goods.

Appendix B
Biographies of Major Personalities

Adams, Charles Francis, Jr. (1835–1915): Historian and railroad expert. Grandson of former President John Quincy Adams and chair of the Massachusetts Board of Railroad Commissioners in 1875.

Adams, Henry (1838–1918): Historian and writer. Brother of Charles Francis Adams, Jr.

Addams, Jane (1860–1935): Humanitarian and peace activist, Addams founded the Chicago settlement Hull House in 1889, which became a model for similar settlements nationwide.

Alger, Horatio (1832–1899): Unitarian minister who wrote a series of successful novels for young boys beginning in 1867.

Alger, Russell Alexander (1836–1907): In 1897, Alger became war secretary under President McKinley. He resigned in 1899 amidst criticism of his management of the military during the Spanish–American War. Elected a U.S. senator from Ohio, 1902.

Arthur, Chester Alan (1830–1886): A former lawyer, Arthur was named New York Port Authority collector in 1871 by President Grant. In 1877, during the Hayes administration, Arthur's management of the Port Authority was investigated by federal authorities and he was suspended from his post. Arthur was nominated by the Republicans for the vice presidency in 1880, sharing the ticket with James Garfield. When President Garfield was assassinated in 1881, Arthur succeeded him as president and became a reform leader known for taking a hard line with politically corrupt officials. He did not receive the party's nomination to a full term of office in 1884; the nomination went instead to James G. Blaine.

Barton, Clara (1821–1912): Founder of the American Red Cross.

Beecher, Henry Ward (1813–1887): Minister of New York's Pilgrim Congregational Church. Became key figure in mid-1870s scandal when named by a parishioner as the principal defendant in an adultery trial. Brother of novelist Harriet Beecher Stowe.

Bell, Alexander Graham (1847–1922): Scientist who invented the telephone; educator of the deaf.

Bellamy, Edward (1850–1898): Utopian Socialist and promoter of the Social Gospel, the obligation that citizens had to make positive changes in social institutions as a means of improving the lives of all citizens. Author of popular novel *Looking Backward*, published in 1888.

Beveridge, Albert J. (1862–1927): Republican senator from Indiana. Supporter of U.S. territorial expansion into the Pacific. Author of a joint resolution (S.R. 53) that established U.S. authority over the Philippines.

Blaine, James G. (1830–1893): A native of Maine, Blaine was elected to the House of Representatives in 1863 and became Speaker of the House in 1869. In 1881, President Garfield named Blaine secretary of state. He failed to win his party's nomination for U.S. president in 1876, but he received the Republican party bid in 1884. Although he lost the election, he served later as secretary of state during the administration of President Benjamin H. Harrison.

Booth, John Wilkes (1838–1865): Assassin of President Abraham Lincoln.

Bowles, Samuel, II (1826–1878): Journalist and outspoken Massachusetts newspaper editor. Publisher of the *Springfield Republican*.

Brace, Charles Loring (1826–1890): New England Protestant minister and reformer.

Brooks, Phillips (1835–1893): Liberal theologian and reformer. Rector of Trinity Episcopal Church, Boston, Massachusetts.

Bryan, William Jennings (1860–1925): Democratic nominee for president who ran unsuccessfully against McKinley in 1896. Bryan, a vehement supporter of free coinage of silver, also had the support of Populists in the election, but this was not sufficient to elect him to the presidency.

Carnegie, Andrew (1835–1919): Owner of the Homestead, Pennsylvania, Carnegie Steel Company, millionaire and philanthropist.

Catt, Carrie Chapman (1859–1947): A leader of the woman suffrage movement and a president of the National Woman Suffrage Association.

Clemens, Samuel (1835–1910): Known by his pen name, Mark Twain, Clemens's books and short stories reflected U.S. life in a way that was particularly unique. Twain was, and is, considered one of the nation's best writers. He wrote the best-selling *Tom Sawyer, The Adventurers of Huckleberry Finn* and with coauthor Charles Dudley Warner, *The Gilded Age.*

Cleveland, Grover Stephen (1837–1908): Staunch supporter of civil service reform and one-time governor of New York, Cleveland was elected president of the United States in 1884. His opposition to high protective tariffs and his support of a sound money policy were faulted by critics, but his honest approach to politics generally appealed to millions of Americans. He won re-election to the presidency in 1892 after a four-year hiatus, during which Benjamin Harrison served as chief executive.

Cody, William Frederick ("Buffalo Bill") (1846–1917): Buffalo hunter, sharpshooter, Indian scout for the 5th U.S. Cavalry and popular rodeo entertainer.

Colfax, Schyler (1823–1885): Vice president of the U.S. during the first administration of President Grant. Implicated in the Credit Mobilier scandal.

Conkling, Roscoe (1829–1888): New York Republican, elected to Congress in 1858. Outspoken foe of fellow Republican James G. Blaine.

Cooke, Jay (1821–1905): Investment banker and railroad expert. Head of financial house that failed and precipitated the panic of 1873.

Cullom, Shelby M. (1829–1914): Governor of Illinois, 1876–83 and Republican senator who sponsored the Interstate Commerce Bill signed into law in 1887.

Custer, George Armstrong (1839–1876): Former Civil War general who achieved fame as an Indian fighter. Was killed during spectacularly risky raid at the Little Bighorn River in 1876.

Darrow, Clarence (1857–1938): Democrat and opponent of America's imperialistic expansion.

Davis, Richard Harding (1864–1916): Journalist and correspondent for Hearst newspapers during the Spanish–American war.

Debs, Eugene V. (1855–1926): Labor leader and organizer of the American Railroad Union; later head of the Socialist Labor party.

Dewey, George (1837–1917): Naval commander and hero of the battle of Manila Bay during the Spanish–American War.

Dodge, Grenville Mellen (1831–1916): Chief engineer during construction of the transcontinental railroad in 1869. Head of the Dodge Commission in 1898 which investigated actions of the U.S. Army in the Spanish–American War.

Douglass, Frederick (1817–1895): Author of *Up From Slavery*, former slave and tireless spokesman for black Americans' civil rights.

Du Bois, W. E. Burghardt (1868–1963): Became African-American professor of sociology at Atlanta University in 1897. A founder of the Niagara movement and the National Association for the Advancement of Colored People (NAACP).

Dunne, Finley Peter (1867–1936): News editor and creator of the satirical character "Martin Dooley" in the *Chicago Evening Post* in 1893.

Eddy, Mary Baker (1821–1910): Founder of the Christian Science religion.

Edison, Thomas Alva (1847–1931): Ohio-born inventor of the light bulb, electrical conduction systems, the motion picture camera and the gramophone, or phonograph.

Ely, Richard T. (1854–1943): Professor of economics at Johns Hopkins University. A founder of the American Economic Association.

Fish, Hamilton (1808–1893): Secretary of state under President Ulysses S. Grant. Through a series of careful negotiations, he helped restore amicable relations between the U.S. and Great Britain following the Civil War.

Ford, Henry (1863–1947): Founder of the Detroit Automobile Company in 1899, he was the first to perfect a mass assembly system of automobile manufacture.

Frick, Henry Clay (1849–1919): Plant manager at the Homestead, Pennsylvania, Carnegie Steel Company.

Garfield, James A. (1831–1881): An Ohio Republican who served in both the House and Senate. Garfield was elected to the presidency in 1880. He was assassinated in July 1881 by Charles Guiteau, a disgruntled would-be appointee.

George, Henry (1839–1897): Economic reformer, promoter of the single-tax and author of the books *Poverty and Progress* and *Social Problems.*

Gladden, Washington (1836–1918): Congregational minister and promoter of the Social Gospel.

Glidden, Joseph F. (1813–1906): Inventor of barbed wire.

Godkin, Edwin Lawrence (1831–1902): Journalist and editor. Godkin was publisher of the *New York Evening Post.* A Mugwump and supporter of the gold standard, Godkin was editor of the *Nation,* a popular monthly.

Gompers, Samuel (1850–1924): Union organizer and founder and president of the American Federation of Labor for 41 years, until his death in 1924.

Grant, Ulysses S. (1822–1885): After his tour of duty as commander of the union army, Grant was named secretary of war under President Andrew Johnson. Grant was elected president of the United States in 1868. He served for two terms and was considered by most to be a better military officer than political leader.

Greeley, Horace (1811–1872): Editor of the *New York Tribune* and Liberal Republican nominee for president in 1871.

Hanna, Mark (1837–1904): Campaign manager for William McKinley in the 1890 congressional elections and the 1896 presidential elections. Was himself elected to the U.S. Senate in 1898.

Harrison, Benjamin (1833–1901): The grandson of the nation's ninth president, William Henry Harrison, Benjamin Harrison was active in the Republican party in Indiana. He was elected senator in 1880 and in 1888 received the party's nomination for president. He defeated Grover Cleveland in 1888 by garnering 233 electoral college votes to Cleveland's 168. The incumbent Harrison was renominated by the Republican party in 1892, but was defeated by Cleveland in that election.

Harvey, William H. ("Coin") (1851–1936): Free-silver proponent, founder of the Patriots of America society in 1895 and author of *Coin's Financial School,* published in 1894.

Hay, John Milton (1838–1905): Hay was appointed secretary of state by president McKinley. Hay also served as secretary of state for President Theodore Roosevelt, and was an author of the Hay–Paunceforte Treaty.

Hayes, Rutherford Birchard (1822–1893): A Republican congressman from Ohio from 1865 to 1867, Hayes was elected to three terms as governor of Ohio beginning in 1868. Subsequently, although Hayes garnered less than a majority of popular votes in the 1876 presidential election against Democrat Samuel J. Tilden, he became the nation's 19th president. Congress intervened in the disputed election, because Tilden was judged to have only 184 electoral college votes to Hayes's 185. Part of this decision resulted also in the Compromise of 1877, guaranteeing removal of federal troops from the South in exchange for delivering the election to Hayes.

Hearst, William Randolph (1863–1951): Owner and publisher of the *San Francisco Examiner.* Bought the *New York Morning Journal* to begin competing with Joseph Pulitzer's *New York World.*

Hobart, Garret A. (1844–1899): Vice president under William McKinley, Hobart served during McKinley's first term in office. His death paved the way for Theodore Roosevelt to be McKinley's running mate in 1900.

Holmes, Oliver Wendell (1841–1935): U.S. Supreme Court Justice from Massachusetts.

Howard, Oliver O. (1830–1909): General and military commander of the Washington Territory during the federal government's attempt to clear out Native-American populations to make way for white settlements.

Howells, William Dean (1837–1920): Author of several popular novels, including *The Rise of Silas Lapham,* which detailed life in the Gilded Age. Howells's realism was considered a new approach to fiction in the latter part of the 19th century.

Ingersoll, Robert Green (1833–1899): Illinois attorney general who became a Radical Republican following the Civil War, and who was famous for his political oratory, particularly in issues dealing with the South and its role in the U.S.

Jackson, Helen Hunt (1831–1885): Writer who spoke eloquently of the plight of the Indian. Best known for *Century of Dishonor* (1881), the novel *Ramona* (1884) and also for her writings on the training of children.

James, Henry (1843–1916): Novelist in the realist tradition, and satirist of late-19th century lifestyles. Author of *The Bostonians*; brother of philosopher William James.

James, William (1842–1910): American philosopher, pragmatist, and anti-imperialist. Author of *The Varieties of Religious Experience*; brother of novelist Henry James.

Johnson, Andrew (1808–1875): With a long history of congressional service, and as the Democratic governor of Tennessee, Johnson was chosen as Abraham Lincoln's vice-presidential running mate in 1864. Johnson assumed the presidency when Lincoln was assassinated in 1865. A Radical Republican Congress soon found him unwilling to guide the nation according to its wishes, and throughout the immediate postwar years the effectiveness of the executive branch was in serious jeopardy. Congress sought to eliminate any interference with its actions by the highly inept Johnson, who faced a Senate impeachment trial in 1868. Johnson was acquitted on a one-vote margin, and after he had stepped down from the presidency he was re-elected to the Senate in 1875.

Kelley, Florence (1859–1932): Close associate of Jane Addams and leader in settlement house work. One of the first woman graduates of Cornell University in 1882.

Kelly, Oliver Hudson (1826–1913): Founder of the Patrons of Husbandry in 1867, which grew into the national Granger movement. Under Kelly's leadership, the nation's farmers gained a political voice and helped change federal agricultural policies.

Lloyd, Henry Demarest (1847–1903): Popular journalist whose exposés of Standard Oil won him a large following. His famous attack on trusts, *Wealth Against Commonwealth*, was published in 1894. In it, Lloyd urged greater control of business by the federal government.

Lodge, Henry Cabot (1850–1924): Republican senator from Massachusetts. Strong proponent of foreign expansion.

McCormick, Cyrus Hall (1809–1884): Founder and owner of the McCormick Harvester Works.

McCoy, Joseph Geating (1837–1915): Cattleman who made Abilene, Kansas, a depot for cattle-loading onto the Kansas & Pacific Railroad bound for the Chicago stockyards.

McKinley, William (1843–1901): A Republican from Ohio, McKinley served in Congress from 1876 to 1891, except for the period 1883 to 1885. A supporter of big business, he favored protective tariff legislation, the most comprehensive of which was known as the McKinley Tariff of 1890. In 1892 he was elected governor of Ohio, and received his party's nomination to the presidency in 1896. He won re-election in the 1900 race against William Jennings Bryan. McKinley was shot and killed by an assassin, L.F. Czolgosz, in September 1901.

McParlan, James (1844–1919): Pinkerton detective who successfully infiltrated the secret society, the Molly Maguires. Through McParlan's efforts, the group's leaders were brought to trial and the organization soon lost all power.

Mahan, Alfred Thayer (1840–1914): Historian and naval officer who published *The Influence of Sea Power on the French Revolution*, and *The Influence of Sea Power upon History, 1660–1783*, a book credited with focusing the nation's interest on a strong naval force as the basis of imperial power.

Miller, Samuel Freeman (1816–1890): A Kentucky native, Miller was named U.S. Supreme Court Justice in 1862 and served in that capacity until 1890. He was most widely known for his majority opinion in the 1873 Slaughterhouse Cases, in which he upheld the right of states to grant corporate monopolies.

Moody, Dwight Lyman (1837–1899): Founder of the Moody Bible Institute in Chicago, Illinois. Established the Sunday School movement.

Morgan, John Pierpont (1837–1913): A banker, considered among the most able of all American financiers. Under Morgan's direction, the U.S. Steel Company was formed, the first billion-dollar company.

Morton, Julius Sterling (1832–1902): In 1893, Morton became agriculture secretary when appointed by President Cleveland to that cabinet post. Although a westerner, he did not support the farmers' movements, and he opposed state regulation of railways.

Nast, Thomas (1840–1902): Cartoonist for the *New York Tribune*.

Olmsted, Frederick Law (1822–1903). Architect and landscape planner. Designed Central Park in New York City and the Boston Public Gardens.

Olney, Richard (1835–1917): A corporate and railroad lawyer who defended the Whiskey Trust from charges of having violated the Sherman Anti-Trust

Act. In 1893, President Cleveland appointed Olney attorney general, a post he held until 1895, when he was named secretary of state.

Page, Walter Hines (1855–1918): Editor of the *Atlantic Monthly*. Supportive of U.S. imperialism in the 1890s.

Powderly, Terence V. (1849–1924): Leader of the Knights of Labor.

Powell, John Wesley (1834–1902): Surveyor whose *Report on the Arid Regions of the U.S.* encouraged westward expansion.

Pulitzer, Joseph (1847–1911): Publisher of the *New York World* and competitor of William Randolph Hearst; founder of the Pulitzer prizes.

Pullman, George M. (1831–1897): President of the Pullman Company, a manufacturer of railway sleeping cars, where workers began the American Railway Union strike of 1894.

Rockefeller, John D. (1838–1919): Founder of Standard Oil of Ohio, millionaire and philanthropist.

Roosevelt, Theodore (1858–1919): In 1901, after the death of President William McKinley, then-Vice President Roosevelt assumed the presidency. He was reelected on the Republican ticket in 1904. Having made a reputation for himself as an energetic, take-charge administrator while Civil Service Commissioner, Roosevelt became Assistant Secretary of the Navy in 1897. He was a "rough rider" during the Cuban Revolt, and was elected governor of New York in 1898. He was chosen as McKinley's running mate in 1900.

Schurz, Carl (1828–1906): A Liberal Republican who was named secretary of the interior under President Hayes in 1877.

Seward, William (1801–1872): Secretary of state under President Andrew Johnson. His dealings with Russia enabled the United States to purchase Alaska for $7.2 million.

Sheridan, Phillip H. (1831–1888): Secretary of war under President Grant, and a former Union general who was involved in the removal of Native Americans from their ancestral lands.

Sherman, William Tecumseh (1820–1891): Noted Civil War general whose efforts in the years following the war were aimed at clearing the westward regions of uncooperative Indians. He was named President Grant's second secretary of war in 1869.

Starr, Ellen Gates (1859–1940): Social worker. A colleague and close friend of Jane Addams, Starr helped found Hull House in Chicago, Illinois.

Stephens, Uriah (1821–1882): Founder of the Knights of Labor in 1869.

Stevens, Thaddeus (1792–1868): Radical Republican leader and U.S. representative from Pennsylvania. An outspoken critic of President Andrew Johnson and an opponent of Johnson's attempts to soften the intent of Reconstruction policies. Led the Radical Republicans in passing the four Reconstruction Acts.

Strong, Josiah (1847–1916): Protestant minister, general secretary of the Evangelical Alliance, and author of *Our Country* and *The New Era*, books detailing the growth of American Protestantism and the city.

Sullivan, Louis (1856–1924): Architect, often referred to as the inventor of the skyscraper.

Sumner, Charles (1811–1874): Massachusetts senator. Leader of the Radical Republicans along with Representative Thaddeus Stevens (R-Pennsylvania).

Sumner, William Graham (1848–1910): Episcopal priest, sociologist, economist and later a professor at Yale University. Proponent of laissez-faire business practices, opponent of protective tariffs. A critic of the Social Gospel.

Sunday, William Ashley ("Billy") (1862–1935): Revivalist and itinerant Protestant minister.

Sylvis, William (1828–1869): Union organizer for the Iron Molders Union. Helped found the National Labor Union in 1866.

Thomas, Martha Carey (1857–1935): President of Bryn Mawr College in Pennsylvania, Thomas was one of the first women to head a women's college in the U.S.

Tilden, Samuel Jones (1814–1886): Democratic governor of New York who ran against Rutherford B. Hayes in the 1876 presidential race. Tilden was respected as a reformer who fought corruption and was known for his successful defeat of the Tweed Ring in New York City.

Trevellick, Richard A. (1830–1895): Cofounder, with William Sylvis, of the National Labor Union.

Turner, Frederick Jackson (1861–1932): Historian and author of the frontier thesis.

Tweed, William Marcy ("Boss") (1823–1878): Political boss and head of the "Tweed Ring," a network

Lillian Wald, New York City social worker. Courtesy of the Library of Congress.

of corruption in the upper echelons of New York City government. "Boss" Tweed was ultimately sent to prison for his illegal dealings.

Vanderbilt, Cornelius (1794–1877): Entrepreneur and railroad magnate. Known as "Commodore" because of his early success in the shipping industry. Vanderbilt controlled the New York Central Railroad.

Waite, Morrison R. (1818–1888): Chief justice of the U.S. Supreme Court.

Wald, Lillian D. (1867–1940): Leader of the well-known Henry Street Settlement in New York City and associate of social reformer Jane Addams.

Ward, Lester Frank (1841–1913): Sociologist. Challenger of William Graham Sumner's philosophy, promoter of Populism and William Jennings Bryan.

Washburne, Elihu B. (1816–1887): The first of two secretaries of state to serve under President Grant, Washburne was named to his post in 1869 and was considered instrumental in re-establishing more amicable relations between Great Britain and the U.S. following the Civil War.

Washington, Booker T. (1856–1915): Former slave, founder of the Tuskegee Institute in Alabama, and author of the "Atlanta Compromise." In this statement, Washington expressed his belief that black Americans required vocational training as a means of becoming economically self-sufficient. A close associate of William E.B. Du Bois during the 19th century.

Wells, David A. (1828–1898): Economist and well-respected analyst of the effect of industrialization on America.

White, Stanford (1853–1906): Chicago architect.

Whitman, Walt (1819–1892): One of the United States' most widely recognized poets. Wrote numerous poems concerning the Civil War and several praising President Abraham Lincoln, including "O Captain! My Captain!"

Woodhull, Tennessee (1846–1923), and Victoria Woodhull Claflin (1838–1927): Sisters and popular clairvoyants who established a brokerage house on Wall Street in the early 1870s.

Wright, Frank Lloyd (1869–1959): Architect who invented a new approach to design in American architecture, one that addressed nature and environment. After an apprenticeship with Louis H. Sullivan, he opened his own architectural firm in 1893 in Oak Park, Illinois.

Appendix C
Maps, Charts and Graphs

1. How the United States Constitution May Be Amended

2. Year of Admission to the Union

3. The End of Reconstruction

4. The Presidential Election of 1876 (Electoral Vote)

5. Early Pacific Railroad Lines

6. Population per Square Mile in the American Frontier, 1860

7. Miles of Railroad Track Operating, 1866–1886

8. Agriculture in the United States, 1860–1890

9. Mining of Natural Resources in the United States, 1860–1890

10. The Election of 1868

11. Native American Lands and Tribal Locations, 1890

12. Women in the American Labor Force, 1890 (Indians Not Included)

13. Population of the United States, 1860–1893

14. Population Growth Among Principal Midwestern Cities, 1880–1890

15. European Emigration to the United States, 1820–1920

16. U.S. Patterns of Settlement, 1890

17. Location of Sioux Indian Reservations, 1890

1. How the United States Constitution May Be Amended

	Methods of Ratification	
	Legislatures in three–fourths of the states	Ratifying conventions in three–fourths of the states
Two–thirds vote in both houses of Congress	Usual method used	Used only once—for Twenty-first Amendment
National constitutional convention called by Congress at request of two–thirds of the state legislatures	Method still unused	Method still unused

Methods of Proposal

2. Year of Admission to the Union

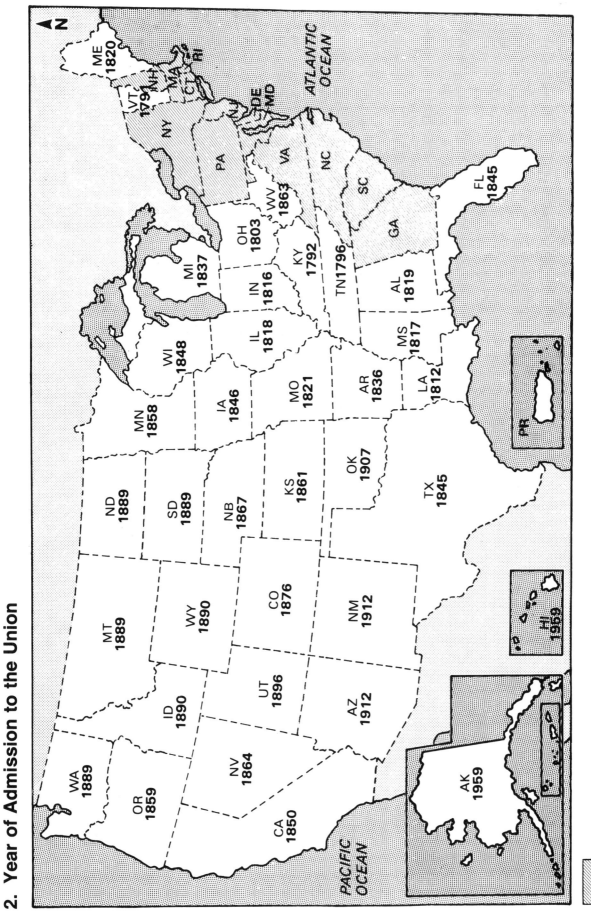

ME 1820
VT 1791
NH
MA
CT
RI
NY
PA
NJ
DE
MD
VA
NC
SC
GA
FL 1845
WV 1863
OH 1803
KY 1792
TN 1796
AL 1819
MS 1817
MI 1837
IN 1816
IL 1818
WI 1848
IA 1846
MO 1821
AR 1836
LA 1812
MN 1858
ND 1889
SD 1889
NB 1867
KS 1861
OK 1907
TX 1845
MT 1889
WY 1890
CO 1876
NM 1912
WA 1889
ID 1890
UT 1896
AZ 1912
OR 1859
NV 1864
CA 1850
AK 1959
HI 1959
PR
ATLANTIC OCEAN
PACIFIC OCEAN

Original colonies

3. The End of Reconstruction

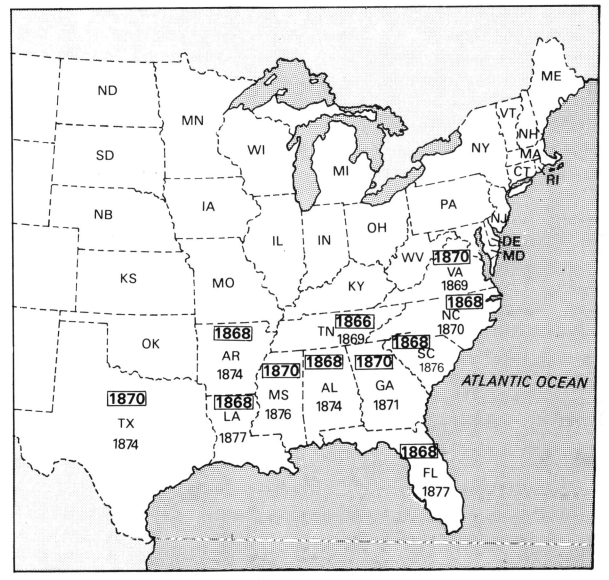

Dates in bold—Readmission to the Union
Dates in light—End of Carpetbagger Government

4. Presidential Election of 1876 (Electoral Vote)

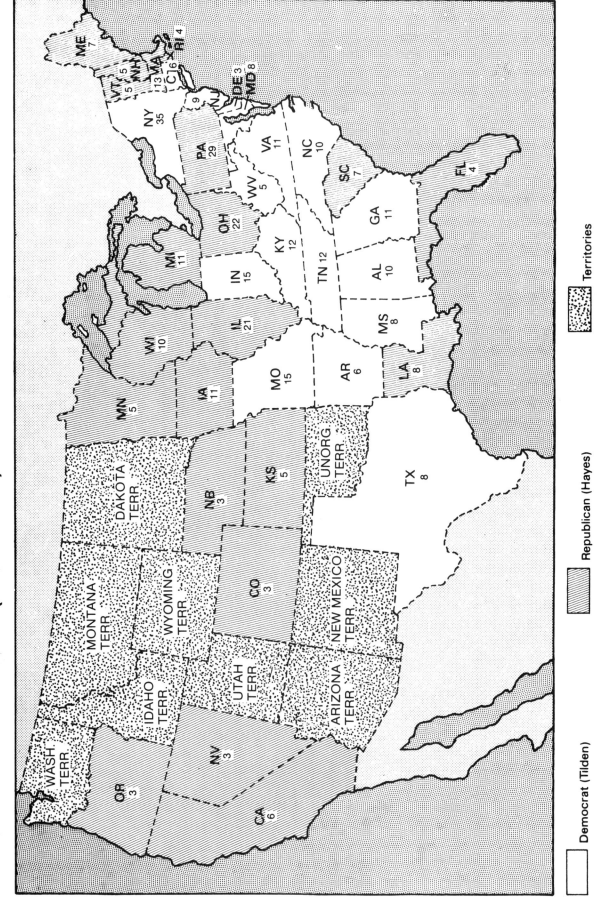

Democrat (Tilden)

Republican (Hayes)

Territories

226

5. Early Pacific Railroad Lines

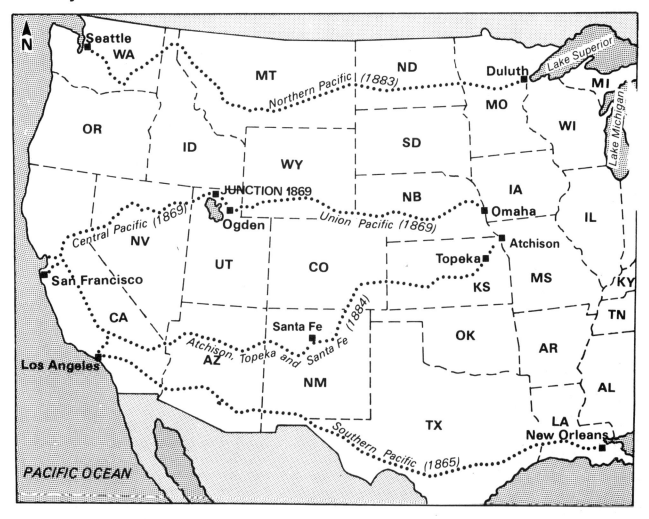

6. Population per Square Mile in the American Frontier, 1860

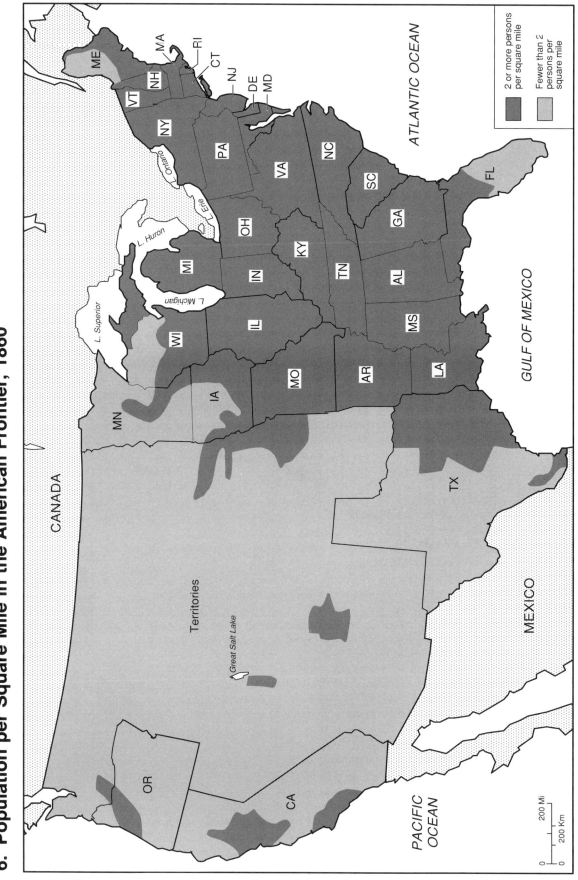

2 or more persons per square mile

Fewer than 2 persons per square mile

ATLANTIC OCEAN

GULF OF MEXICO

PACIFIC OCEAN

CANADA

MEXICO

Territories

Great Salt Lake

L. Superior

L. Huron

L. Michigan

L. Erie

L. Ontario

ME
NH
VT
MA
RI
CT
NJ
DE
MD
NY
PA
VA
NC
SC
GA
FL
OH
KY
TN
AL
MS
IN
IL
MI
WI
MO
AR
LA
IA
MN
TX
OR
CA

200 Mi
200 Km

7. Miles of Railroad Track Operating, 1866–1886

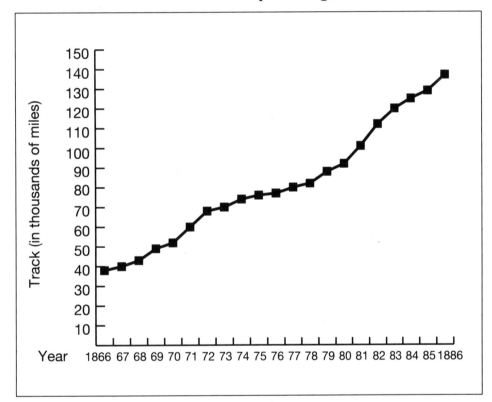

8. Agriculture in the United States, 1860–1890

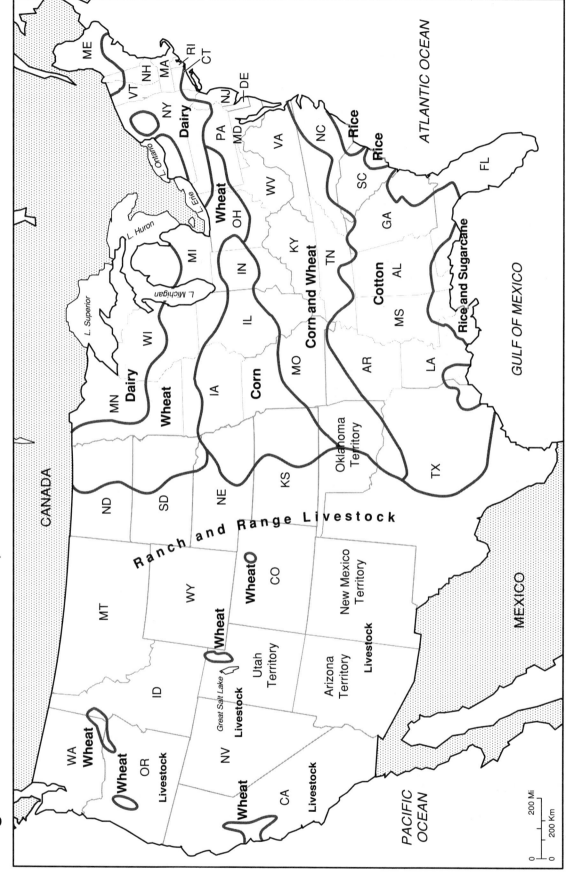

9. Mining of Natural Resources in the United States, 1860–1890

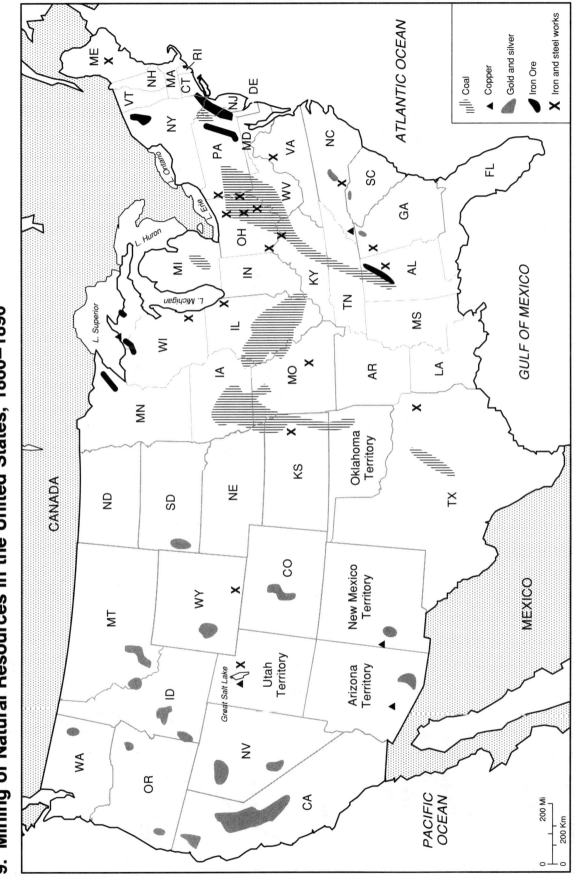

Legend	
Coal	
▲	Copper
	Gold and silver
	Iron Ore
✗	Iron and steel works

ATLANTIC OCEAN

GULF OF MEXICO

PACIFIC OCEAN

CANADA

MEXICO

L. Ontario
L. Erie
L. Huron
L. Superior
L. Michigan

Great Salt Lake

ME
NH
VT
MA
CT
RI
NY
NJ
DE
PA
MD
WV
VA
NC
SC
GA
FL
OH
IN
KY
TN
AL
MS
LA
MI
IL
WI
IA
MO
AR
MN
ND
SD
NE
KS
Oklahoma Territory
TX
CO
WY
MT
New Mexico Territory
Arizona Territory
Utah Territory
ID
NV
WA
OR
CA

200 Mi
200 Km

10. The Election of 1868

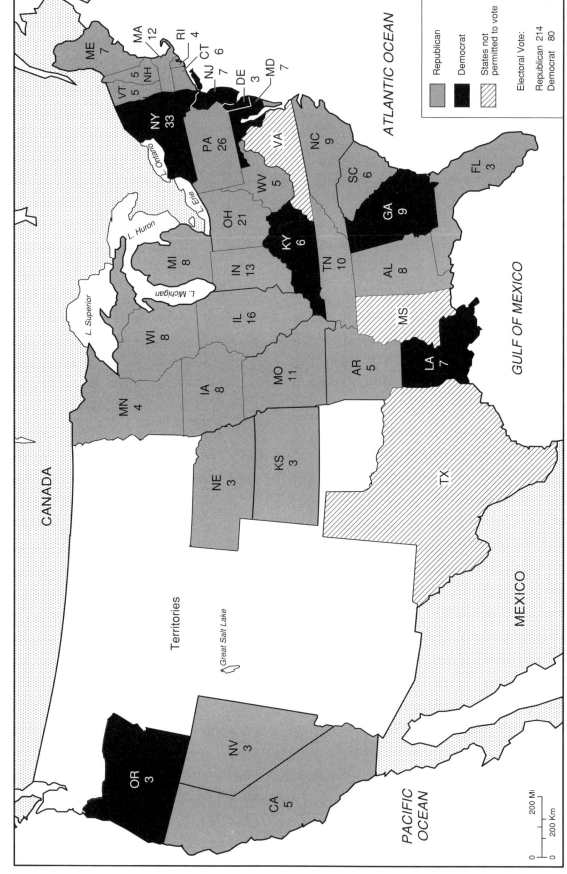

Electoral Vote:
Republican 214
Democrat 80

Republican
Democrat
States not permitted to vote

ATLANTIC OCEAN

GULF OF MEXICO

PACIFIC OCEAN

MEXICO

CANADA

Territories

Great Salt Lake

L. Superior
L. Huron
L. Michigan
L. Erie
L. Ontario

ME 7
MA 12
RI 4
CT 6
NH 5
VT 5
NJ 7
DE 3
MD 7
NY 33
PA 26
VA
NC 9
SC 6
FL 3
WV 5
OH 21
KY 6
TN 10
GA 9
AL 8
MI 8
IN 13
IL 16
MS
AR 5
LA 7
WI 8
MO 11
IA 8
MN 4
NE 3
KS 3
TX
NV 3
OR 3
CA 5

200 Mi
200 Km
0
0

11. Native American Lands and Tribal Locations, 1890

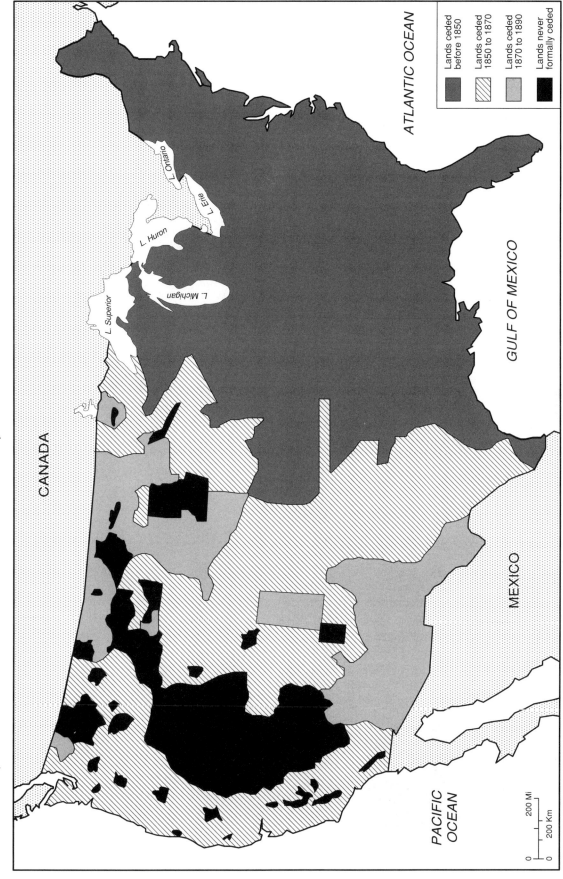

CANADA

L. Superior

L. Huron

L. Michigan

L. Ontario

L. Erie

ATLANTIC OCEAN

GULF OF MEXICO

MEXICO

PACIFIC OCEAN

	Lands ceded before 1850
	Lands ceded 1850 to 1870
	Lands ceded 1870 to 1890
	Lands never formally ceded

200 Mi

200 Km

12. Women in the American Labor Force, 1890

| | MARITAL STATUS | | | | |
Age	All Marital Status	Single and Unknown	Married	Widowed	Divorced
all ages	18.9	40.5	4.6	29.3	49.0
15–24	29.0	37.3	6.4	53.5	50.0
25–34	17.2	55.0	4.8	55.0	56.0
35–44	13.2	48.1	4.5	50.1	54.2
45–54	12.9	41.0	3.9	37.0	44.5
55–64	12.0	32.3	3.0	24.5	32.9
65	8.3	17.7	2.3	11.0	18.1
unknown	30.8	44.0	14.2	39.2	58.2

SOURCE: U.S. Department of Commerce, Bureau of the Census

13. Population of the United States, 1860–1893

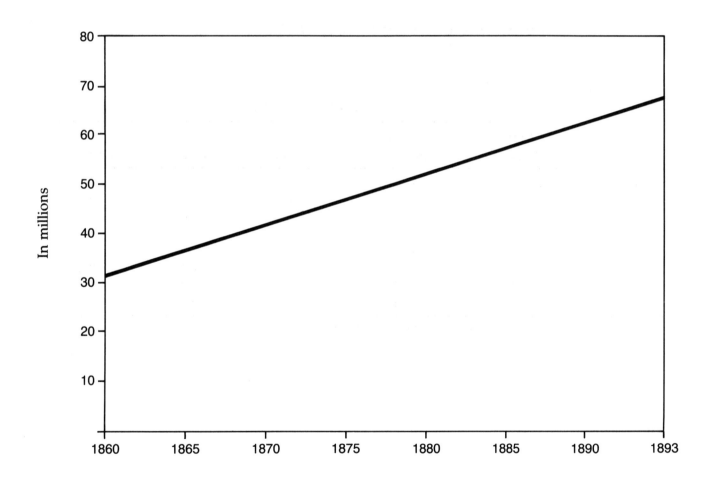

14. Population Growth Among Principal Midwestern Cities, 1880–1890

CITY	YEAR		(PERCENT INCREASE)
	1880	1890	
Chicago	503,125	1,099,850	119%
Minneapolis	46,887	164,738	251%
St. Paul	41,473	133,156	221%
Kansas City	55,781	132,710	138%
Denver	35,029	106,773	205%

15. European Emigration to the United States, 1820–1920

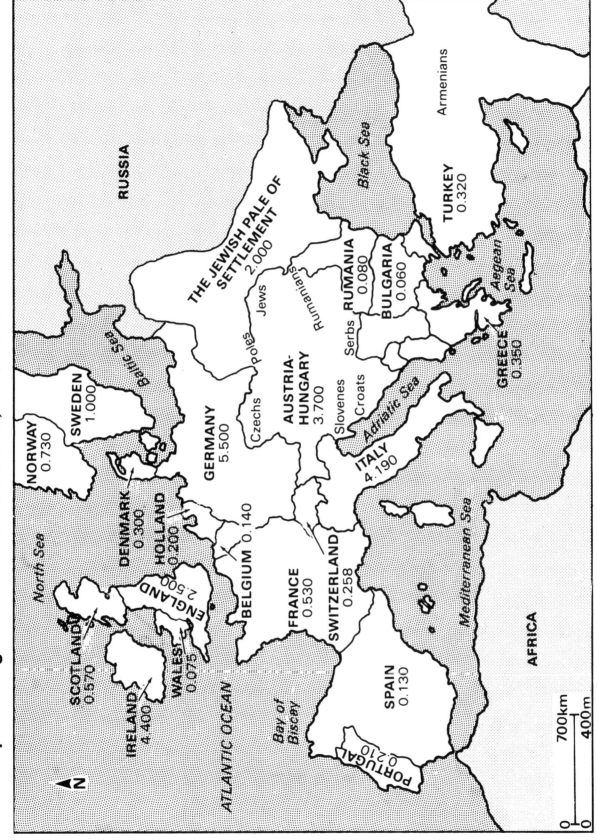

Figures are given in millions

RUSSIA

THE JEWISH PALE OF
SETTLEMENT
2.000

Armenians

Black Sea

TURKEY
0.320

RUMANIA
0.080

BULGARIA
0.060

Jews

Rumanians

Serbs

Aegean Sea

NORWAY
0.730

SWEDEN
1.000

Baltic Sea

Poles

Czechs

GERMANY
5.500

AUSTRIA-
HUNGARY
3.700

Slovenes

Croats

Adriatic Sea

ITALY
4.190

GREECE
0.350

North Sea

DENMARK
0.300

HOLLAND
0.200

BELGIUM 0.140

FRANCE
0.530

SWITZERLAND
0.258

Mediterranean Sea

ENGLAND
2.500

SCOTLAND
0.570

IRELAND
4.400

WALES
0.075

ATLANTIC OCEAN

Bay of
Biscay

SPAIN
0.130

PORTUGAL
0.210

AFRICA

N

700km

400m

0

0

237

16. U.S. Patterns of Settlement, 1890 (Indians Not Included)

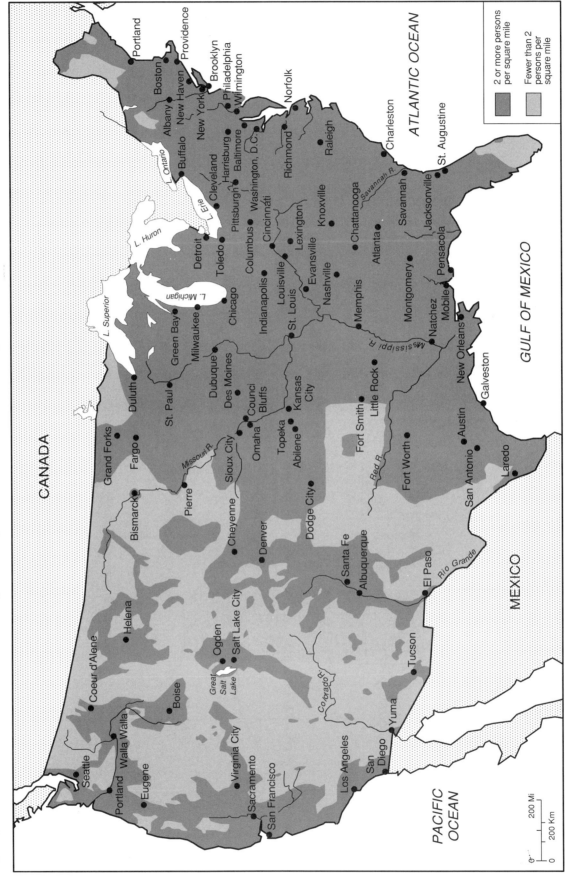

Legend:
- 2 or more persons per square mile
- Fewer than 2 persons per square mile

CANADA

MEXICO

ATLANTIC OCEAN

GULF OF MEXICO

PACIFIC OCEAN

Portland, Boston, New Haven, Providence, Albany, Brooklyn, New York, Buffalo, Philadelphia, Wilmington, Baltimore, Washington, D.C., Harrisburg, Cleveland, Pittsburgh, Norfolk, Richmond, Raleigh, Columbus, Cincinnati, Lexington, Knoxville, Chattanooga, Charleston, St. Augustine, Jacksonville, Savannah, Pensacola, Atlanta, Montgomery, Mobile, Natchez, New Orleans, Detroit, Toledo, Chicago, Louisville, Evansville, Nashville, Memphis, Indianapolis, St. Louis, Green Bay, Milwaukee, Dubuque, Des Moines, Council Bluffs, Kansas City, Topeka, Abilene, Little Rock, Fort Smith, Galveston, Austin, Laredo, San Antonio, Fort Worth, Duluth, St. Paul, Sioux City, Omaha, Dodge City, Santa Fe, Albuquerque, El Paso, Grand Forks, Fargo, Bismarck, Pierre, Cheyenne, Denver, Tucson, Yuma, Helena, Ogden, Salt Lake City, Virginia City, Boise, Coeur d'Alene, Walla Walla, Seattle, Portland, Eugene, Sacramento, San Francisco, Los Angeles, San Diego

L. Ontario, L. Erie, L. Huron, L. Michigan, L. Superior, Savannah R., Mississippi R., Missouri R., Red R., Rio Grande, Colorado R., Great Salt Lake

200 Mi
200 Km

17. Location of Sioux Indian Reservations, 1890

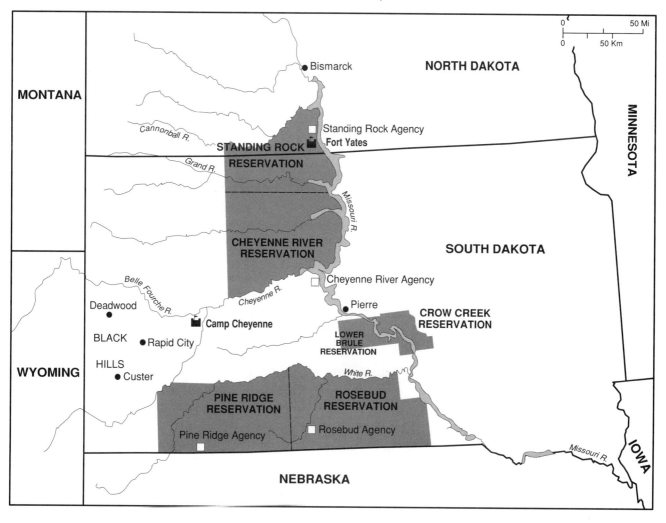

18. Presidential Election of 1896 (Electoral Vote)

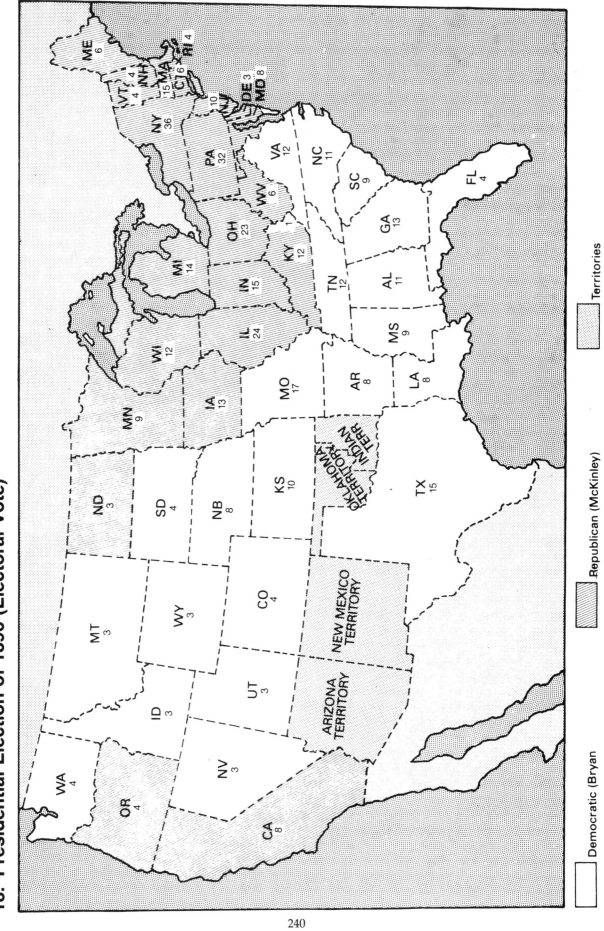

State	EV
ME	6
VT	4
NH	4
MA	15
RI	4
CT	6
NY	36
PA	32
NJ	10
DE	3
MD	8
VA	12
NC	11
SC	9
FL	4
GA	13
WV	6
OH	23
KY	12
MD	1
TN	12
AL	11
MS	9
MI	14
IN	15
IL	24
WI	12
IA	13
MO	17
AR	8
LA	8
MN	9
ND	3
SD	4
NB	8
KS	10
TX	15
WA	4
OR	4
MT	3
WY	3
CO	4
ID	3
UT	3
NV	3
CA	8

OKLAHOMA TERR.
INDIAN TERR.
NEW MEXICO TERRITORY
ARIZONA TERRITORY

Democratic (Bryan

Republican (McKinley)

Territories

240

19. Dates of Statehood, 1867–1896

Nebraska	March 1, 1867
Colorado	August 1, 1876
North Dakota	November 2, 1889
South Dakota	November 2, 1889
Montana	November 8, 1889
Washington	November 11, 1889
Idaho	July 3, 1890
Wyoming	July 10, 1890
Utah	January 4, 1896

20. Spanish–American War, 1898—Pacific Campaign

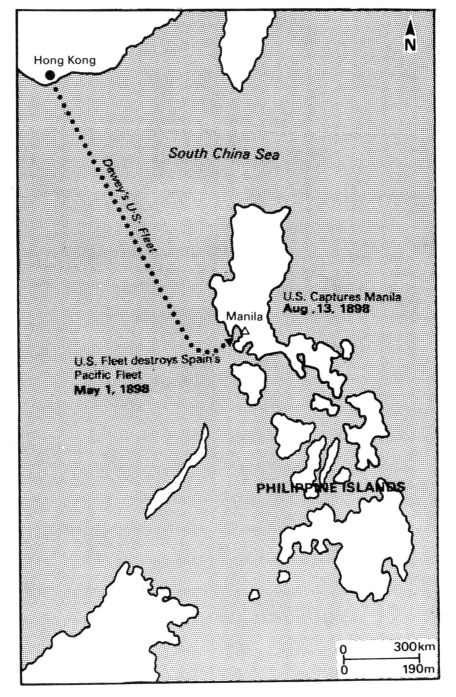

21. Spanish–American War, 1898—Caribbean Campaign

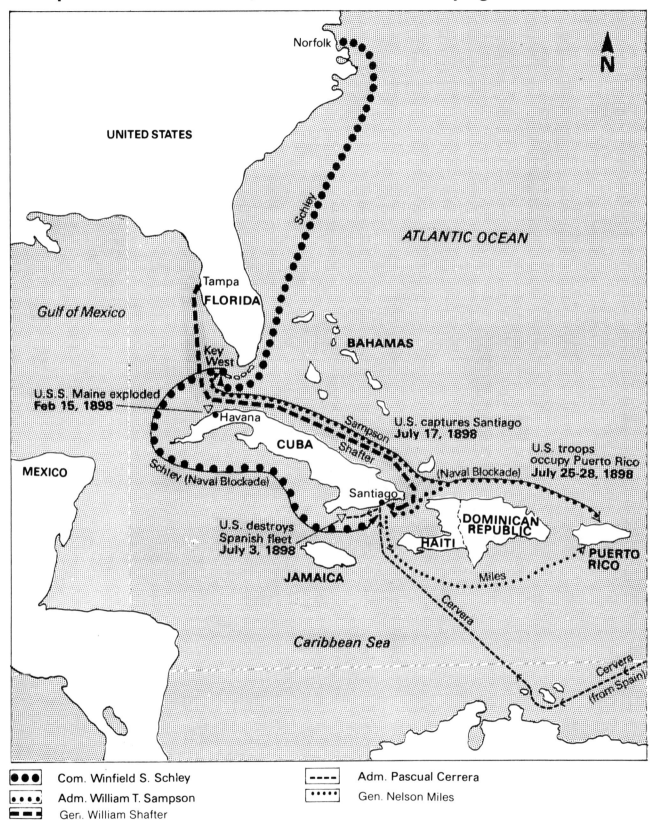

●●●	Com. Winfield S. Schley	----	Adm. Pascual Cerrera
●●●●	Adm. William T. Sampson	●●●●●	Gen. Nelson Miles
– – –	Gen. William Shafter		

22. Immigrants to the United States, by Regions of Origin, 1860–1900

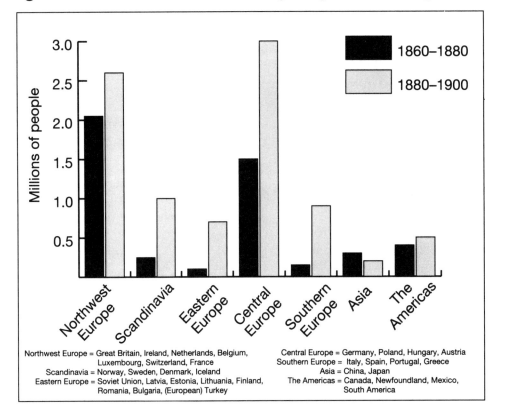

Northwest Europe = Great Britain, Ireland, Netherlands, Belgium,
Luxembourg, Switzerland, France
Scandinavia = Norway, Sweden, Denmark, Iceland
Eastern Europe = Soviet Union, Latvia, Estonia, Lithuania, Finland,
Romania, Bulgaria, (European) Turkey

Central Europe = Germany, Poland, Hungary, Austria
Southern Europe = Italy, Spain, Portugal, Greece
Asia = China, Japan
The Americas = Canada, Newfoundland, Mexico,
South America

23. Presidential Elections, 1868–1900: Candidates and Party Affiliation, Distribution of Popular and Electoral Votes

1868	ULYSSES S. GRANT	Republican	3,012,833	214
	Horatio Seymour	Democratic	2,703,249	80
1872	ULYSSES S. GRANT	Republican	3,596,745	286
	Horace Greeley	Democratic	2,843,446	66
1876	RUTHERFORD B. HAYES	Republican	4,036,572	185
	Samuel J. Tilden	Democratic	4,284,020	184
1880	JAMES A. GARFIELD	Republican	4,449,053	214
	Winfield S. Hancock	Democratic	4,442,032	155
	James B. Weaver	Greenback-Labor	308,578	
1884	GROVER CLEVELAND	Democratic	4,874,986	219
	James G. Blaine	Republican	4,851,981	182
	Benjamin F. Butler	Greenback-Labor	175,370	
1888	BENJAMIN HARRISON	Republican	5,444,337	233
	Grover Cleveland	Democratic	5,540,050	168
1892	GROVER CLEVELAND	Democratic	5,554,414	277
	Benjamin Harrison	Republican	5,190,802	145
	James B. Weaver	People's	1,027,329	22
1896	WILLIAM McKINLEY	Republican	7,104,779	271
	William J. Bryan	Democratic; Populist	6,502,925	176
1900	WILLIAM McKINLEY	Republican	7,219,530	292
	William J. Bryan	Democratic; Populist	6,356,734	155

24. Percentages of American Women in Various Occupations, 1870 and 1900

	1870	1900
Service	49.7	38.4
Private household	48.9	10.2
Personal service (excluding private household)	.81	28.2
Clerical/kindred	1.3	8.6
Crafts and Manufacture	19.4	25.4
Professional/Technical	5.6	11.2
Agriculture	21.6	15.9
Managerial/Official	.03	.2
Totals	97.6	99.7

SOURCES: U.S. Department of Commerce, Bureau of the Census

25. Participation Rates of Men and Women in the American Labor Force, 1900

AGE	MALE	FEMALE
10–15	26.1	10.2
16–20	76.8	32.3
21–24	93.1	30.8
25–34	96.3	19.9
35–44	96.6	15.6
45–54	95.5	14.7
55–64	90.0	13.2
65	68.4	9.1
age unknown	59.6	24.2
total	90.5	20.6

SOURCE: U.S. Department of Commerce, Bureau of the Census

26. United States Currency, 1866–1898

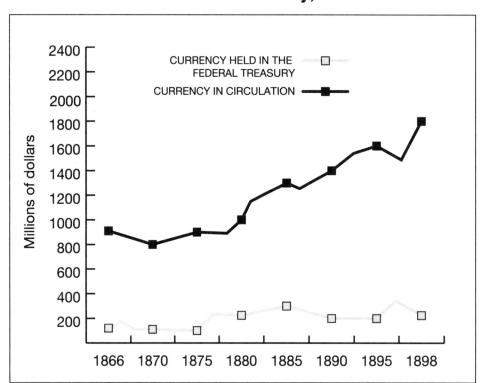

27. Election Patterns, 1868–1900

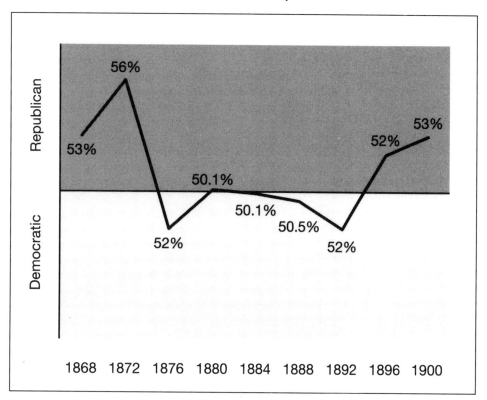

28. American Public School Enrollment, 1870–1900

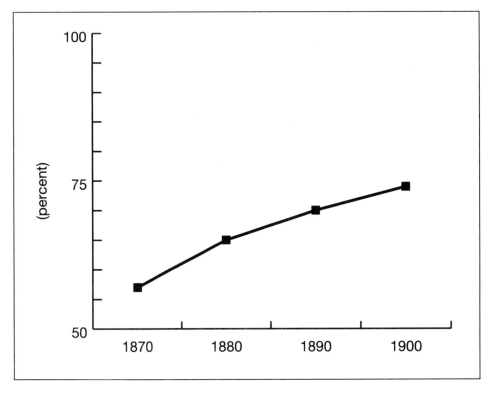

29. Growth in Foreign Imports and Exports, 1870–1900

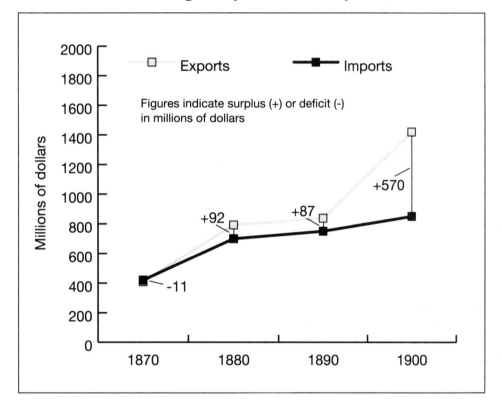

30. U.S. Presidents, Years of Election and Cabinet Members, Years of Appointment, 1865–1901

President		Vice-President		Secretary of State		Secretary of Treasury		Secretary of War	
17. Andrew Johnson Unionist	1865		1865	Wm. H. Seward		Hugh McCulloch	1865	E. M. Stanton U. S. Grant L. Thomas J. M. Schofield	1865 1867 1868 1868
18. Ulysses S. Grant Republican	1869	Schuyler Colfax Henry Wilson	1869	E. B. Washburne Hamilton Fish	1869 1873	Geo. S. Boutwell W. A. Richardson Benj. H. Bristow Lot M. Morrill	1869 1873 1874 1876	J. A. Rawlins W. T. Sherman W. W. Belknap Alphonso Taft J. D. Cameron	1869 1869 1869 1876 1876
19. Rutherford B. Hayes Republican	1877	William A. Wheeler	1877	W. M. Evarts		John Sherman	1877	G. W. McCrary Alex. Ramsey	1877 1879
20. James A. Garfield Republican	1881	Chester A. Arthur	1881	James G. Blaine		Wm. Windom	1881	R. T. Lincoln	1881
21. Chester A. Arthur Republican	1881			F. T. Frelinghuysen	1881	Chas. J. Folger W. Q. Gresham Hugh McCulloch	1881 1884 1884	R. T. Lincoln	1881
22. Grover Cleveland Democratic	1885	T. A. Hendricks	1885	Thos. F. Bayard		Daniel Manning Chas. S. Fairchild	1885 1887	W. C. Endicott	1885
23. Benjamin Harrison Republican	1889	Levi P. Morton	1889	James G. Blaine John W. Foster		Wm. Windom Charles Foster	1889 1892	R. Proctor S. B. Elkins	1889 1891
24. Grover Cleveland Democratic	1893	Adlai E. Stevenson	1893	W. Q. Gresham Richard Olney		John G. Carlisle	1893 1895	D. S. Lamont	1893
25. William McKinley Republican	1897	Garret A. Hobart Theodore Roosevelt	1897 1901	John Sherman Wm. R. Day John Hay		Lyman J. Gage	1897 1897 1898	R. A. Alger Elihu Root	1897 1899
26. Theodore Roosevelt Republican	1901	Chas. W. Fairbanks	1905	John Hay		Lyman J. Gage	1901	Elihu Root	1901

Attorney General	Postmaster General	Secretary of Navy	Secretary of Interior	Secretary of Agriculture
				Cabinet status since 1889
James Speed 1865 Henry Stanbery 1866 Wm. M. Evarts 1868	Wm. Dennison 1865 A. W. Randall 1866	Gideon Welles 1865	John P. Usher 1865 James Harlan 1865 O. H. Browning 1866	
E. R. Hoar 1869 A. T. Ackerman 1870 Geo. H. Williams 1871 Edw. Pierrepont 1875 Alphonso Taft 1876	J. A. J. Creswell 1869 Jas. W. Marshall 1874 Marshall Jewell 1874 Jas. N. Tyner 1876	Adolph E. Borie 1869 Geo. M. Robeson 1869	Jacob D. Cox 1869 C. Delano 1870 Zach. Chandler 1875	
Chas. Devens 1877	David M. Key 1877 H. Maynard 1880	R. W. Thompson 1877 Nathan Goff, Jr. 1881	Carl Schurz 1877	
W. MacVeagh 1881	T. L. James 1881	W. H. Hunt 1881	S. J. Kirkwood 1881	
B. H. Brewster 1881	T. O. Howe 1881 W. Q. Gresham 1883 Frank Hatton 1884	W. E. Chandler 1881	Henry M. Teller 1881	
A. H. Garland 1885	Wm. F. Vilas 1885 D. M. Dickinson 1888	W. C. Whitney 1885	L. Q. C. Lamar 1885 Wm. F. Vilas 1888	N. J. Colman 1889
W. H. H. Miller 1889	J. Wanamaker 1889	Benj. F. Tracy 1889	John W. Noble 1889	J. M. Rusk 1889
R. Olney 1893 J. Harmon 1895	W. S. Bissell 1893 W. L. Wilson 1895	Hilary A. Herbert 1893	Hoke Smith 1893 D. R. Francis 1896	J. S. Morton 1893
J. McKenna 1897 J. W. Griggs 1897 P. C. Knox 1901	James A. Gary 1897 Chas. E. Smith 1898	John D. Long 1897	C. N. Bliss 1897 E. A. Hitchcock 1899	James Wilson 1897
P. C. Knox 1901	Chas. E. Smith 1901	John D. Long 1901	E. A. Hitchcock 1901	James Wilson 1901

31. Chief Justices of the United States Supreme Court, 1865–1901

NAME	BORN	DIED	HOME	GRADUATED
Chase, Salmon Portland	1/13/1808	5/7/1873	Ohio	Cincinnati College, Dartmouth
Waite, Morrison Remick	11/29/1816	3/23/1888	Connecticut	Yale
Fuller, Melville Weston	2/11/1833	7/4/1910	Illinois	Bowdoin Harvard Law School

APPOINTED BY	CONFIRMED	LANDMARK DECISIONS
Lincoln	12/6/1864	Ex parte Milligan Ex parte Garland Ex parte McCardle Texas v. White Hepburn v. Griswold Knox v. Lee Slaughterhouse Cases
Grant	1/1/1874	Minor v. Happersett United States v. Reese United States v. Cruikshank Munn v. Illinois Peik v. Chicago & Northwestern Railroad Co. Stone v. Farmer's Loan & Trust Co. Hall v. DeCuir Pensacola Telegraph Co. v. Western Union Co.
Cleveland	7/20/1888	United States v. Texas California v. Southern Pacific Co. United States v. E. C. Knight Co. Pollock v. Farmer's Loan and Trust Co. United States v. Wong Kim Ark Loewe v. Lawlor

32. Associate Justices of the United States Supreme Court, 1865–1901

NAME	BORN	DIED	STATE	COLLEGE	LAW SCHOOL
Wayne, James Moore	c. 1790	7/5/1867	Georgia	Princeton	private study
Catron, John	c. 1786	5/30/1865	Tennessee		private study
Nelson, Samuel	11/10/1792	12/13/1873	New York	Middlebury	private study
Grier, Robert Cooper	3/5/1794	9/26/1870	Penn.	Dickinson	private study
Clifford, Nathan	8/18/1803	7/25/1881	Maine	Haverhill	private study
Swayne, Noah Haynes	12/7/1804	6/8/1884	Ohio	Quaker Academy	private study
Miller, Samuel Freeman	4/5/1816	10/13/1890	Iowa	Transylvania U.	private study
Davis, David	3/9/1815	6/26/1886	Illinois	Kenyon	Yale Law School
Field, Stephen Johnson	11/4/1816	4/9/1899	California	Williams	private study
Strong, William	5/6/1808	8/19/1895	Penn.	Yale	Yale Law School
Bradley, Joseph P.	3/14/1813	1/22/1892	New Jersey	Rutgers	private study
Hunt, Ward	6/14/1810	3/24/1886	New York	Union Col.	private study

APPOINTED BY		REASON FOR LEAVING DATE			
		CHIEF			
PRESIDENT	DATE	JUSTICE	DIED	RESIGNED	LANDMARK DECISIONS
Jackson	1/9/1835		1867		Scott v. Sandford Ex parte Milligan
Jackson	3/8/1837				Scott v. Sandford
Tyler	2/14/1845			1872	Scott v. Sandford Ex parte Milligan Hepburn v. Griswold Knox v. Lee
Polk	8/4/1846			1870	Scott v. Sandford Ex parte McCardle
Buchanan	1/12/1858		1881		Ex parte Milligan Ex parte Garland Hepburn v. Griswold Ex parte Virginia
Lincoln	1/24/1862			1881	Ex parte Milligan Hepburn v. Griswold Knox v. Lee Slaughterhouse Cases
Lincoln	7/16/1862	1890			Ex parte Garland Hepburn v. Griswold Slaughterhouse Cases
Lincoln	12/1/1862			1877	Hepburn v. Griswold Slaughterhouse Cases
Lincoln	3/10/1863			1897	Ex parte Garland Paul v. Virginia Munn v. Illinois Bradley v. Fisher
Grant	2/18/1870			1880	Knox v. Lee Stauder v. W. Va. Ex parte Virginia
Grant	3/21/1870		1892		Knox v. Lee Slaughterhouse Cases Civil Rights Cases
Grant	1/9/1873			1882	Slaughterhouse Cases United States v. Reese Reading RR v. Penn.

NAME	BORN	DIED	STATE	COLLEGE	LAW SCHOOL
Harlan, John Marshall	6/1/1833	10/14/1911	Kentucky	Centre Col.	Transylvania U.
Woods, William Burnham	8/3/1824	5/14/1887	Georgia	W. Reserve, Yale	private study
Matthews, Stanley	7/21/1824	3/22/1889	Ohio	Kenyon	private study
Gray, Horace	3/24/1828	9/15/1902	Mass.	Harvard	Harvard Law School
Blatchford, Samuel Milford	3/9/1820	7/7/1893	New York	Columbia	
Lamar, Lucius Quintus Cincinnatus	9/17/1825	1/23/1893	Miss.	Emory	private study
Brewer, David Josiah	6/20/1837	3/28/1910	Kansas	Wesleyan, Yale	Albany Law School
Brown, Henry Billings	3/2/1836	9/4/1913	Michigan	Yale	Yale Law School, Harvard Law School
Shiras, George, Jr.	1/26/1832	8/2/1924	Penn.	Ohio U., Yale	Yale Law School
Jackson, Howell Edmunds	4/8/1832	8/8/1895	Tennessee	W. Tenn. Col., U. of Va., Cumberland	private study
White, Edward D.	11/3/1845	5/19/1921	Louisiana	Mt. St. Mary's, Georgetown	private study

APPOINTED BY		REASON FOR LEAVING DATE				
PRESIDENT	DATE	CHIEF JUSTICE	DIED	RESIGNED	LANDMARK DECISIONS
Hayes	10/29/1877				Plessy v. Ferguson Hennington v. Georgia Champion v. Ames United States v. Texas Northern Securities Co. v. United States
Hayes	12/21/1880				United States v. Harris Presser v. Illinois United States v. Lee
Garfield	5/12/1881				Bowman v. Chicago & N.W. Railway Co. Hurtado v. California Yick Wo v. Hopkins
Arthur	12/20/1881				Mayre v. Parsons Poindexter v. Greenhow Bowman v. Chicago & N.W. Railway Co. Chicago, Milwaukee & St. Paul RR v. Minn.
Arthur	3/27/1882				Chicago, Milwaukee & St. Paul RR v. Minn. Counselman v. Hitchcock In re Neagle
Cleveland	1/16/1888				Chicago, Milwaukee & St. Paul RR v. Minn. In re Neagle United States v. Texas
Harrison	12/18/1889				Reagan v. Farmers Loan & Trust Co. Kansas v. Colorado Muller v. Oregon In re Debs
Harrison	12/29/1890				Pollock v. Farmers Loan & Trust Co. Plessy v. Fergusson Downes v. Bidwell Holden v. Hardy
Harrison	7/26/1892				Pollock v. Farmers Loan & Trust Co.
Harrison	2/18/1893				Pollock v. Farmers Loan & Trust Co.
Cleveland	2/19/1894	1910			United States v. E. C. Knight Co. Adair v. United States

NAME	BORN	DIED	STATE	COLLEGE	LAW SCHOOL
Peckham, Rufus Wheeler, Jr.	11/8/1838	10/24/1909	New York	Union	private study
McKenna, Joseph	8/10/1843	11/21/1926	California	Collegiate Institute	

APPOINTED BY		REASON FOR LEAVING DATE			
PRESIDENT	**DATE**	**CHIEF JUSTICE**	**DIED**	**RESIGNED**	**LANDMARK DECISIONS**
Cleveland	12/9/1895				Lochner v. New York Allgeyer v. Louisiana Maxwell v. Dow Ex parte Young
McKinley	1/21/1898				Adair v. United States Adams v. Tanner Bunting v. Oregon Pettibone v. Nichols

33. U.S. Possessions and Territories to 1903

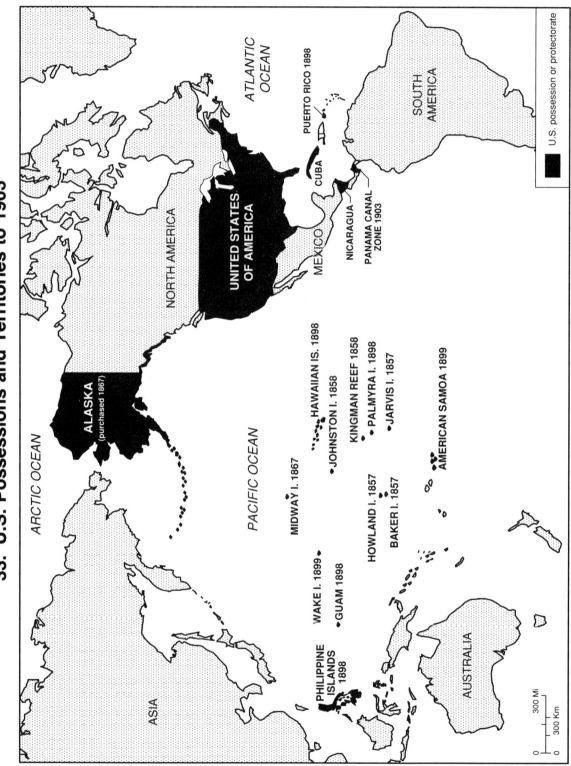

ARCTIC OCEAN

ASIA

NORTH AMERICA

ATLANTIC OCEAN

ALASKA
(purchased 1867)

UNITED STATES OF AMERICA

PUERTO RICO 1898

CUBA

MEXICO

NICARAGUA

PANAMA CANAL ZONE 1903

SOUTH AMERICA

PACIFIC OCEAN

MIDWAY I. 1867

HAWAIIAN IS. 1898

JOHNSTON I. 1858

KINGMAN REEF 1858

PALMYRA I. 1898

JARVIS I. 1857

HOWLAND I. 1857

BAKER I. 1857

AMERICAN SAMOA 1899

WAKE I. 1899

GUAM 1898

PHILIPPINE ISLANDS 1898

AUSTRALIA

U.S. possession or protectorate

300 Mi
300 Km

Bibliography

Ahlstrom, Sydney E., *A Religious History of the American People*. New Haven: Yale Univ. Press, 1972.

Baltzell, E. Dibgy, *The Protestant Establishment*. New York: Vintage Books, 1966.

Bartlett, John, *Familiar Quotations*, 12th ed. Boston: Little Brown, Brown, 1951.

Baxandall, Rosalyn; Gordon, Linda; and Reverby, Susan (eds.), *America's Working Women*. New York: Vintage Books, 1976.

Boorstin, Daniel J., *The Americans: The Democratic Experience*. New York: Vintage Books, 1974.

Bowman, John S., and Zoss, Joel, *Diamonds in the Rough*. New York: Macmillan, 1989.

Callow, Alexander B., Jr., *American Urban History*, 2d ed. New York: Oxford Univ. Press, 1973.

Campbell, A.E., *Expansionism and Imperialism*. New York: Harper & Row, 1970.

Carruth, Gorton, et al., *The Encyclopedia of American Facts and Dates*, 7th ed. New York: Crowell, 1979.

Cashman, Sean Dennis, *America in the Gilded Age*. New York: New York Univ. Press, 1984.

Current, Richard N., and Garraty, John A., *Words that Made American History, Colonial Times to the 1870's*. 2d ed. Boston: Little, Brown, 1965.

Current, Richard N., and Garraty, John A., *Words that Made American History, Since the Civil War*, 2d ed. Boston: Little, Brown, 1965.

Davis, Allen F., *American Heroine*. New York: Oxford Univ. Press, 1973.

Davis, Allen F., and Woodman, Harold D., *Conflict or Consensus in American History*. Boston: D.C. Heath, 1966.

Degler, Carl N., *The Age of the Economic Revolution 1876–1900,* 2d ed. Glenview, Illinois: Scott, Foresman, 1977.

DeNovo, John A. (ed.), *The Gilded Age and After.* New York: Scribner's, 1972.

Dubofsky, Melvyn, *Industrialism and the American Worker, 1865–1920.* Arlington Heights, Illinois: AHM, 1975.

Elliott, Stephen P., *A Reference Guide to the United States Supreme Court.* New York: Facts on File, 1986.

Fairman, Charles, *Mr. Justice Miller and the Supreme Court.* New York: Russell & Russell, 1939.

Garraty, John A. (ed.), *Labor and Capital in the Gilded Age.* Boston: Little, Brown, 1968.

Gianakos, Perry E., and Karson, Albert, *American Diplomacy and the Sense of Destiny.* Vol. 1, *The Initial Thrust, 1885–1900.* Belmont, California: Wadsworth, 1966.

Ginger, Ray, *People on the Move.* Boston: Allyn & Bacon, 1975.

Grob, Gerald N., and Billias, George Athan, *Interpretations of American History,* 2d ed., vol. II, New York: Free Press, 1972.

Handlin, Oscar, *The Americans.* Boston: Little, Brown, 1963.

Higham, John, *Strangers in the Land.* New York: Atheneum, 1975.

Hofstader, Richard, *The American Political Tradition.* New York: Vintage Books, 1948.

Hoogenboom, Ari, and Hoogenboom, Olive, *The Gilded Age.* New Jersey: Prentice-Hall, 1967.

Howe, Frederic C., *The Confessions of a Reformer.* New York: Quandrangle Books, 1967.

Johannsen, Robert W., *Reconstruction 1865–1877.* New York: Free Press, 1970.

Josephson, Matthew, *The Politicos 1865–1893.* New York: Harcourt, Brace & World, 1963.

Kelley, Robert, *The Shaping of the American Past,* 2d ed. Englewood Cliffs, N.J.: Prentice-Hall, 1978.

Kennan, George F., *American Diplomacy, 1900–1950* Chicago: Univ. of Chicago Press, 1951.

Lockwood, Alan L., and Harris, David E., *Reasoning with Democratic Values: Ethical Problems in United States History.* Vol. 2, *1877 to the Present.* New York: Teachers College Press, 1985.

Lodge, Henry Cabot, *Early Memories.* New York: Scribner's, 1913.

Maddow, Ben, *A Sunday Between Wars.* New York: W.W. Norton, 1979.

Matthaei, Julie A., *An Economic History of Women in America.* New York: Schocken Books, 1982.

Morgan, H. Wayne (ed.), *The Gilded Age.* Syracuse: Syracuse Univ. Press, 1970.

Myers, Robert Manson (ed.), *The Children of Pride.* Vol. 3, *The Night Season.* New Haven: Yale Univ. Press, 1972.

Paradis, Adrian, *The Labor Reference Book.* New York: Chilton, 1972.

Paterson, Thomas G. (ed.), *American Imperialism and Anti-Imperialism.* New York: Crowell, 1973.

Powderly, Terence V., *Thirty Years of Labor 1859–1889.* New York: Augustus M. Kelley, 1967.

Roche, John P. (ed.), *American Political Thought from Jefferson to Progressivism.* New York: Harper & Row, 1967.

Schlesinger, Arthur M., Jr., (ed.), *Almanac of American History.* New York: Putnam's, 1983.

Sicherman, Barbara, and Green, Carol Hurd (eds.), *Notable American Women: The Modern Period.* Cambridge, Mass.: Belknap Press, 1980.

Slotkin, Richard, *The Fatal Environment.* New York: Atheneum, 1985.

Smith, Page, *The Rise of Industrial America.* New York: McGraw-Hill, 1984.

Sochen, June, *Herstory—A Woman's View of American History.* New York: Alfred, 1974.

Tuchman, Barbara, *The Proud Tower.* New York: Macmillan, 1966.

Van Voris, Jacqueline, *Carrie Chapman Catt: A Public Life.* New York: Feminist Press, 1987.

Warner, Sam Bass, Jr., *Streetcar Suburbs.* New York: Atheneum, 1976.

Weinstein, Allen, and Wilson, R. Jackson, *Freedom and Crisis: An American History*, Vol. 2, *Since 1860.* New York: Random House, 1978.

Zaitzevsky, Cynthia, *Frederick Law Olmsted and the Boston Park System.* Cambridge, Mass.: Belknap Press, 1982.

INDEX

Names and page numbers in bold refer to biographical entries; numbers in italics refer to illustrations and captions.